A TRANSLATIONAL TURN

LATINX AND LATIN AMERICAN PROFILES
Frederick Luis Aldama, Editor

A TRANSLATIONAL TURN

Latinx Literature *into the* Mainstream

MARTA E. SÁNCHEZ

University of Pittsburgh Press

Published by the University of Pittsburgh Press, Pittsburgh, Pa., 15260
Copyright © 2018, University of Pittsburgh Press
All rights reserved
Manufactured in the United States of America
Printed on acid-free paper
10 9 8 7 6 5 4 3 2 1

Cataloging-in-Publication data is available from the Library of Congress

ISBN 13: 978-0-8229-6551-0
ISBN 10: 0-8229-6551-8

Cover art: Alfredo Ramos Martínez, *Mixtecas Primitivas*, c. 1942, private collection,
©The Alfredo Ramos Martínez Research Project, reproduced by permission.
Cover design: Melissa Dias-Mandoly

For Gabo and Paul—el futuro.
May they continue to see the world through the lens of two languages.

CONTENTS

PREFACE

One of my most enjoyable experiences as a professor of Chicano and Latino literatures was the engagement and enthusiasm I heard in my students' voices when they expressed strong and varying opinions about "Spanglish" and other forms of the English-Spanish language contact phenomena ("The two should be kept separate!"; "Mixture is great because this is the way we speak!"). My students' reactions about this subject really resonated with me for professional and personal reasons. As a scholar and professor, I was interested in the convergence of Latinx literature, bilingualism, multilingualism, and in what is known today as the planetary tent of world literatures (or language landscapes at the heart of literature and translation). But I know why I found their responses so compelling: I was recalling my own experiences with language and bilingualism, especially my role of interpreter/translator for my immigrant Spanish-monolingual maternal grandmother when I was young. My grandmother was a permanent fixture of our household growing up. She was born in Durango, Durango, moved to Chihuahua, Chihuahua, and from there crossed the Mexico–U.S. border into El Paso in 1921. While a massive immigrant population was crossing the Atlantic from Europe to the East Coast (1901–1930), she and many others crossed into El Paso, the Ellis Island of the Southwest, when Mexican immigration mushroomed in the second decade of the century. *El paso* translates as "the pass" or more literally "the step," that connotes for me the proximity of Mexico and the United States. She "stepped" through an open border after the Mexican Revolution (1910–1917), even before the establishment of the Border Patrol (1924), with her young daughter, my mother, who learned English in El Paso and became a bilingual speaker. From El Paso, they came to settle in a Mexican community in east Los Angeles where my two brothers and I heard, and sometimes spoke, an interactive mode of the two languages. This mixture, quite ordinary for us, was and still is for Spanish monolingual and English monolingual speakers a disorienting experience.

When I first encountered the translation of English-language Latino texts to Spanish in the early 1990s, I was teaching Chicano literature in the Spanish section of the Literature department at UCSD. The classes I was teaching were for Spanish majors and minors. Everything—the class lectures and discussions, writing and oral assignments, and nonfiction readings—were in Spanish, though English was the base language of some texts, often mixed in with Spanish words, phrases, and sentences. After all, this was Chicano literature, the cultural expression of women and men whose "original" language already represented a specific cultural condition of hybridity and bilingualism. Such teaching practices appeared odd to some people unacquainted with this literature: "You teach Chicano literature written in English in Spanish!" Using texts written in English, discussing and writing about them in Spanish made perfect sense to me, but I had to admit I understood how it would seem somewhat disorienting to outsiders.

So, when I encountered the translation of narrative texts by Latinos and Latinas to Spanish—instead of feeling relief and joy that now I could draw up a list of readings exclusively in Spanish—the disorienting experience I had encountered among outsiders became a disorienting experience to me. Why teach Latino literatures in translation, especially when they seemed to be translated into monolingual Spanish, when I could teach them in their original print language, a mixture of English and Spanish? I decided to teach the texts in their first English version and continue to replicate for my students the bilingual and multilingual world out of which Chicano and the other Latino literatures and cultures emerged. I knew well that the Spanish vernacular and different forms of spoken and written "Spanglish" used by the authors of Latino literatures, by women and men, primarily of working-class background, was not the standard varieties of

Spanish spoken and heard in the capitals of Spain, Mexico, and Spanish-speaking nations of the Global American South.

The long and short of it was that I became engrossed with the subject of Spanish-to-English translation, already in place at the time, on the one hand, and English-to-Spanish translation by mainstream presses, on the other hand. The former translation had always been the result of efforts by independent minority presses. The latter, a phenomenon of the decade of the 1990s, was new and unconventional for several reasons. First of all, the children of Mexican ancestry who are born here and speak Spanish, or enter the country from Spanish-language countries, are rapidly disabused for speaking Spanish and are encouraged to learn English. Yet, mainstream presses, responding to changing business market demands, began to take on the translation of Latino literature with bilingual features into the language that U.S. political and linguistic policies forbid because endorsers of these policies deem Spanish dangerous and disturbing. The second reason why this translation to Spanish of English-language Latino narratives appeared odd was because it occurred in a country that represents its national belonging as linked to a single tongue, national community, and geography of the nation-state.

I liked to remind my students then and myself now of what Marc Shell and Werner Sollors said in their *Multilingual Anthology of American Literature* (2000)—that the United States always has had an immense though unrecognized multilingual presence. Its inhabitants and literature are not only the offshoots of several linguistic mother tongues; they are "the result of the interaction of many linguistic and cultural trajectories, which are felt also in the many 'impure' linguistic elements—be they code switching, translated metaphors, or non-idiomatic expressions" (Shell and Sollors 8), present in everyday speech and literature. This linguistic diversity is even more intense now.

This book is a preliminary study about the translation of Latino narratives; about border crossings (both actual and metaphoric), code-mixing, bilingualism, and multilingualism. More than theorizing, it is about exemplifying translation and bilingualism/multilingualism implicit in language and culture. Some citizen groups in the United States might desire a pre-Babel universe of what they perceive to be English monolingualism, but the future is not monolingualism; the linguistic ecology here and in the major cities and suburban outskirts of the global world is bilingual and multilingual.

I make two notations about terminology. First, I use the "United States" and "U.S. American" instead of "America" and "American" because I hold the term "America" to represent the Hemispheric Américas, North and South, much more than only the United States. I resist the almost perennial usage of the term as synonymous for only the United States or as standing in for all the

Américas, a synecdoche, the part for the whole, the one for the many. A term
in Spanish, "Usamericano," offers a good solution because it more accurately
captures the specificity of an inhabitant of the United States. My alternatives
in English come closest to it. Secondly, the terms *Latino* and *Latina* (also *Chicano* and *Chicana*) are of Spanish-origin, gender-specific, locked in a gender
binary, as are "she" and "he" in the English language. They are all noninclusive
of the trans binary realities that permeate our lives today. Some have proposed Latin@, Latinus, and Latinx as more inclusive terms, but while these
terms are useful in moving beyond the gender binary, they can sometimes
appear as overly abstract when they designate real life people. Still, as I am
sensitive to the need to mark gender and transgender specificity and inclusive-
ness in language, I use the gender-neutral Latinx (pronounced "La-teen-ex")
or Chicanx when these terms describe objects, for example, "the Latinx population" or "Latinx narratives." When *Latino* or *Latina* are nouns, referring
to real life women and men who identify as such, I use Latinos/as, Latinas
and Latinos, and the feminine and masculine forms interchangeably, shifting
from one to the other to avoid always privileging the designation of the male
power structure. I am aware that all attempts to blur gender divisions and the
hierarchies they imply in our language use are limited and imperfect.

The book's cover shows three brown indigenous women. They represent for
me a multiplication of La Malinche, the Mayan pre-Columbian woman who
(history and legend tell us) translated between the Old and the New World,
making possible the communication between the two. The preeminent translator, she is a fitting figure of the subject matter of this book about translation,
languages, border crossings, bilingualism, and multilingualism. The women
are turning, as if in dialogue. Their "turning" signals the various turns of the
macro turn in my title. The first is the turn in the marketplace during the last
decade of the twentieth century and the aughts, by U.S. mainstream presses
to publish Latinx narratives in English; second, the turn by these presses to
translate English Latinx texts to Spanish, an unprecedented event; third, the
turn by these presses to publish these translations predominantly for a domestic audience, with some spillage into the transnational Spanish-language
market. The translation of Latinx narratives is an intra-national translation,
within the same nation-state; this fourth turn interrupts the direction taken
by most literary translation—from one national border to a different national border. This book also deals with a fifth turn, the twists and turns in the
translations themselves; for example, the erasure of their bilingualism, their
multilingualism, and the effects lost.

ACKNOWLEDGMENTS

My conversations with Stephanie Jed, my colleague from UCSD and good friend, have been invaluable to me for support and inspiration. Her suggestions have enriched my work. I thank Michael Davidson from UCSD for reading and believing in my work. I am grateful to Ana Celia Zentella for encouraging me to rethink some key concepts, and to Sandy Dijkstra for cheering me on as I worked to contact New York presses. I appreciate Nicolás Kanellos, Director of Arte Público, and his staff for answering my questions. My conversations with Antonia Meltzoff, always enjoyable, made me examine why I wanted to write this book. I also thank Frederick Aldama at Ohio State University for his enthusiasm about my project and my editor Josh Shanholtzer and Alex Wolfe, editorial and production director, at University of Pittsburgh Press for seeing it through the editing and publishing phases. I also thank the anonymous readers whose comments helped to improve the initial draft of the manuscript.

Paul Espinosa's undying love and support has kept me sane during anxious moments—he always believed that I would finish this book. I also thank

Marisa and Jaime, and especially Gabo, age six, and Paul, age four, for giving me joy and keeping me engaged in the routine of everyday life while working on this book.

Chapter 3 and Chapter 5 are extended and reworked versions of *Pocho en Español: The Anti-Pocho Pocho*, first published in *Translation Studies* (2011), and "'I May say Wetback but I Really Mean '*Mojado*': Migration and Translation in Ramón 'Tianguis' Pérez's *Diary of an Undocumented Immigrant*," first published in *Perspectives: Studies in Translatology* (2013). They are reprinted by permission of the publisher Taylor & Francis LTD. (www.tandfonline.com).

A TRANSLATIONAL TURN

SETTING THE STAGE

1979. Nuevo Laredo, a small Mexican city on the Mexican side of the Mexico–U.S. border. Ramón Pérez, a nineteen-year-old bilingual Zapotec Indian from Oaxaca, is waiting to cross into Texas. Before making his way hundreds of miles north to the border, Pérez had been a *guerrillero* in a peasant rebellion in the southern Mexican state of Oaxaca. He and his fellow *compañeros* had been fighting to defend their communal lands against encroachment by multinational agribusiness companies in the 1970s. Their leader, Florencio Medrano-Mederos, *el güero*, is assassinated in 1979. Pérez and his compañeros are arrested, tortured, and released from prison. Pérez cannot return to San Pablo de Macuiltianguis, his indigenous village, because his actions as a guerrillero have compromised its safety. His actions have made the village vulnerable to government attack. Desperate to leave Mexico, he contacts Dick Reavis, a white, bilingual, Anglo-American journalist and editor he had met earlier in the 1970s when *Texas Monthly* sent Reavis to cover the Zapotec rebellion. Pérez had been Reavis's guide through the treacherous mountains of Oaxaca. They became friends. By 1979, Reavis lives in Houston.

Waiting to cross, Pérez, with $100 in his billfold and $550 sewn into the lining of his jean jacket, misjudges. Thinking that no one will steal his clothes, he takes off his jacket, falls asleep, and is robbed. Later, he attempts the precarious crossing, but his group is caught by *la migra* (the U.S. border patrol). They interrogate everyone, confine them in cells for a day, and then return them to the Mexican side. Reavis has been a shadow presence thus far,[1] but now decides to become more involved in Pérez's journey. He crosses *la frontera*. He locates and pays a *patero* (literally a "duck-man") to ferry Pérez clandestinely across the north bank of the Rio Grande/Rio Bravo. He tells him where he will wait on the U.S. side. After a perilous river crossing, Pérez meets Reavis in a little-known spot near Laredo, Texas. They drive through this road until they arrive in Houston. Here, Pérez begins the life of an undocumented worker in the United States. His journey will take him to other areas of the Latinx Southwest over the next seven years. In 1986, aware of the impending passage of the most comprehensive immigration reform bill in several decades that might provide him legal status, Pérez ironically decides to return to Mexico.

When Pérez returns to Mexico after his seven-year sojourn in the United States, Reavis suggests he write his memoir. To encourage a novice writer, he offers to pay Pérez a dollar per page.[2] Pérez writes a draft manuscript that he calls "Diario de un mojado," and Reavis translates it to English, calling it *Diary of a Wetback*. Pérez "crosses" the border in several ways. First, he chooses to cross the river. Second, he "is crossed" by Reavis, in the sense that he could not have done it without Reavis's help; the latter travels to the border to direct his crossing. Then, a third way, Reavis translates his story. Few source texts and translations provide as tight a nexus between the author and the translator: the translator literally crosses his subject across national borders and discursively when he translates his subject's work. The translator orchestrates the author's actual crossing and several years later transfers him, metaphorically, between two sovereign countries.

Years after, Pérez in Mexico and Dick in the United States, conduct a transnational epistolary relationship, sending the manuscript back and forth, editing and improving it. Their task completed, Reavis, unable to convince Mexican houses to publish the Spanish original,[3] takes his draft-translation to Houston's Arte Público press that rewrites the title of the memoir and publishes it as *Diary of an Undocumented Immigrant* (1991), probably because a Latinx press would deem "wetback" an ethnic slur, which would be off-putting to its Latinx audience. Twelve years later, Pérez's manuscript is published by Arte Público using the original title, *Diario de un mojado* (2003).[4] Pérez's title (and book) runs a full circuit of translation: from Pérez's *mojado* to Reavis's "wetback" (Spanish to English), then to the press's rewriting of "wetback" to "undocumented immigrant" (English to English), and finally a full return from "undocumented immigrant" to its original mojado in Spanish (English to Spanish).

Pérez told me this story, the same story he narrated in *Diario/Diary*, when I visited him in Jalapa, Vera Cruz in 2011, where he has made his home. His story provides a context situation for this book. His story is a metaphor of inextricable connections between migration and translation, translator and translation, Spanish and English languages, and source and translated texts. These thematic pairs are the major sets of parameters that guide the text-centered analyses around three imaginative narratives and their translations classified under the wide and porous net of U.S. Latinx literature. The literary narratives are the Chicano novel *Pocho* ([1959] 1970, 1984) by José Antonio Villarreal and the mainland Puerto Rican memoir *When I Was Puerto Rican* (1993) by Esmeralda Santiago, and, of course, the Mexican-Latinx *Diario de un mojado* (2003). The corresponding translations are *Pocho en Español* (1994) by the Chicano Roberto Cantú, *Cuando era puertorriqueña* (1993) by the author, Santiago, herself, and *Diary of an Undocumented Immigrant*.[5] The first two textual pairs, *Pocho/Pocho en español* and *When I was Puerto Rican/Cuando era* are from English to Spanish; the third, *Diario* and *Diary* is from Spanish to English. However, the latter follows the same pattern of the first two texts (from English to Spanish) in that the publication of the translation precedes that of the original. These texts offer examples of both Spanish-to-English and English-to-Spanish translations because it is important to recognize a bidirectional movement in the translation of Latinx literature. The translation of Latinx narratives had been primarily a one-way street (Spanish to English), but in the 1990s, the translation of Latinx narratives became a two-way street (English to Spanish).

The central questions of this book are the following: What does it mean for the New York multinational mainstream presses to translate English-language Latinx texts to Spanish within the same nation-state? What happens to the bidirectional, multilingual features of Latinx narratives when they are translated to Spanish? When mainstream presses take on the translation of Latinx narratives already in English (as Random House, HarperCollins, and other publishing houses did in the 1990s) they take on products emerging from Latinx communities that have a history of colonization, conquest, and annexation. Notably, they translate the products of acculturated populations into the language suppressed, "forgotten," in the colonization. So, what happens when these multilingual texts from historically marginalized cultures are commissioned for translation into Spanish? Likewise, does the translation to English of narratives into Spanish keep the two languages separate? Or does some slippage of the original linguistic features manifest itself in the translation text? What happens when a narrative, written in Spanish, in a country where it is the primary language, enters a national space where Spanish is a minor language and undergoes translation to English? As translation changes the status of the texts, does the translation retain the untranslatable words and expressions and other multilingual variants explicit or submerged in the original texts? Or does it flatten these marks of difference, and linguistically make the texts captive to the cultural matrices of standard Spanish or English, depending on which direction the translation goes? Does it matter if works are translated inside the same nation-state for domestic audiences, or across national borders for "foreign" readers?

Whether coming from outside or inside the nation-space, Spanish-to-English literary translation (not English-to-Spanish) is the more commonplace occurrence when these two languages are in play. I borrow the aphorism "dog-bites-man" from journalism to denote the ordinary occurrence of Spanish-to-English translation. The "dog-bites-man" angle represents the direction we expect language transference to take in multilingual countries where English is the dominant language, such as the United States. Such translation of Latin American narratives has occurred since the nineteenth (Allen, "Will to Translate" 83; Lomas, "Thinking-Across," 13)[6] and early twentieth century by New York publishers for a domestic market. Notable examples of the late twentieth century are the 1960s and 1970s watershed translations of Latin American "boom" narratives.

Spanish-to English translations of Latinx literary texts first began in the 1970s—not by mainstream presses but by alternative Latinx presses. Tomás Rivera's . . . *y no se lo tragó la tierra* (*And the Earth Did Not Swallow Him*), the first Chicano novel translated to English, was published in a bilingual format edition in 1971, republished by Arte Público in 1987 with a new translation by Evangelina Vigil Piñón, in print to this day. Rolando Hinojosa Smith's Spanish language *Klail City y sus alrededores*, winner of Cuba's prestigious Premio Casa de las Américas in 1976, was initially published in Cuba and translated in a bilingual edition as *Generaciones y semblanzas* in 1977, translated by Rosaura Sánchez. It was republished as *Klail City* (*Klail City y sus alrededores*) by Arte Público Press in 2014.[7] Both first editions are Spanish on the left-side page and English on the right-side page. If it is true that the Western eye goes to the right-side page, making this side primary, then the publishers of these first editions must have wanted to emphasize the translated tongue, suggesting that the bilingual edition was primarily for the English-dominant reader. The later editions of Rivera's novel are sequential Spanish-English presentations; the 2014 *Klail City* edition, alternatively, is a sequential English-Spanish format.

English-to-Spanish translation is the new contrarian translation, the "man-bites-dog" angle of this book. The reversal of the aphorism denotes an unusual occurrence: English-to-Spanish translation goes contrary to expectations, given the long tradition of Spanish-to-English translation by mainstream U.S. publishers. These translations are transnational, even counternational because they overturn the linkage between the English language and the United States. When the source narratives, ironically, cross over into the English-language mainstream, they are translated to Spanish by the major commercial presses (like Random House and HarperCollins) that initiated this translation, mainly (but not exclusively) for a U.S. market. The translations are especially unexpected because authors of Latinx literature come from marginalized communities that have been pressured, historically, to adopt English as a sign of their assimilation. Such endeavors have yielded a bumper crop of reverse crossover translations from 1990 to 2010. I discuss this "new" and contrary-to-expectations phenomenon in chapter 2.

All three texts dramatize acts of migration, either by the protagonist or the protagonist's immediate family members. The migration routes imply deep changes in the writer's/protagonist's ancestral roots. One deeply important area of change is language. All three writers are "language migrants" (Besemeres 10) either because they did the migrating themselves, for example Santiago and Pérez, or because they were brought up to speak their migrating parents' language at home and then drawn into English through schooling, for example Villarreal (Yildiz calls the latter "postmigrants"; Yildiz 170). They are all bilingual and their literary language is not their mother tongue. Villarreal and Santiago are U.S. American writers from working-class backgrounds whose first language was Spanish.[8] Pérez is a Zapotec Indian Mexican whose mother tongue is Zapotec but is literate in Mexican Spanish. All three come from ethnic groups in the United States and Mexico that have been dispossessed of their mother tongue in confrontation with a dominant national language.

Acts of translation are generally thought of as acts of crossing over from one nation-state, culture, and language to a different nation-state, culture, and language; acts of migration are encounters with the "foreign," as are acts of translating literary texts because they involve the interaction of different languages and cultures. The social processes of migration and translation can result in the assimilation of "foreign" persons and texts to make them fit the cultural norms of what is designated "native" (say, English), or they can result in allowing nonnative persons and texts to maintain traces of their "foreign" selves (say, non-English). Put another way: a translator can bring the source text closer to the reader or she can bring the reader closer to the source text.

My preference is the latter. My interest is to uncover the contradictory moments in which the "foreign" elements of these writers' texts cross over into a reader's experience in both directions, from Spanish to English and English to Spanish.

I bring to the fore the tensions and contradictions posed when U.S. Latinx narratives are translated from English to Spanish and Spanish to English. I discuss both source and translation texts as interdependent coequals, as opposed to the historical hierarchical relationship between the author and original text as the prime generators of meaning, and the translator and the translation text as imitators and imitative, producing a derivative product. Especially in the Anglo-American tradition, the author is the originator of meaning, the primary mover, the creator of the original text; the translator and translation text are secondary, subordinate to the author and the original text. The author and his work are "authentic"; the translator and his work are copies. They merely transmit, supposedly, a meaning already present before their existence. Seen as such, translation is perceived as a second-rate activity. Robert Wechsler in *Performing Without a Stage*, laments that derivativeness has defined the translator's work (7). The translator, he says, is a "performer without a stage" (7). Actors are praised (or condemned) for embodying a role in a play, a dancer for interpreting a choreographer's composition, a pianist for interpreting a musical score, a singer for interpreting a songwriter's piece. Translators are not, who also interpret and perform a written composition. An actor, a dancer, a pianist, or a singer must operate in different mediums than the playwright, the choreographer, the musical composer, or the songwriter, a reality that contributes to establishing the independence of their medium; but the translator's work takes the same form of the author's—it is also writing. This is one reason why it is underappreciated, a translator translating is "nothing but ink on a page" (7). This hierarchical relationship also has masculine–feminine implications. Lori Chamberlain does an excellent critique of the masculinist tradition in theories of translation in "Gender and the Metaphorics of Translation." She uncovers the metaphors of gender bias and their implications that maintain the hierarchical relationship of the author as originator (masculine) and the translator as a secondary and derivative force (feminine) in translation theory since the seventeenth century.

I read original and translation texts in tandem not to insist upon the old adage that a translation is no substitute for the original. Rather, I do it to show that a translation is only a translation in relation to a source text, or in some cases, in relation to its other translations.[9] Except in classroom settings on translation, source and target texts usually are not read together, but translation raises important issues about language difference and language transference that can only be confronted if both the original and translated texts are side by side. Consider that both translations of *Pocho* and *When I Was* had a prior text to consult, but *Diary of an Undocumented Immigrant* stood alone in the book marketplace for twelve years before *Diario* was published. This text thus went from Spanish to English in terms of translation, and then from English to Spanish in terms of publication. Chapter 5 demonstrates the prime moment of cultural and linguistic complexity enacted in this text that was delayed because there was no antecedent to the translation available until twelve years later.

STRUCTURING TERMS

The original versions of many Latinx narratives with English as a linguistic base, in the case of the first two texts, contain overtly bilingual and multilingual features. The terms bilingual and multilingual are important, and I use them throughout the book. In the twentieth century, the term "bilingual" has been linked inextricably with Spanish and English languages with mainland Puerto Ricans and in the context of U.S. immigration specifically with Mexican Americans, the two largest subgroups of the U.S. Latinx population. Historically, the term described East Coast German immigrant communities responsible for establishing the country's first bilingual schools. (Mexicans are sometimes referred to as the "new Germans"). More often, "bilingual" is thought of as limited to two languages, but some scholars of language consider "bilingual" as the broader category that subsumes "multilingual." Despite its prefix, "multilingual" is commonly used when two linguistic phenomena are in play (Clyne 301).[10] The meaning and usages of the terms overlap, but I emphasize multilingual because Spanish is not the only "other" language spoken in this country (bilinguals speaking other languages exist here and elsewhere in the world). I situate Spanish speakers within the multilingual history of the United States and a global world.

I also stress multilingualism to differentiate it from multiculturalism. The term "multilingual" more powerfully than "multicultural" puts the stress on language: if one is "multilingual," one is necessarily "multicultural," whereas the reverse is not necessarily so. Though the two are inextricably bound, cultural diversity stresses racial diversity and its relation to power, instead of language diversity which is also embedded in relations of power, given that different languages are assigned different amounts of power in specific situations. Shell, in "Babel," observes that America falters "always between its horror of race slavery and the ideal of race blindness and prefers to emphasize racial difference instead of language difference" (Shell 119). The homegrown movement of multiculturalism of the 1980s paid little attention to multilingualism, and the interest in transnationalism of the 1990s on through the twenty-first century, also failed to implement a national awareness or support for linguistic diversity. In their introduction to the *Multilingual Anthology of American Literature*, Shell and Sollors call language a "blind spot" of the modern multicultural age of the 1980s, because languages are seldom factored into the multicultural equation (4). In the context of globalization, categories such as "transnational," "transethnic," "multiethnic," "multinational," and "multicultural" are abundantly attended to; but "translingual," "multilingual," or "interlingual" remain largely untapped domains. It is ironic that the interest in the "other" implied by both multiculturalism and transnationalism (albeit in different ways and for different reasons) fails to promote the interest and support for the study of languages spoken by those "others," either at levels of social practice (the everyday ability to communicate in a language) or academic scholarship (language study).

Epithets like "bilingual," "bilingual education," and "bilingual population" in the United States and elsewhere are most often attached to speakers of ethnic minority groups, frequently to those who mix two languages. This is one reason why, as Joshua Fishman asserts, bilingualism is traditionally thought of as a negative condition, "a stumbling block" to the modern image of progress, peace, and posterity (42). Seldom are the social attitudes and references to bilingualism positive. Though multilingualism is an everyday practice in the United States and elsewhere in the world, Aneta Pavlenko tells us in *Emotions and Multilingualism* that in "traditionally monolingual communities, bilinguals are often viewed with suspicion. . . in conflict with themselves, or as individuals whose shifting linguistic allegiances imply shifting political allegiances and moral commitments." (esp. 23–24). In an article titled "We have Room but for One Language Here," she states that the fiction of English monolingualism remains the symbol of Americanness in the narrative of U.S. national identity (164). Lei Wei, in "Dimensions of Bilingualism," explains that the dominant belief about bilinguals among educators and even linguists up until the 1960s, was that they were insufficiently competent in either language, presumably lacking in both ("semilingual"), or one language interfering with the ability to learn the other (19–21). Though these attitudes are still with us, he finds evidence of change in favor of bilingualism, as U.S. society perceives and recognizes that it can increase a person's employability and social mobility (Wei 18–24).

I develop three paradigms of translation for the three texts I discuss in the book: *international*, *transnational*, and *transborder* translation. International translation, the normative type of translation, occurs between different nation-states with different national languages and cultures, move from one national language of one nation-state to a different national language of a different nation-state. Usually, they are done with monolingual readerships in mind. A German or Japanese novel translated into English in the United States or Britain is an example. I develop my next two categories against this normative type of translation. Transnational translation presumes a source text that is multilingual, involving the copresence of two or more languages. These translations are done within the same nation-state that the original text is written, published, and read; but they also move into global spaces, sometimes commissioned and published by "foreign" presses, especially when the translating language is a global language, such as Spanish or French. The translations of *Pocho* and *When I Was* are transnational translations. The translation of *Diario* is a transborder translation: it falls in-between these two kinds of translations. While the writing of the source text is fully on the Mexican side of the border, the publication, translation, and audience of both source and translated texts are in the United States.

Pocho and *When I Was* offer examples of external multilingualism, or the movement between two different languages within the same text, and internal multilingualism, varieties within English or Spanish (Walkowitz 41). They are openly bidirectional, multilingual narratives. Yet they are translated into a standardized Spanish that suppresses the terms of its dialects. For example, *Pocho en Español* contains regionalisms of northern Mexico, but it is still translated into highly literate Spanish. The translations replace instead of supplement the dimensions of external and internal multilingualism. *Diario/Diary*, my third pair of source translation texts, from which I take my opening anecdote, reverses this process because the translation language (English in this case) reveals the simultaneity of two different languages. More specifically, the central term (*mojado*) of the source text interrupts the monolingual flow of the core scene in the translation text. My readings of the translation texts expose the potential of multilingualism that connects the source and target-language texts.

One premise of this book is that no language is strictly speaking unilingual—all languages are mixed; they have "high" and popular registers: vernacular speech, dialects, idioms, slang, borrowed words from other languages. It is highly important to keep in mind, therefore, that English-to-Spanish and Spanish-to-English translation is not about just going from one discreet language into another discreet language (from language A to language B, so to speak) as though languages were singular flat planes, stable blocks or objects, or isolated units that do not mix or touch each other. As one scholar put it, languages are talked about as if they were apples and oranges (Sakai 73). Talking about languages this way may be unavoidable, but the downside of such a perspective is to obscure from view the linguistic complexity and variety of any one language. What is even more at stake is the complexity and variety when two languages are involved in the translation of a literary text in two languages.

For example, if we think of translation as a substitution of one national language for another, or as a cultural technology that establishes communication between two apparently monolingual entities that, at the same time, allow the textual entities to maintain their monolingualism on either side of the translational divide (Bandia 424),[11] then *Diario/Diary* would be most likely refracted through monolingual frames of a Spanish "original" and an English translation. We would be reading it through a lens of translation, and *Diary* subsequently would be a monolingual conversion of *Diario*. On the other hand, if we read attentively and realize that the translator himself is capturing the author's Mexican mojado (the "wet one," because he crossed the river) and the translator's U.S. English slang "wetback" in a simultaneous presence, then we are in the realm of multilingualism (Grutman, "Multilingualism" 182). The English translation text surpasses the limits of translation and moves into multilingualism: the simultaneous presence of two languages within the same text.

In all respects, I visualize the two languages, English and Spanish, not as demarcated entities closed off from one another, but as discontinuous and shifting phenomena that lead to language contact, intersections, and mixing. Languages are social, not general abstract things; they are specific, spoken by specific communities in contact with other specific communities; they vary according to how people who speak them vary.

THE LITERARY TEXTS AND THEIR TROPES: POCHO, JÍBARO, AND MOJADO

My three narratives are inaugural texts. *Pocho* and *When I Was Puerto Rican* are "firsts," for different reasons, in their respective literary communities (i.e., the two Spanish-language origin communities, Chicanx and Puerto Rican, with the longest histories in the United States). *Pocho* was the first Chicanx novel written in English of the modern period, published in the pre-Chicanx movement years by Anchor Doubleday in 1959. It is the first, and perhaps the only one since that time, to make the pocho a foundational figure of Chicanx literature. The novel has remained viable, steadily appearing on syllabi of Chicanx literature courses, Chicanx studies, and Latinx studies since its second printing in 1970, when the world had prepared for it a fit audience—an active readership during the university campus militant years. It was then that Chicanos/as demanded to read relevant material from their specific histories.

Pocho is a multilingual text not because Villarreal offers words or phrases in Spanish immediately followed by their English counterparts (say in the typical way of one-on-one translation in bilingual texts), nor does he use intrasentential code-mixing, the alternation of Spanish and English at the word, phrase, clause, or sentence level. It is a dual language text because he chooses to appropriate the English language and varieties of vernacular Spanish to produce what Frances Aparicio called "sub-versive" narrative texts (795): texts with "undercover" meanings that reveal an author's bilingual and bicultural sensibilities by encoding references to lived realities beneath English, for example, deliberately filling Spanish syntax with English words, making their awkwardness apparent even to English readers. These are also examples of borrowing, "where the English element is [willfully] incorporated into the Spanish system" (Valdés 125). Such a bilingual technique joins two different languages, what Stavans calls "verbal promiscuity," a linguistic form "that refuses to accept anything as foreign" ("Introduction" 9, 15), showing us just how interdependent and interactive, in partnership or in conflict, the two languages and cultures are. In this sense, *Pocho* is important as a precursor to the advanced bilingual techniques, for example the variations of intrasentential code-mixing that emerged as a self-conscious literary style in the 1960s and 1970s, when the Chicano poet Alurista (1947), the dramatist Luis Valdez (1940), and the Puerto Rican poets Miguel Algarín (1941) and Miguel Pinero (1946–1988) began to write poetry in formats of vernacular Spanish and English.

In contrast to Villarreal's *Pocho*, Santiago's narrative (1993) is not a chronological first in the modern history of mainland Puerto Rican literary narratives. *Down These Mean Streets, Nilda* by Nicolasa Mohr, and *Family Installments* by Edward Rivera were all published years ahead of *When I Was*, in 1967, 1973, and 1982, respectively. It is the first, however, by a Puerto Rican woman—who was born on the island and came of age on the mainland—to take the identity of the island's jíbaro and twist this figure's gender and geographical location to make it central to the formation of her female literary identity: a *jíbara norteamericana*. While Piri Thomas in *Down These Mean Streets* exposed racially-charged linguistic terms (*moyeto, blanco, negro, moreno, trigueño*) commonly used by young Puerto Rican men of his time in a New York urban context to refer to African and Anglo Americans, Santiago is the first to take the marginalized figure of island rurality and transpose it to an urban Puerto Rican mainland literary narrative. Similarly, to pochos or pochas, jíbaros and jíbaras were a source of shame to middle-class, educated, island Puerto Ricans, an attitude internalized by working-class Puerto Ricans and jíbaros/as themselves, because they were judged to speak Spanish badly ("bad speech"). Such pejorative attitudes are not unknown today among those who judge bilingual English-Spanish speakers to speak Spanish "badly" because they mix Spanish with English and vice versa. The linguistic judgment often goes together with class-based, racial, ethnic, and gender stereotypes of *puertorriqueños/as* and Chicanos/as. *When I Was* offers various linguascapes of multilingualism, for example, translations of dialectal speech and transliteration.

Diario, the third text, is a "first" in that it presents a case of a Zapotec Indian and Spanish-speaking Mexican male, the author himself, who flees Mexico in the late 1970s for political reasons. He leaves behind his Zapotec Indian communal identity and his identity as a Zapotec guerrillero and becomes the Mexican mojado/"wetback." It is this marginalized identity that Pérez makes the primary trope of his book. *Diario* is the first text in the history of Spanish-to-English translation done by Latinx presses to describe the mojado experience in a sustained way through the eyes of a literate, Spanish-writing Zapotec Mexican.[12] Together with its translation text, it brings into relief a transborder nexus of translation and migration. The two acts are inseparably linked, at both literal and metaphoric levels.

These texts present three hybridized cultural figures of marginalization—Villarreal's pocho; Santiago's jíbaro or jíbara, and Pérez's mojado[13]—central to the histories of migration of Chicanos/as, Mexicans, and Puerto Ricans. These ciphers carry emotionally-charged connotations given the strong histories of racialization in the respective national contexts of these groups (the United States, Puerto Rico, and Mexico). They have been used pejoratively, but the recipients of the verbal sting have turned them and given them a liberating force. They turned the stigma of difference into the prestige of distinction. Like other idiomatic terms (pocho, mojado, and jíbaro/a), they are born "untranslatable" (Yildiz 31), yet, as Barbara Cassin explains in her introduction to *Dictionary of Untranslatables*, untranslatables are "expressions . . . syntactical or grammatical turns one keeps on (not) translating" (xvii). In other words, untranslatables are paradoxes: one has no choice but to translate them even though they impede translation, no choice but to make them intelligible though impossible to capture the full extent of their meaning in the native culture. In chapters 3, 4, and 5, I tell the story of these terms: their etymologies, their histories of usage, and their respective meanings.

Briefly, the pocho or pocha is specific to Chicano-Mexican cultural histories. It incorporates ethnicity and social class, but above all it indexes linguistic behavior: it refers to someone who mixes English and Spanish or simply someone judged to speak Spanish "brokenly." As a rule, the person to whom the term is attributed (and sometimes will assume self-consciously) grows up in the southwestern United States. The term points to an individual who is the *result of generational migration*. The term jíbaro is a Puerto Rican identification, more generally Caribbean: the "white" peasant who lived and worked in the Puerto Rican highlands as opposed to the slave population that inhabited the coastal areas. Mojado is a term of clandestine migration, for whoever crosses from Mexico into U.S. territory without legal authorization and for whom the material reality of the identity is created *at the moment of crossing* water, specifically the Rio Bravo/Rio Grande, though it also through the years has come to be used more generally to include those who cross by land or more seldom by plane. Unlike pocho and mojado, the jíbaro (mostly male) became a national icon, after World War II for a specific group of island Puerto Rican intellectuals and nationalists. Coded as connected to the Spanish colonial past, it represents the national soul, primordial, and preindustrial Puerto Rico.

CHAPTER OUTLINE

Chapter 1 introduces the "new" translation of English texts to Spanish in the context of the development of the U.S. Spanish-language market in the last two decades of the twentieth century. Initially published in the English-language mainstream, *Pocho* and *When I Was*, along with many other texts in the 1990s by Latino men and women, did a reverse crossover, by which I mean from the English-language mainstream into Spanish translation. Other narratives, including Arte Público Press's best-seller *The House on Mango Street*, had been published first in English by Latinx presses, subsequently taken up and republished by mainstream presses, and then translated to Spanish. While there can be no absolute differentiation in a global world between inside (national) and outside (foreign), I argue that the mainstream presses involved in the translation of Latinx narratives envision, primarily, a domestic consumer market for their products. I explain *who* commissioned the translations, *why*, and *for whom* and why I think this direction in translation is a contrarian one—indeed unprecedented—in the context of a country that represents itself and is represented as a monolingual nation. The reverse crossover narratives (*Pocho* and *When I Was*) and the publication of the English translation *Diary* prior to the Spanish original *Diario* fit the three paradigms of translation: international, transnational, and transborder translations. I restate briefly. International translations cross national borders and involve different national languages and cultures; they aim to address monolingual audiences. Transnational translations occur within nations with multilingual histories and traditions and, at the same time, are connected to global markets that tend to "flatten" languages into monolingual unities. Transborder translations are neither fully international nor transnational—they are published for audiences inside a country other than their own national audience or country. Lastly, I offer one example of the loss of a multilingual effect from Junot Diaz's *Drown* in the translation *Negocios.*

To underscore the importance of Spanish today in the United States, made up of many variants of Spanish spoken by the different Latinx communities (Mexican-American, Puerto Rican, Cuban, Dominican, Central American), I highlight in chapter 2 the unique features of Spanish that, since the 1980s, have given it a "new" status: for example, the depth of its historical roots; its perennial subordinate position to English; and its size, scope, and concentration. To emphasize this new status, I compare the status of Spanish during the Latin American literary boom that occurred within the nation-state model of the 1960s and 1970s, and the many-faceted Latinx boom (beyond literature) that occurred in the era of the transnationalism of the 1990s. I discuss the new communications technologies that have made Spanish a global language and the second national language of the United States. These conditions undermine its past definition as a foreign language. Market economic forces in a U.S. national space, at once connected to broader global processes, drove large New York publishing houses (and smaller publishers too, but on a lesser scale) to conduct contrary-like translation. Concurrently, U.S. ideological nativist forces continued to lobby for the ideal of a monolingual nation and the elimination of the presumed dangers posed to it by the "little" languages (other than English) of ethnolinguistic groups, the "wild little people" (Fishman 45), or linguistic minorities, who need bilingual services.

The centerpieces of the book are chapters 3, 4, and 5. In them I offer a way to read these texts that reveals the multilingual forms flattened by translation practices that prioritize rendering texts into the standard format of national languages. I think it important that we see and retain these multilingual forms. I favor an approach that makes readers aware of the translator and the translation itself. The translator makes a rhetorical turn that jars the predominant language choice and style of the rest of the text and that I interpret as a move that makes him or her visible. It is a translator's inadvert slip that causes a disfiguration in the text, and these are precisely the moments of rupture that I look for in these texts. The translator lays her or himself bare and we recognize a mutual agency of the author and translator functions. The goal is not to arrange everything into a bicameral relationship of author-creator and translator-imitator, English and Spanish, domestic and foreign. I want to locate traces of the translator's voice in the author's voice and vice a versa, traces of the foreign in the familiar. I want to privilege moments of linguistic diversity. These disfigurations may be awkward and some readers might take them as signs of failure upon encountering them. But they are failures only if we assume that fluency is the main value, only if we assume the translation should sound like the original, without "betraying" itself as a translation. To my mind, they are successes—productive failures—because they interrupt the impression of language as a coherent whole.

In the chapters that follow, I capture the interlocking pressures between the source and translated texts. The title of the first translation—*Pocho en Español*—epitomizes the central issue I take up in chapter 3. How is one to translate the source text when half of the translation title *en Español* signals a standardized formal Spanish? How should one translate a novel, whose central character is the pocho, into the language of the oppressive culture, because the pocho or pocha do not speak Spanish "properly" according to the ideal norms of Spanish, or, worse, mixing the two languages in forms of Spanglish, "el hablar mocho de los pochos" (chopped-up Mexican American speech) (Zentella, "Bilinguals and Borders" 15). The rhyme *mocho* and pocho in this formulaic utterance highlights the common denominator of the two terms: to be in a state of having been cut. One common colloquial usage of mocho is *te dejaron mocho* (they cut off too much hair) when commenting on someone's haircut for example. Likewise, *pocho/a* imply a state of being cut off from the center of gravity: the Mexican nation, its culture and language, implying a tinge of betrayal. The title signals a ready-made trap. Translator Cantú attributes to the character of the pocho a grammatically correct Spanish that he/she never spoke in the first place. Gone is the literal translation Villarreal uses in the novel's narration and dialogue to enact linguistic mixing, and no counterpart or analogous language appears in its stead. While Villarreal wrote *Pocho* in minimalist English prose—simple, straight-forward, unadorned—Cantú adopts a standard variety of prestige Spanish—excess, abundance, efflorescence. My reading exposes the contradiction of taking the pocho out of the pocho and finds a disfigurement in the text that goes against the elevated language that pervades the translation.

My reading of Santiago's source-translation pair—the focus of chapter 4—grapples with the question of how Santiago had to remember, to *unforget* the *forgetting*, the language she inherited at birth (Spanish). The process was not smooth or easy. It required her to create multilayered voices in her "English I" and "Spanish I," at levels of plot and rhetorical strategies. In the original, she uses external multilingualism (a movement between English and Spanish) to translate local idioms to her monolingual mainland audiences; in the English and Spanish texts, she employs internal multilingualism (varieties within one language) to produce transliterative effects to stress the idea that she is heard differently by different audiences. But the most intriguing tension occurs in *Cuando era* between standard Spanish and Spanglish, or what she calls *es-*

panglés in her introduction to this text where she admits that she mistook the standard Spanish expected of her by the Spanish publishing world—the press, her editors, and some in her audience—for Spanglish. She confesses, "el idioma que ahora hablo, el cual *yo pensaba que era el español*, es realmente el espanglés" (The language I speak now, the *one I thought was* Spanish, is really Spanglish [my emphasis, xvi]). In the translation, her jíbara self, the dialect she spoke and heard on the island in her childhood before the migration, and the code-switching she used as a teenager on the New York mainland after the migration, surface, become visible. In other words, the translation text brings to the foreground the forms of multilingualism erased in the source text. Translation becomes a site of potentiality, and not just a derivative copy of the original. Ironically, the translation becomes an agent of creativity complementing the source text that preceded it. This turnaround resists the usual hierarchy that attributes the creative power to the original and the derivative quality to the translation.

The source and target language texts of chapter 5, *Diario/Diary*, offer a different scenario of interdependent tensions between original and translation texts. For one thing, unlike the first two texts that enjoy a solid geographical place, published and translated within the same nation-state, *Diario* exists in a space-in-between two nation-states. Its cultural and literary roots are not located permanently in a single territorial or national space, though they lie more on one side than the other. Then, too, the pair is different in that *Diary* (1991), the translation, premiered in the United States twelve years before the Spanish original *Diario* was published in the United States in 2003. If readership rather than time of publication decides which text is the "original," the translation is the original because it was read before the source text. This upset the conventional "order of things," though differently than the previous text-pairing, the usual hierarchy that gives the original prime status over the translated text, usually published subsequently. What is most significant, however, about the relationship of this third pair of texts is that they reconfigure a transborder-transnational discursive field that is rooted in a nexus of migration and translation. Pérez "washes" his bilingual identity when his translator takes the responsibility of literally translocating him across the waters of the Rio Grande. Pérez is a translated man. Reavis reinterprets Pérez's mojado identity, one that comes from a long line of migrating men from his Zapotec community ("Somos un pueblo de mojados" [we are a village of wetbacks]), turning him into the Anglo, racialized "wetback." But the target text creates its own multilingual textual space, no longer translation or the substitution of one national language for another, but multilingualism or the contiguity of two terms in a simultaneous presence.

This book joins three areas of scholarly research that came together with the English-Spanish and Spanish-English translation of narratives by Latinas and Latinos during an almost twenty-year span (1990–2010) in the United States. This is the first study to put the three fields of inquiry—language and literary studies, Latinx studies, and translation studies—into conversation. Languages are the medium of literary expression, the raw material of literary studies and studies on translation, yet language systems often are passed over in silence and separated from the teaching and learning of literature in literary studies. Similarly, English and Spanish language systems receive thin and scattered attention in Latinx studies.[14] Likewise, the convergence of English and Spanish in Latinx contexts is seldom an object of serious inquiry in studies on translation. Scholars of Latinx studies fail to establish contact with those in translation studies and vice versa. Linking these disciplines is important to understanding the role language plays in promoting equality and dialogue between different language communities of people who live and have lived in the United States and the global world.

When commercial mainstream presses initiated the translation of a substantial number of Latinx narratives in English (with overtly bidirectional, multilingual features) to Spanish, they redirected and widened the long-standing, one-way street of Spanish-to-English translation into a bidirectional translational activity. This bidirectional activity underscores the need to fill the perceived vacuum in literary, Latinx, and translation studies. Latinx studies and translation studies have common developments and interests—each is a mainstream university subject; each is an interdisciplinary and independent discipline; each has expanded and diversified its methods and approaches since their institutional origins. While translation studies emerged unto the world stage in the 1970s, Latinx studies did so a bit later; and both came into their own in the 1990s. The subject of code shifting or language alternation (methods, functions, meaning) is well known in Latinx studies; contrastively, bilingualism and multilingualism in non-Latinx language contact situations has been an important focus of translation studies. While the first avoids the relationship of language contact to translation, even though code-mixing and code shifting as it operates in Latinx literature at times is translation, the second, given its interest in multiple languages, has almost no research on translation in a Latinx context. Latinx literature and translation are, generally, discussed independently of each other. Translation seems to belong to translation studies, except for researchers who do not always define themselves working in translation studies but have made important contributions to the area.[15] Language contact in Latinx literature has been an absent area of study in translation studies. Why?

One reason for the separation in these research disciplines is that ordinary and literary bilingualism in Latinx culture is largely an intranational phenomenon in the United States while translation studies is oriented primarily to English and other source languages in a global context. Susan Bassnett called for a cultural "turn" in translation studies in the 1990s (123), that is, for a change in approaches to studying translation, but the turn—this is the second reason—included primarily those literatures traditionally studied by translation scholars. The cultural "turn" did not turn wide enough to encompass Latinx literature, and, conjointly, scholars of Chicanx-Latinx literature have kept the study of translation at arm's length. Yet, a third reason may be that Latinx literature has emerged as an English-dominant discipline in the academy, even though Spanish-speaking communities are at its base.

The 1990s, the decade of the cultural "turn" in translation studies, saw the establishment of a series of alliances among translation studies and postcolonial theory (Niranjana, Robinson [Review, *Translation and Empire*]), translation studies and gender studies (Chamberlain), and translation studies and power (Cheyfitz, Rafael, and Tymoczko). But as far as I know no study to date has emerged to bring together Latinx studies and translation studies. The emergence of the translation to Spanish in the 1990s by U.S. mainstream presses of English Latinx literary texts with multilingual features provides an opportunity to lay the groundwork for a dialogue between the two disciplines. I want to begin to break down boundaries between these disciplines.

In the world of transnational communications and global relations, the ability to read and speak different languages, to understand and appreciate translation's role, and to generate knowledge about practices of translation become more necessary and important. Historically, the Mexican-origin population has required services in translation and interpretation but even more so today among the most recent arrivals from the New World Spanish Americas, in educational, medical, civic, and legal social networks. In the academy, some literary and cultural studies scholars have had to confront translation in researching nineteenth- and early twentieth-century Chicanx and Latinx literature and history. Yet, notwithstanding, its institutionalization since the 1980s, Chicanx-Latinx literary and cultural studies scholars have not focused overtly and directly on translation or multilingualism as a central concern. Therefore, this book is about three imaginative narrative texts and their translations in a long list of intranational Latinx translations from English to Spanish (less long in Spanish to English translations but no less important). My book is an exploratory attempt to inject the subject of translation into Latinx Studies about this translational phenomenon. It lies squarely in the middle of current debates around language, bilingualism and multilingualism, race and immigration policies, and other issues of vital national and global import.

CHAPTER 1

REVERSE CROSSOVER LATINX NARRATIVES

English-to-Spanish Translations in a U.S. Market

At a certain moment, a moment that extends from the early 1990s to the first decade of the twenty-first century, something unusual happened in the historical evolution of Latinx literature. This unusual event is the translation of English-language Latinx narratives into Spanish by New York mainstream presses for audiences at home and abroad. The unusualness of this event is heightened by the fact that these same presses had not published this literature in *any* language prior to the 1990s—only small Latinx presses had published it. Now commercial presses were not only publishing it in the original English. These presses were also commissioning its translation into Spanish. One might argue that the publication of Latinx literature in Spanish is a logical outgrowth of a long standing historical record of publication in Spanish in the United States. However, the surprising element is *who* was doing it.

Commercial presses interrupted the long-standing historical record in Spanish-language publication.[1] This was truly a turning point, especially for literature instructors of my generation who moved into the academy after the civil rights struggle and took on an intellectual and political project to legitimate Latinx literature as worthy of study and publication (1965–1985)—no matter the language. It was a landmark moment for mainstream presses to publish this literature for the first time *in English*. What wonder, then, to see mainstream presses publish, almost simultaneously, translations into Spanish. Indeed, it was a strange reversal to see Latinx literature published in the language suppressed in the colonization of Mexican American and Puerto Rican Latinx groups, the language "forgotten" as one result of the colonial experience, prohibited over time by U.S. processes of linguistic assimilation and "English-only" legislations that began in the 1980s in California and continue in many states today!

In the late 1960s to the mid-1980s, small ethnic presses with tiny but committed staffs and limited budgets took the combined opportunity and risk to publish the majority of Mexican American and Puerto Rican mainland literature (both poetry and prose) in English and Spanish. They did not undertake Spanish translations of Latinx literary narratives at that time. It was not until the 1990s that they translated a modest number of their 1970s single Spanish-language texts to English. The two major small presses that survived the tempestuous Civil Rights era are the Bilingual Review of Tempe, Arizona and Arte Público of Houston, Texas. The Bilingual Review published Aristeo Brito's 1976 novel *El diablo en Texas* in a bilingual edition titled *The Devil in Texas (El diablo en Texas)* in 1990. It also published Miguel Méndez's 1974 *Peregrinos de Aztlán* as *Pilgrims in Aztlán* in 1992[2] and in 2002, it published a Spanish translation of Ron Arias's *The Road to Tamazunchale* ([1978] 1987) (*El camino de Tamazunchale*). Arte Público Press published translations of *Odisea del Norte* (1999) by Mario Bencastro (*Odyssey to the North* 1998) and the rediscovered narrative *Las aventuras de don Chipote, o, Cuando los pericos mamen* (1998) (*The Adventures of Don Chipote, or, When Parrots Breastfeed* 2000) by Daniel Venegas.[3] It published translations of Alejandro Morales's *The Brick People* (1988) (*Hombres de ladrillo* 2010) and Graciela Limon's *In Search of Bernabé* (1993) (*En busca de Bernabé* 1997). In 1991, they premiered the English translation *The Diary of an Undocumented Immigrant* of Ramón "Tianguis" Pérez's manuscript "Diario de un mojado," written in Mexico. Subsequently, twelve years later, they published the Spanish version in 2003. This book thus did a complete turnaround: translation from Spanish to English followed by publication from English to Spanish, all in the United States. As I explained in the previous chapter, this narrative represents the core themes of my book: the inextricable connections between migration and translation, Spanish and English, and source and translated texts. Pérez's narratives are the case study of chapter 5.

Set against the Spanish to English translation by newspaper and small publishing houses in the United States for more than a century, the English-to-Spanish translation and publication of literary narratives by mainstream presses in the 1990s is noteworthy for three reasons: because mainstream presses only began to publish this literary fiction *in English* in the 1990s—a belated event since the majority of Latinx authors had used English as the base language of their individual narratives since the mid-twentieth century; because mainstream presses up until the 1990s had no history of substantial publication in Spanish, much less translation into the language; and lastly, because the production of this literature's translation to Spanish originated in the United States, a country that is supposedly made up of a people who speak (or should speak) one and only one language that links them to one another in the imagined collectivity of "one nation" or "one culture."

Writing in 2002, María Carreira, a professor of Spanish at California State University, Long Beach, and an expert on heritage languages, noted that "[w]hile ten years ago there were sixty US companies publishing in Spanish, today there are approximately 600 such companies, including HarperCollins, Random House, and Lectorum" (Carreira 42).[4] What is notable about Carreira's statement is not only the increase in the number of companies publishing in Spanish in the United States from 1990 to 2010 but even more striking is *who* was doing it, *for whom*, and *why*? In this chapter, I turn to address these aspects: *who, for whom*, and *why* of the reverse crossover of Latinx narratives from English to Spanish. The reverse crossover of English to Spanish translations, a unique U.S. phenomenon, requires me to develop two "new" paradigms of translation in the context of Latinx narratives. I call these paradigms *transnational* and *transborder translations*. I develop them against the normalized paradigm of translation which I call *international translation*. International translation involves literary texts from the national language of one nation-state to a different national language of another nation-state. The "new" paradigms of translation involve literary narratives published and translated in the same nation-state but whose publishing details and potential readerships go beyond the nation-state. In publishing and translating these narratives, mainstream presses broke with their previous publication practices and, more importantly—if only temporarily—with the model of the "one country–one language" nation-state. They do not, however, necessarily lead to a recognition and respect for the multilingual aspects of Latinx narratives. They did not construct an audience of bilingual consumers. The paradigm of translation for Latinx narratives turned into unilingual Spanish translation, eviscerating the multilingual specificity of the narratives. This, I believe, is what is at stake—the abilities of presses, editors, markets, and translators to capture the multilingual features of texts in transnational, transborder translations. The future of translation of Latinx narratives is staked on the lessons we learn from these translations. I offer a full-bodied example of the loss of multilingual specificity in the last section of this chapter and develop its various mutations in chapters 3, 4, and 5.

WHO? FOR WHOM?

HarperCollins and Random House, two multinational publishing houses with a major presence in the First World and with no history of publishing Latinx literature in English prior to the 1990s, became full participants during the last decade of the twentieth century in publishing Mexican American and Puerto Rican mainland literature and the newest branches of Latinx narratives (Cuban, Dominican, and Central American). By then, the urtexts of Mexican American and Puerto Rican literatures in English, published during the 1970s and 1980s, mostly products of small press publication, a select few by mainstream presses, had gained canonical status. Examples are . . . *y no se lo tragó la tierra* (. . . *and the Earth did not Swallow Him*) by Tomás Rivera, *With His Pistol in His Hand* by Américo Paredes, *Pocho* by José Antonio Villarreal, *Bless Me, Ultima* by Rudy Anaya, *The House on Mango Street* by Sandra Cisneros, and *Down These Mean Streets* by Piri Thomas.[5] These presses not only took on publishing Latinx narratives in English but were at the vanguard of a publishing-translating project in Spanish, with stated commitments to its growth and sustainment. They developed their individual, national Spanish-language imprints: HarperCollins launched Rayo (Rayo means "flash" of lightning) in 2000 and Random House founded Vintage Español in 1994. These imprints remained energetically viable from the 1990s on through the first decade of the twenty-first century. However, since Spanish is both a national and a global language, U.S. presses established transnational alliances with national Spanish foreign presses to obtain the economic benefits of the global market. Rayo launched a joint venture with the Barcelona-based publishing giant Grupo Planeta in 2006 (Bardales 5); Vintage Español formed an alliance with Alfaguara, the literary imprint of Grupo Santillana of Spain and Latin America (Bearden, "Buenos días" 77+). In 2009, it reached an agreement with its Spanish partner company, Random House Mondadori, to copublish Spanish titles for an audience in the United States ("Vintage Español Enters . . ." 2009).[6] These alliances allowed them to participate in the global Spanish-language market, while carving a space in the domestic market at the same time for the circulation of English-language Latinx literature in translation. U.S. presses would now oversee translations into Spanish of Latinx narratives for the national market and reprint and distribute editions of literature from Spain and Latin America. "The books will be marketed and sold in the United States by HarperCollins" (Bardales 5).

In 2004, HarperCollins announced a significant expansion through the Rayo imprint of its publishing activity for the Latinx market. The word "Latino"[7] in the press-release title is indicative of an inside market: "HarperCollins Publishers Expands Rayo Publishing Program Offering Greater Range of Titles to *Latino* Market" (HarperCollins Publishers, emphasis added). The U.S.-born René Alegría, named publisher and editorial director of Rayo in 1999, said in the same press release: "With Rayo, we have been able to impact how Hispanics in America are perceived, both as a literary community and as a fully integrated portion within American society" ("HarperCollins Publishers . . ." 2004, 2). Assuming Alegría uses "America" to designate the United States, a common practice among U.S. Americans, and not the American hemisphere, which I believe "America" more accurately names, he is suggesting that presses are looking for Latinx ("Hispanic") Spanish-reading consumers *inside* the United States as a profitable target market. He also suggests he considers the Spanish language an asset for improving the perception of Latinos and Latinas in the United States and for their incorporation into its society. I inquired more specifically about the target market for the translations of Latinx narratives to Spanish in 2006. Raymond A. García, an associate publisher at HarperCollins Rayo with a background in marketing strategy, business development, and advertising, answered my question this way: "The market is the Spanish-dominant, 1st generation Hispanic book buying community. Today, US publishers' distribution and sales for books in Spanish, both original and translated fiction and nonfiction, have grown exponentially. For us, the demand is domestic" (email correspondence, July 26, 2006). In 2005, Carmen Ospina wrote in *Críticas* about Vintage Español's plans to expand its publishing activities to include reprints of Latin American originals and translations to Spanish of Latinx narratives. She designated its target audience inside the country. In "Random House Expands Spanish Line . . ." she stated: "The new Vintage Español line will be designed specifically with U.S. Latinos in mind" (Ospina 5).

In an email query about Latinx publications in Spanish, Johanna Castillo, vice president and executive editor at Atria Books, told me that Atria Español was created in 2005 to publish "original titles in Spanish for the U.S. Spanish market." Atria, she said, publishes eight to ten titles in Spanish a year. They "publish the Spanish edition of an original or a book in translation (English-to-Spanish) when there is either a demand from the readers" or "it makes sense for the U.S. Spanish marketplace" or "the topic is relevant for the U.S. Spanish reader." Castillo added that a book in Spanish translation, generally, "sells 30% to 50% of the English edition total sales."[8] One of Atria Books' Latinx titles was the well-received *Across 100 Mountains* (2006) by Reyna Grande and translated by Grande to Spanish one year later (*A través de cien montañas*);

a second title was Grande's memoir, *The Distance Between Us* (2012), translated as *La distancia entre nosotros* in 2013, also by Grande.

The business practices of large mainstream houses, like Random House and HarperCollins, broke with the one nation–one language model, shifting from listing no books in Spanish (except for children's literature in facing-page bilingual editions or short narrative verses in both languages on a single page, as in Dr. Seuss books) to owning a hefty, in-house, in-country list of literary acquisitions—both ebooks and print books—in Spanish. Listings included translations of memoirs by American celebrities, such as *Mi Vida* (My Life) (2005) by former President Bill Clinton and *La otra cara de América* by the bilingual-biliterate popular Univision television anchor Jorge Ramos, first published by Mexico's Grijalbo in 2000. The translation (*The Other Face of America*) was issued by HarperCollins Rayo in 2002 and reprinted by Random Mondadori 2004 for Spanish-language markets. Listings also included fiction originals in Spanish by canonical, bestselling Latin American authors, for example, Gabriel García Márquez's, *Memorias de mis putas tristes* (2004) and Isabel Allende's *La casa de los espíritus* (2001)—no translation necessary.[9] The break with the one nation–one language model made it difficult to establish a clear line between what originated outside (the global world) and what inside (the nation), since all products were in Spanish, both a global and a national language. For example, a Latin American boom foreign literary novel like *Cien años de soledad*, translated into *One Hundred Years of Solitude*—the international standard practice of translation of the one nation–one language model—was released in the 1990s directly *in Spanish*. Meanwhile, a native inside product like José Antonio Villarreal's classic Chicano novel *Pocho*, the subject of chapter 3, was translated *from English* and published in Spanish (*Pocho en Español*). Such doings apparently challenge the one nation–one language model because foreign texts, those from Latin America, were launched untranslated into the U.S. marketplace, as though they were native products; Latinx texts, the native products, in contrast, were translated and treated like foreign material.

In 2004, HarperCollins Rayo issued a statement in both English and Spanish on its website: "Rayo will publish books that embody the diversity within the Latinx community, in both English and Spanish-language editions, connecting culture with thought, and invigorating tradition with spirit" (Ospina, "HarperCollins To Expand").[10] The unmeasured abstraction "connecting culture with thought, and invigorating tradition with spirit" no doubt has linguistic capital for a particular economic market, but the key word here is "diversity," a feature of the Latinx population that makes it a challenging market to gauge and measure. Latinos and Latinas are vastly diverse linguistically in terms of competency levels, registers of Spanish spoken, and length of time in the United States. The competency range is far more complex than the bipolar frame of monolingual English and monolingual Spanish. The range includes English-dominant speakers, speakers of both English and Spanish with various levels of linguistic and cultural bilingualism, and low-income, Spanish-dominant speakers with often little education and experience in reading literate Spanish. It also includes different dialects and Spanish regionalisms (Mexican American or Chicanx, Puerto Rican, Cuban, Dominican, and Central American).

So, who is the target consumer audience of the "Spanish-language editions" the website refers to? Certainly, these readers will not be dominant-English speakers, nor will they be limited bilingual readers either. Although the latter may be the largest, most established, wealthiest, and most educated segment of the Latinx population, they still might be insufficient in reading Spanish. Neither would the readership be Spanish-dominant speakers from Spain and Latin America living in the United States, educated or not, with little cultural competency to understand the sociocultural and linguistic nuances of Latinx literature.

Logically, the most ideal audience is a bilingual-biliterate educated audience with an interest in buying and reading Latinx literature, in and out the United States, capable of reading literate Spanish. The sad reality is that the texts are not overtly translated for a bilingual-biliterate audience, since the main register of communication of these translations is monolingual Spanish. The hypertranslation of *Pocho*, (chapter 3) is a clear example. It is a translation that may be thought to "improve" on the original, "washing away" the original's bilingual play. In reality, mainstream presses do not take up the challenge of addressing a bilingual audience. They substitute English monolingualism for Spanish monolingualism. They turn toward a Spanish monolingual practice and hence fail to take the opportunity to acknowledge a domestic multilingual audience of different Spanishes in the United States. This is hardly evidence of a growing multilingual conscience on the part of mainstream presses. A global turn to one, homogenous Spanish language "flattens" things; it makes a transnational translation subject to the forces of a global Spanish. Even the small press translation of *Diario* and *Diary* looks for the lowest common denominator because translation favors the Anglicized version ("wetback") as opposed to the "foreign" (*mojado*), a subject I take up in the final chapter.

WHY ENGLISH-TO-SPANISH TRANSLATION?
AN UNPRECEDENTED EVENT

Given the worldwide context of the English language—its global spread and diffusion—and the reality that the United States is an English-language coun-

try, why translate Latinx literature already in English? Brian Lennon notes in
In Babel's Shadow, "virtually all books published for distribution in the United States by U.S. trade publishers are published in English, for a readership
that by market mandate is presumed monolingual in English" (9). From this,
and the fact that prestige and power accompanies a dominant language, it is a
short leap to understand why English is (for now) the most translated national language.[11] To use a monetary metaphor, English is the world's strongest
linguistic currency, the language with the most perceived and actual market
value in the global economy.

Is not, then, the translation of Latinx narratives already in English initiated by U.S. mainstream presses contrary to the "order of things"? How does
one explain this unprecedented event and why was the period between 1990
and 2010 an especially fertile time for the publication and translation of Latinx narratives? The catalyst for this unexampled translation is the result of the
confluence of the dramatic growth rate of native births among U.S. Latino/as
and the intensification of transnational movements. Add to these events, the
global and local situation of the Spanish language in the United States.

Spanish is the second most widely spoken language in the world, with approximately 4.5 million first-language speakers; the number increases to above
5 million if second-language English speakers are included (Spanish-language
domains). Twenty-nine countries have at least one million Spanish speakers
(Spanish-language domains), including England, Germany, Canada, and
Equatorial Guinea, a former colony of Spain. In the 1980s there were between
10 and 11 million speakers of Spanish in the United States; by 2000, there were
about 22 million, and by 2011 the figure was 35 million. The increase is 233
percent (López, "What is the Future"). The 1980s marked the highest rates of
migration and immigration from Spanish-language countries to the United
States. The rise in births of a Latinx native population and the three million
Spanish-language immigrants legalized through the 1986 amnesty law, in
addition to those entering the country in the 1990s during the aftermath of
the law's passage, also increased the number of consumers with familiarity
of Spanish, especially those, say, fifteen years of age and older. The number of
immigrants and first-generation parents who speak Spanish at home to their
children—37,579,787—spoke Spanish or Spanish creole in the home in 2011
(Ryan, "Language Use" 3), and students enrolled in high school and college
courses in Spanish (Flaherty, "Not a Small World")[12] are factors that also help
to explain this never-before-seen translation phenomenon. By the mid-1990s,
the numbers of Spanish as the second most spoken language in private and
public spaces, as the most present in the plurality of non-English languages in
the United States, had doubled since the 1980s. The initial moment of migra-

tion for the fictional characters in *Pocho* and *When I Was* occurred in the early and mid-twentieth century, but Pérez's testimony in *Diario* about his border crossing and stay in the United States belongs to the intense migration of the final two decades of the twentieth century. The translation and publication to Spanish of the three texts I discuss in this book occurred in the 1990s.

It is not only demographics that explain why mainstream presses would translate Latinx literary texts from English and publish reprints of Latin American texts in Spanish. It is also the history and staying-power of the Spanish language itself in the United States, especially where it is an integral part of the linguistic landscape—California, New Mexico, Texas (Shell, "Babel" 123), and Florida and New York on the East Coast. Enough people already speak Spanish to make the language a sustainable force. There is also the belief that "Spanish speakers have a historical 'right' to the land, a belief that might also pertain to French speakers in Louisiana and Navaho speakers in Arizona." (Shell, "Babel" 123) All this impacts the mainstream perception of the presence and extent of the Spanish language, even though not all U.S. native-born Latinos and Latinas are speakers of Spanish, and speakers of a language are not necessarily readers of that language.

A few landmark events of cultural importance motivated mainstream presses to enter the Spanish-language market. The Cuban American writer Oscar Hijuelos was the first Latinx writer to win the Pulitzer Prize in 1990 for his second novel, *The Mambo Kings Play Songs of Love* (1989). This award catapulted him onto bestseller lists and earned him international acclaim. The translation *Los reyes de mambo tocan canciones de amor* was published in Spain in 1990 and the United States in 1996.[13] In 1992–1993, Doubleday released the Mexican writer Laura Esquivel's *Como agua para chocolate* in Spanish in a U.S. market (Bearden, "Esquivel's Spanish Primer" 40).[14] The release the same year of the film *Like Water for Chocolate* buttressed the success of the book. By 1994, 70,000 hardcover copies and 63,000 paperback copies in Spanish had been sold (Bearden, "Esquivel's Spanish Primer" 40). These two turning-point events, Esquivel's book and Hijuelos's prestigious prize, were encouraging for mainstream publishers to seriously consider venturing into the Spanish-language market. In 1992, Grand Central Publishing published *Bendíceme, Última*, a debut translation of the 1972 award-winning novel *Bless Me, Ultima* by the New Mexican writer Rudy Anaya. Sandra Cisneros literary career also offered a "first"—the first Latina writer to obtain a New York literary agent to help sell her work. Her first novel, *The House of Mango Street* (1988), was a best seller for Arte Público Press, but when she finished her second book, a collection of short stories titled *Woman Hollering Creek*, publishing ownership of her work went from a small publisher to a mainstream publisher (*Woman Hollering Creek* was translated as *El arroyo de la llorona* [1996]). The agent not only sold the manuscript of *Woman Hollering Creek* to Random House, but also negotiated a hardcover edition of the stories and a paperback reprint of her first novel *The House on Mango Street* (Stavans, "Bilingual Nation" 399–400). The package deal also included a Spanish version with a bilingual title.[15] To add to its luster, *La casa en Mango Street* carried a translation credit for the celebrated Mexican author, Elena Poniatowska. These were significant crossovers: from small publisher to mainstream publisher (English) and from the customary Spanish-to-English translation to the curious translation-in-reverse (English-to-Spanish) by a mainstream publisher. Cisneros's success produced a ripple-effect: Ana Castillo (*The Mixquiahuala Letters*), Julia Alvarez (*How the García Girls Lost Their Accents*), and Denise Chavez (*Face of an Angel*) were also signed by Random House, and Alvarez's and Castillo's narratives were translated to Spanish (See Alvarez, *De cómo* and Castillo, *Las cartas*). The four appeared in a 1994 issue of *Vanity Fair* dubbed as "The Four Amigas: Latina Literature's New Doyennes" (Shnayerson 128).

The publication in Spanish of celebrated Latin American authors, such as García-Márquez, Laura Esquivel, and Isabel Allende, and the success of the Spanish-language television industry enjoyed by Spanish-language viewers in the United States in the thirty years prior to the 1990s led presses to seek ways to cater to a growing Spanish-language, culturally-specific market. Mainstream presses began to project to themselves an image of a community of Spanish-language Latinx consumers. From a marketing perspective, reaching a Spanish-language audience is a wise business decision. The monumental growth of a population is bound to alter the practices of commercial, for-profit businesses that want to create and cultivate what it perceives to be an emergent Spanish-language audience in the United States. Did the audience of Spanish readers imagined by presses begin suddenly to read books in Spanish, demanding that presses produce books in this language? In other words, did readers lead the presses? Or, did presses take note of the migratory and demographic trends, as well as in the sustainability of Spanish and the cultural first-time events I have outlined, an opportunity to sell books in Spanish to an audience of Spanish readers in print and electronic platforms? In other words, did presses lead the readers? It is probably a combination of both, but I suspect it has more to do with the latter than the former, a situation having to do with profit.

We can surmise that all these factors, in addition to the general perception created by global and transnational marketing and advertising agencies of "Latinos are hot," and "a bandwagon to jump on," are reasons *why* some major

U.S. presses would shift their practices to take on the publication of Latinx literature in English and even attempt its translation to Spanish.

TYPES OF TRANSLATION

The three paradigms of translation refer to the world of publishing and not to the translator's creative acts or styles. Before the 1990s, U.S. presses took responsibility for English translations of novels in, say, German, French, or Japanese, and were usually published in the country of the respective national tongue. The "original" text belonged to one national patrimony and the translation text to a different national patrimony. National languages remained contained more easily than today inside their national borders: Spanish, for example, was over "there," English was "here." I call this paradigm of translation between different national languages *international translation*. International translation, a mode of communication across the divide of national (monolingual) borders of different nation-states, depended on the conceptualization of one nation-state sealed off from other nation-states. Nation-states, it is supposed, have nothing in common with their neighbors, as though separation from one another were a fact of life (Casanova, *World*, 104–106). Yet one nation's singularity is dependent on their relational differentiation to other nation-states (Casanova, *World*, 36). In international translation, the source language is the national language of the country the original text is translated *out of* and the target language is the national language of the country the original text is translated *into*.

Practiced, of course, by translators with bilingual competencies, international translation is assumed to cater to monolingual audiences. Sometimes, it moves between global languages (English-to-French or English-to-Spanish), or between smaller national languages (German-to-Japanese).[16] Late twentieth-century examples of Spanish-to-English international translation are the numerous translations of Spanish-language Latin American "boom" authors in the 1960s and 1970s, particularly Gabriel García Márquez and Manuel Puig.[17] Then, U.S. cultural philanthropic institutions and university presses initiated the translation and publication of Latin American literature from a foreign (*their* Spanish) language into the national language (*our* English) of the audience for whom the translation was done. Works in Spanish were "foreign," published elsewhere, not here, especially not by mainstream presses. At that time, one could still perceive Spanish as a language "outside" the United States. International translation is business as usual. The conditions of publishing international translation involve business negotiations between a press in the text's home country and a press in the foreign translating country that aims to assimilate the literary piece as its own, recontextualizing it in a new place and time, repositioning it for a potential new audience. The crucial point is that languages in an international paradigm of translation (from language A to language B) are considered monolingual and existing in a dichotomous relationship of foreign/native, native/non-native readers, insiders/outsiders, separated by sovereign borders.

Naoki Sakai, a translation studies theorist and an expert in Japanese history who writes about the historical development of the Japanese and Chinese languages, explains that international translation implies the unity of languages (73 and 83). He, on the other hand, argues against the idea of "unity of languages" in which each language is external to another, bounded and separated by national borders. Rhetorically, he asks, "[i]s language a countable, just like an apple and an orange and unlike water? (73). "By what measures can you distinguish one from another, and endow each with a unity or body?" (83). The "unity of language" idea (or monolingualism) is tied to the concept of the nation-state. The two entities—unity of language and nation state—are coterminous, emerging at the same time in the late eighteenth century, as noted by Yildiz (3).[18] Benedict Anderson in his much-cited *Imagined Communities* also sees language as a major characteristic of nation-making. Anderson suggests that the imagined community in which strangers—those who never meet—imagine themselves attached to a shared exclusive group is based on natural ties, as if those who belong to the collective's sanctioned social group had a biological unchosen claim to the national language (141–146), as if they "owned" this language as property. "It is always a mistake to treat languages in the way that certain nationalist ideologues treat them—as *emblems* of nation-ness, like flags, costumes, folk-dances, and the rest" (Anderson 133). Jacques Derrida in his influential *Monolingualism of the Other*, also argues that languages are not property, not countable objects, to which one has an automatic right (30, 65).

Latinx narratives are different in that they are domestic narratives in English, translated to Spanish inside (mostly) the United States, sold in both national and global markets. This kind of translation, one I call *transnational translation*, does not imply nations as bounded monolingual linguistic communities. It involves multilingual texts and multilingual societies and occurs within an intercultural, national space where the realities of the global world are folded into it. These transnational translations are connected to a global world because they represent cultures that have ongoing communication with home communities outside the United States. *Pocho* and *When I Was*, the case studies I take up in chapters 3 and 4, are transnational translations.

Transnational translation is not a question of translating from an "original" text in one national language to a text in a different national language, as is true of international translation. Transnational translation and multilingual writing ideally keep readers from separating languages into native and foreign; they block equivalency between one language and one nation. Depending on how it is done, transnational translation potentially can disrupt dyads of foreign/native that characterize international translation because it deals with texts, minimally, in two languages that are indigenous to one nation-state. Roberto Cantú, the translator of *Pocho*, and Esmeralda Santiago, translator of her own text, *When I Was*, recoded their "originals" in the United States where both translations were published. Latinx texts by Anglophone writers are translated for audiences mostly inside the continental United States, but the translations are also read elsewhere; for example, Santiago's *Cuando era* is read in Puerto Rico. Esmeralda Santiago told me that the translation is required reading for schools in Puerto Rico (Interview June 13, 2014). Books by Oscar Hijuelos, Sandra Cisneros, and others have been published and sold in Spain, and books by Junot Díaz (*Drown* [*Negocios*] and *The Brief and Wondrous Life of Oscar Wao* [*La breve y maravillosa vida de Óscar Wao*]) are read in translation in the Dominican Republic. Presses commissioning transnational translation have roots inside the country of the translation text. HarperCollins and Random House, for example, decided to support the translation of Latinx literature already in the national language into Spanish. True, Spanish is the non-English language associated with the largest ethnic segment of the market industry, but Latinx educational levels, and of the general U.S. population, do not suggest high Spanish literacy rates. These tend to decrease with each generation, with competency loss greatest by the third generation of immigrant communities. Nonetheless, Latinas and Latinos of all generations recognize its importance (See P. Taylor). With the transnational translation of Latinx writers, one could no longer ignore the fact that Spanish was "inside" (a U.S. minority–majority language) and "outside" (a global language) the country. The outside permeates the inside and vice-versa.

The translation of *Diario* into *Diary* is neither the same old, same old international translation nor completely a transnational Spanish-to-English translation. It repeats elements of both but with a difference. Its production bears aspects of the standard international translation because Pérez wrote it in Mexico in the language of its national home; yet it deviates from it because the original text has never been acknowledged, that is published, by a Mexican press. It is not fully inside its own nation, not a fully settled Mexican text, as were the boom novels before translation, whether Mexican, Colombian, Peruvian, etc. Similarly, *Diary* fits into transnational translation because it is published and translated in the United States for a U.S. audience,[19] as were the other Latinx narratives. Both author and text found a voice and audience

outside the home country, across the border. It differs from other Latinx narratives, however, in that the target text was published twelve years before the
source text. This means that it functioned like an "original"—it was published
first and read for twelve years before the "real" original existed in book format.
Originality in this case is determined, one might say, by the act of reading, not
by the date of publication. When the original appeared, it did so after its English-language version. *Diary* fits neither paradigm fully. This text sits within
a third paradigm I call *transborder translation*, a bridge text in-between two
broad structures of translation, in-between two nations that for centuries have
been and are historically linked.

Transnational translation produces a tension in the publishing of Latinx
and Latin American literature, not there at the time of the translation of the
Latin American boom writers of the 1960s and 1970s. Some of the "boom"
translators expressed this tension. Eliot Weinberger, translator of the Mexican
poet Octavio Paz, and Gregory Rabassa, the "translator's translator" of Latin
American fiction, both seem to lament the rise of multiculturalism (their code
term for Latinx literatures and culture) because they claim it has led presses
to substitute Latinx literature (in English or translated) for Latin American
literature. Writing in the twenty-first century, Weinberger claims that "multiculturalism" is "the worst thing to happen to translation" (4) and Rabassa says
"it has let some questionable partners into the tent" (44). Though I agree with
them that multiculturalism's critique of Eurocentrism did not lead to what
Weinberger calls a "new internationalism" (he means an interest and com-
mitment to the study of languages and translation of non-U.S. literatures),
I would not go so far as to imply, as I think they do, that Chicanx and other
Latinx writers have an easier entry than Latin American writers into publication or translation.

THE LOSS OF THE CODE SWITCH

The peculiar challenge that Latinx narratives pose but that transnational
translation does not always confront is how to capture their multilingual features without flattening them into a single standard language. This is what is
at stake. The unique feature lost is often the code switches and their effects. We
will see a variety of examples in chapters 3 and 4, but let me begin by giving
one example of this loss by considering one instance of translation of a short
story by Junot Díaz. Diaz's literary debut was launched by his best-selling
Drown, a collection of eleven short stories, published in 1996 and translated
in 1997 as *Negocios* (Díaz, *Negocios*), also the title of the final story in the
anthology. Efraín Barradas writes a review, "Telémaco Criollo" (1997), of the
Spanish-born Eduardo Lago's translation. Let's take a look at the example Bar-

radas uses from the story to show what happens to the author's code switch when translated (1997, 75).

> Homero y Josefa, *tíos of Nilda*, drove home with them from the airport in a cab and gave them the "bedroom." The couple slept in the other room, the "living room" (*Drown*, 196, *sic*, emphasis added).[20]

> Homero y Josefa, *los tíos de Nilda*, fueron a recogerlos al aeropuerto y luego los llevaron a la casa en taxi. Les cedieron el 'aposento' y ellos se quedaron a dormir en el otro cuatro, la 'sala.' (*Negocios*, 173, emphasis added).

The "them" are Nilda and the narrator's father, lovers in the States. They have come to Santo Domingo from New York. Three characteristics stand out in the translation. First, and Barradas notes it, is that Lagos moves *tíos* (uncles) unaltered into the Spanish translation. This word that appears in Spanish throughout *Drown*, is simple enough for any reader of English. Díaz does not take the English reader by the hand, as do some writers when they use one word side-by-side Spanish-English units (*silla* [chair], *niña* [girl]). Díaz prefers to leave his Spanish unmarked. He does not use typographical markings, such as italics, to accent Spanish words as foreign:

> "I don't explain cultural things…For me, allowing the Spanish to exist in my text without the benefit of italics or quotations marks was a very important political move. Spanish is not a minority language. Not in this hemisphere, not in the United States. . . . So why treat it like one? Why 'other' it? Why denormalize it?" (Céspedes 900, 904).[21]

In translating, Lago returns *tíos* unaltered to a Spanish monolingual context. The second characteristic is that Lago returns Díaz's literal translation ("tíos of Nilda," literally "uncles of Nilda" and not "Nilda's uncles") to its standard habitat of correct Spanish (*los tíos de Nilda*). Díaz's words "tíos of Nilda" is an unusual syntax in English because it literally translates Spanish syntax (*de Nilda*). Barradas is pleased that Lago changes the original syntax to make, he says, the Spanish translation smoother than the English original phrasing: "[Lago] cambia la sintaxis original para aligerar [to ease or to lighten] el texto en español" (75). Also pleasing to Barradas is Lago's addition of the *dominicanismo* "aposento" because it gives an "original" touch to his translation ("También introduce . . . un dominicanismo ['aposento'], lo que le da un sentido de originalidad a su traducción" 75), as if Díaz's intent were to create an authentic island Dominican speech for two people visiting the island who have lived on the U.S. East Coast. Barradas laments the loss of *tíos*, since the appearance of tíos in Lago's translation is not the same as *tíos* in Diaz's original, but he celebrates a translation that renders a fluent, smooth, and original reading.

Barradas says that Lago has no choice but to eliminate from his translation the code switch tíos when he translates to Spanish, a switch so important to Diaz's text: ("se ve obligado a eliminar de su versión el cambio de código tan importante en el texto de Díaz" 75). But once he does this, as Barradas specifies, not only does the code-switch and the effect it produces in English disappear in Spanish, but also lost is the literal translation, of Nilda. This, for Barradas, is irresolvable, not only for Lago, he says, but for any translator. "El pasar de una lengua a otra en el texto original tiene un significado que se pierde por completo cuando el texto queda homogeneizado en la traducción" (The significance of moving from one language to another in the original text is lost completely when the text is homogenized in the translation; 75, translation mine). The homogenization of the text in translation is precisely the problematical issue. Why must it be regularized? Díaz is writing in English and tíos is the *narrator's* code switch, not his characters. Nilda and the narrator's father have assimilated some words in English and Díaz is quoting their code switch: "the bedroom" and "the living room" is *their* code switch. He is telling it from their perspective. Even though English is the main language, Díaz puts the words in quotation marks to show that they belong to Nilda and the narrator's father. Díaz distances English, makes it other, even in a text written in the English language.

In addition to translation of a code switch and the correction of literal translation, there is a third characteristic. Lago translates the English switches ("bedroom," "living room"), but, to his credit, he marks them with single quotation marks: 'aposento' and 'sala.' This clues attentive Spanish readers to a "strangeness" of these words, even though they are regular Spanish. This mark of difference is effective, but I suggest a stronger translational option. Lago might have left "the bedroom" and the "living room" of the original story in English to produce a more dramatic code switch effect—a bumpy road to be sure—for Spanish-readers in the Dominican Republic or in the United States. Perhaps, he wanted to avoid the taboo of mixing Spanish and English for his Spanish readers. Perhaps, he was aiming for as much fluency and ease as possible. But had he opted to leave the English in place, he would have produced for Spanish readers a more striking (more noticeable) interruption than the single quotations. Readers are, after all, reading about Nilda and the narrator's father who are from the New York area and have incorporated English words into their Spanish conversation. This is their native speech now. The translation would have gained a touch of bilingual play, even if it meant losing tíos.

Code-shifting has been a central feature of English and Spanish in the United States for a very long time. The rhetorical strategy falls under the umbrella term of Spanglish (or *espanglés*, sometimes *espanglish*, sometimes *inglañol*),[22] designating the various creative linguistic and syntactic combinations of Spanish and English applicable to the speech and writing patterns of the different Latinx communities, ranging in length from one-word, side-by-side units (*muñequita* [little doll]) to intrasentential shifting. The side-by-side units function like translation, or the substitution or replacement of one word for another. The second operates more on a level of contiguity and connection. San Joaquin Valley's Diana García offers one example in her poem, "Posteriors for Posterity" from *When Living Was a Labor Camp*: "And someone shouts/ *mueve la cintura*/and it's not/your waist they desire" (literally "move the waist" 59–60). Juan Felipe Herrera, a former poet laureate of the United States, offers another in the title of a poem, "Watering Cebolla [onion] While My Father Burns Leña [wood]" from *Notebooks of a Chile Verde Smuggler* (2002, 22). Margarita Cota-Cárdenas's *Puppet: A Chicano Novella* (*Puppet: Una novella Chicana*) (1985), one of the few examples in narrative of bilingual literature— not bilingualism in literature—(Rudin 10) is replete with intrasentential shifting (*Dijo que ya casi terminaban* but you had to come in with the guys to finish up, *que también necesitabas traer más adobes para hacerlo bien, que tú sabías* (He said you were just about done but you still had to come in with the guys to finish up, that you still had to bring more adobes to do the job right, *que tú sabías* you knew 4).[23] For Mary Louise Pratt, "multilingualism is translation's mother" ("Translation Studies Forum" 96), meaning that this type of code-shifting fits the "image for multilingualism," a kind of *desdoblamiento*, a multiplying (unfolding) of the self" ("Translation Studies Forum" 96).

Another form of multilingualism is literal translation or source language expressions in Spanish imaged—transliterated—in English. Díaz's "tíos of Nilda" fits this category. When translated literally, proverbs can also provide examples. The saying, "de noche todos los gatos son pardos," translated literally is "at night, all cats are gray" but connotes the sexist observation that at night all women (or men) are alike (any port will do).[24] Another is "trae el nopal en la frente," which literally translated is "she has the cactus on her forehead," and means "she denies she is Mexican but no one believes her because it is so obvious." Broadly, literal translation involves thinking or conceiving an expression in one's first language, then expressing the thought in a second language where the "salient linguistic and rhetorical implants from the first language" are felt and remain visible (Onwuemen 1058).

In chapter 3 on *Pocho* (*Pocho en Español*), we will encounter *pochismos*, usually single English words adapted to Spanish morphology and phonology used specifically by Mexican Americans. In pochismos, there is verbal play in which languages touch and change each other, for example garage turns into *garaje,* yard (patio) into *yarda,* and lunch into *lonche.* Another form is *caló,* urban underworld dialect, argot or slang, associated with *zoot-suit pachuco* culture.[25] Examples are *vato* for "dude," *filero* for "knife," and *mi ruca* for "my broad." While most *pochismos* are discernible to English monolinguals, caló requires familiarity with, and contextual knowledge of, varieties of Spanish dialects. These literary and rhetorical strategies in fictional and social documents are also everyday multilingual oral practices. They are different kinds of defamiliarization or disfiguration of language. In this sense, the three texts covered in this book break out of the traditional monolingual mold of language and participate in the world's multilingual literatures. Yet, what happens to their multilingual characteristics when translated?

The dichotomy of Spanish- and English-language systems as discrete entities obfuscates the tension of the multilingual forms that mark and disrupt the apparent monolingualism of each language. Scholarship on literary multilingualism often involves language combinations involving English, as is evidenced by the portmanteaus of *Taglish* (in the Philippines), *Singlish* (in Singapore), and *Portinglés* (in Brazil), Turkish (in Germany), and varieties of *Eurenglish* all over Europe. To the Welsh linguistic scholar, David Crystal, author of *The Language Revolution*, "English is a vacuum cleaner of a language, readily sucking in words from whichever other languages it meets" (27). Whether English is to function as a threatening "invasive species . . . resisting and supplanting whatever is not written in itself" (Allen, "Translation" 21) or a welcoming lingua franca, changing other languages and simultaneously changed by them, mixed forms are a fact of the global world. According to Crystal, "globally there are probably now more people who use English with some degree of code-switching than people who do not" (30). Languages are shifting and discontinuous linguistic phenomena; strands of different languages, whatever the languages, acclimate to the specific regions and needs of a given population.

The next chapter turns to the "new" status Spanish now holds in the United States. This new status begins in the 1980s and helps to explain why mainstream presses would want to undertake the production of the translation of Latinx literature into Spanish in the 1990s and also why Arte Público would decide to publish an original text in Spanish thirteen years after its translation to English.

CHAPTER 2

THE "NEW" STATUS OF SPANISH IN THE UNITED STATES

There are many permutations of Spanish-English language communication patterns in the Latinx multilingual community. My own family offers a model of one classic pattern. My maternal grandmother, born in Durango, Mexico, was an illiterate monolingual Spanish speaker who crossed the border into El Paso in the early 1920s to work as a domestic in Anglo homes. My mother, born in Chihuahua, Mexico, grew up in El Paso, where she started elementary school. She grew up bilingual and became a U.S. citizen, but her emotional language preference was always Spanish, the language of her self-expression and self-identification. My brothers and I grew up in the 1950s, in Boyle Heights, Los Angeles, speaking Spanish to our 'wuelita and sometimes to our mother, while she and 'wuelita communicated in Spanish. It was inevitable that we would sometimes mix Spanish with English, though my mother did not approve. She did not like hearing one of her friends in Los Angeles say, "Voy para mi house." Primarily, we spoke English with some Spanish among ourselves and to our friends, sons and daughters of first-generation Mexican immigrants. Growing up, I came to know another classic configuration. Some of my high school friends' parents were bilingual (mainly Spanish speakers), yet somehow they chose to encourage their children to speak only English out of fear they would encounter discrimination as they had, or because they felt Spanish would slow their access to the reward system and public fortunes of Anglo society. However, once the schools took over, the shift to English was done, Spanish expunged, apparently repressed, "forgotten." Some of us became English-dominant bilinguals and managed to enhance the Spanish we retained: we studied it in high school, we had exposure to Spanish-speakers in college, and we traveled to Mexico, or another Spanish-language country. My husband and I raised a bilingual-biliterate daughter, not an easy goal to achieve, even for middle-class folks. Young people take in the message of dominant society that English is the prestige language, vital for mainstreaming, and Spanish is a language that does not command the same respect. One must truly be driven by a desire to learn and nourish it, given the lack of incentives and opportunities for the instruction of Spanish, especially among the Latinx population who enter schools in urban areas. Today, I once again experience the challenge *en vivo* with two young grandsons, who will grow up in an even more populous environment of first- and second-generation working-class Spanish speakers than I did.

Today, there is a wide array of Spanish-English communication patterns among the Spanish-language origin U.S. population (Navarro, "Is Spanish"). What these diverse patterns of communication show is that these two languages do not begin and end at a given historical moment, whereby the family's mother tongue with each succeeding generation became buried in the family's history, farther and farther away from the assimilationist tongue, as was the case with many European immigrants. Contrary to the popular view that Latinas refuse to learn English, the number of U.S. Latinx children, the PEW Research Center reported that "some 88% of Latinos ages 5 to 17 said they either speak only English at home or speak English "very well," up from 73% in 2000," and "[a]mong millennial Latinos, aged 18 to 33, 76% said they speak only English at home or speak English very well, up from 59% during the same time period" (Adams, "English is on the Rise"). Since there have been steady influxes of monolingual Spanish-speakers, until recently, generations of families have had close living ties to Spanish.[1] In 2015, the PEW Research Center's 2013 National Survey of Latinos assessed that "about six-in-ten U.S. adult Hispanics (62%) speak English or are bilingual. Among those who speak English, it reported, 59% are bilingual (Krosgstad, "A Majority"). These two languages involve multiplex language structures along a spectrum whose opposites are monolingual Spanish and monolingual English.

In this chapter, I first provide some historical context for the salient features of Spanish in the United States today: its deep historical roots, its asymmetrical relation to English, its size and scope, its geographical concentration, and its national and cultural linguistic variety. I then discuss the "new"—wider and deeper—status of Spanish that begins in the 1980s until the present. I do this within two contexts: the first involves contrasting the Latin American literary boom (1960s and 1970s) that occurred within a nation-state model and the second is the Latinx boom (1990s)—not limited to literature, more inclusive along lines of gender, sexual orientation, and economic class—that occurred within a transnational model. The second context concerns new communication technologies, from the personal computer to wireless internet access, that has made Spanish a global language and repositioned it from a regional to a U.S. national language, though always enveloped in asymmetrical relations of power with English. Third, I ask, should Spanish be called a "foreign" language? I discuss it as a second national language, or majority-minority language, as pointed out by scholars who question its assigned status as a "foreign" language in the United States. I add my voice to these scholars' efforts to legitimate Spanish, and other non-English U.S. languages, as an integral part of the nation's social fabric. Finally, I highlight the tensions between Spanish as the nation's second language and the unquestioned assumption that the United States is a monolingual country. This latter ideological force of "one country, one language, one culture" aims to uphold and invigorate the "order of things": that English is the one and only language of national identity. In preparation of the textual analyses of the Latinx originals and translations in chapter 4, I move toward the affirmation that languages are always in contact, intersecting and mixing with each other.

My intent is not to single out Spanish as some kind of exceptional language, deserving special status—all languages, English included, merit attention and cultivation, though clearly they are assigned different values in the global literary marketplace. Rather, my intent is to recognize the role Spanish has played and is playing in the history and social reality of the United States. It occupies a different place in the history and historical memory of the United States than the other European, Asian, African, and Middle-Eastern languages that make up the United States' multilingual heritage. Today's arguably narrow gap between Spanish and English is a response to the augmentation of three historical transformations in U.S. society: 1) the growth of a U.S.-born Spanish-language heritage population, 2) a constant, multidirectional, worldwide movement of millions of people (and languages) across national borders, especially the new influx of im(migrants) from Spanish-speaking countries that began in the 1970s, and 3) the rise of electronic communication (wireless internet, the personal computer, and social media). All are results of the increased intensity of transnational and global forces since the 1960s. The first two forces have been considered in the previous chapter as prime reasons for the print event that brought to the forefront the "new" place of Spanish in the literary marketplace: the unprecedented translation and publication of English language texts to Spanish by mainstream presses, but also their continuation in lesser quantities by alternative Latinx houses. In this chapter, I consider the third reason.

HISTORICAL CONTEXT: UNIQUE FEATURES OF SPANISH IN THE UNITED STATES

Of all non-English U.S. languages, especially those spoken by the different white European ethnic groups during the nineteenth and twentieth centuries, excepting the Native American languages—Navajo, Lakota, Kumeyaay, Cree—which deserve protection against extinction, Spanish has the deepest historical roots, the most notable longevity, and a resilient persistence. It has diverse national origins and geographical concentration. It has the largest number of speakers after English (in 2013, there were 52 million Latino/as in the United States, though it should be obvious that not all had or maintained actual living ties to Spanish) and the widest scope of national origins (immigrants come from more than 20 Spanish-speaking nations worldwide). Spanish today is a larger, wider, and deeper phenomenon than it was when I grew up.

The Spanish language arrived on the shores of the American western hemisphere when Juan Ponce de León landed in Puerto Rico, making the island "the first part of (what is today) the United States to be settled by [Spanish-speaking] Europeans" (Crawford, *Language* 13). In 1513, he reached the U.S. southern peninsula and called the land Florida, more than a century before the Mayflower in 1620. The city of St. Augustine was founded on Florida's Atlantic coast in 1565. In 1598, Juan de Oñate arrived from Mexico to establish the first Spanish-Mexican settlement in Santa Fe, New Mexico. Missions were established across the Florida panhandle, Georgia, and South Carolina during the 1600s, and a chain of twenty-one missions were founded along the Baja and Alta California coast between 1769 and 1863. Conquest and imperial conflicts of the two wars in the nineteenth century resulted in the colonization of Spanish speakers in what became the U.S. territories: in 1848, the United States annexes a scarce and scattered Spanish-language population in an area almost one-half (1,903,000 square miles) of Mexico's land (Crawford, *Language* 58),[2] and it takes possession of the Spanish-speaking population of Puerto Rico in 1898, when U.S. imperialism sweeps the Caribbean. Military intervention and U.S. expansionism laid the basis for Anglo–Latino social and economic power differentials and language asymmetries between English and Spanish.[3] These ethnic groups developed what Guadalupe Valdés calls "natural" bilingualism as opposed to "elite" bilingualism. According to her, "natural" bilinguals are those who learn to use the majority language of the country they reside in and of "conquered colonized peoples whose original natural language is displaced by the conquering or colonial language" whereas "elite" bilinguals are those who consciously decide to learn a foreign language either through formal study or informal situations of actual communication (Valdés 113–114).

Mexico's civil war (1910–1917) physically displaced a massive number of rural and working-class people (*campesinos* and *peones*) and pushed them to emigrate *hacia el norte*, resulting in the first epic phase of migration of Mexicans, mainly to borderland states but also to the U.S. interior (Cardoso, esp. chapter 3).[4] Operation Bootstrap (*Operación mano de obra*), the economic program of "self-help" designed after World War II to industrialize and economically develop the island, was a major cause for the Great Migration of Puerto Ricans to island cities and the mainland east coast (1945–1965). The accelerated recruitment of Mexican labor to compensate for shortages in agriculture, railroad construction, and the steel industry parallels the period of massive immigration from Europe (1901–1930), the years Douglass Massey has called the "classic era" in his outline of U.S. immigration (633). After 1945, in the postwar era, the number of peoples from the Spanish-language Américas, especially Mexico, increased significantly while immigration from Europe declined steadily. This interruption in immigration from Europe (1930–1961) corresponds to Massey's "long hiatus of limited movement" from Europe (633). Labor shortages during and after the war and the fact that numerical quotas set by immigration law during the 1920s did not apply to Mexicans, although other restrictions did—inspection procedures, the Border Patrol, and deportation (Ngai 7, 71)—brought more Mexican-born immigrants into U.S. society. We only need think of the United States' legally sanctioned *Bracero* program [1942–1964] which stimulated, ironically, illegal immigration (Ngai 147). Many *braceros* (agricultural workers) and unauthorized workers stayed and eventually became permanent inhabitants of U.S. society. Puerto Ricans, U.S. citizens since 1917, left poor barrios and shantytowns on the island for New York's freezing temperatures and garment industry (Zentella, "Language Situation" 140).[5] The major migrations of low-income Mexicans and Puerto Ricans to the Southwest and Eastern areas were historical processes that further reinforced the asymmetry of Spanish, through systems of racial discrimination and prejudice, social control, and segregation, as a language associated with ethnoracial and linguistic minorities.

After 1959 and before 1970, a third Spanish-language group, this time political refugees from the Cuban Revolution (1959), added to the size and scope of cultural-linguistic diversity of the Hispanophone population.[6] Cuba's entering communities to New York represented well-educated and wealthier sectors of Cuban society ("*pequeños comerciantes* of Spanish background" Davila 30). Among them were business owners, advertising executives with prior marketing knowledge and experience, and ties to the U.S. economy (Davila 30–31). As political refugees fleeing a government that the United States tried several times to overthrow, and as part of Cuba's educated middle- and upper-class, they held a firmer footing than Mexicans and Puerto Ricans in U.S. society. In contrast to these longer settled groups, that by this time included at least two generations removed from their parents and grandparents' homeland and whose Spanish had undergone major alterations through its contact with English (from complete loss to varied degrees of bilingualism)—Cubans were not subjects of conquest; their privileged class and political status buttressed the cultural security of their Cuban identity and Spanish language. As one Cuban media industrialist explained, Cubans were not *acomplejados* (ashamed and embarrassed by their [Spanish-speaking] identity"; Davila 32). This generation and later immigrant waves from Cuba intensified and added another layer of geographical concentration to the Spanish language, this time in the Northern and Southeastern parts of the country.

While Mexican Americans, Puerto Ricans, and Cubans underwent generational changes in the speaking and comprehending continuum of Spanish, a new massive influx of Mexican and "new Americans" from Central and Caribbean America (El Salvador, the Dominican Republic, Guatemala, Nicaragua, and Honduras), all primarily of working-class backgrounds, added significantly to the size, the national origins, the geographic concentration, and the cultural-linguistic variety of U.S. Latinas in the late 1970s and 1980s. Civil wars, political and economic instability, gang violence, and poverty were all reasons for pushing the Salvadorans, Guatemalans, Hondurans (the Northern Triangle), and Nicaraguans *hacia el norte*. Following Massey's tripartite model of U.S. immigration (classic era 1901–1930; period of hiatus 1931–1969), the third period, the "new regime of large-scale, non-European immigration" (633) that begins in 1970s until about 2000, marks the formal end of European immigration in the United States. Among U.S. Central Americans, Salvadorans have been poised since 2008 to overtake Cubans for third place in Latinx demographic rankings (López, "Salvadorans May"), after Mexicans and Puerto Ricans. Between 1990 and 2013, they more than tripled in population, from 563,000 to 2 million (López, "Hispanics of Salvadoran Origin"). Six out of ten of the two million Salvadorans here in 2013 were born in the home country, and 89% speak Spanish at home, making them higher in Spanish dominancy than the Latinx population overall (López, "Hispanics of Salvadoran Origin").

Most Dominicans arrived between 1990 and 2000. Their numbers in the continental United States increased from 10,000 in 1960 to 180,000 in 1980 to 1.4 million in 2000, with the bulk settling in Washington Heights (Duany), a demographic growth resulting from immigration influxes and "high fertility rates among Dominican women" (Hernández). Between 1990 and 2013, about 1 million were born in the Dominican Republic and about half a million were U.S. born (López, "Hispanics of Dominican Origin"), insuring, as Salvadorans did, infusions of Spanish; there is a higher amount of Spanish dominancy in Dominican adults (48%) compared with 38% in Latinx adults overall (López, "Hispanics of Dominican Origin"). This wave brought in first-generation Spanish speakers, whose children would have a different relation to Spanish than the sons and daughters, grandsons and granddaughters, of the first-generation of Mexican and Puerto Rican (im)migrants for two reasons: less time in the country and growing up in a time when Spanish is prevalent and pervasive in U.S. mainstream society.

These distinctive features of Latinx immigration help to magnify the social import of the Spanish language in the twentieth century, particularly in the last two decades. Two other distinctions are applicable. First, different national origin-groups brought different languages from different countries during the classic era (1901–1930) of European immigration, but Spanish is the common language spoken by the majority of first generation (im)migrants from the Spanish Americas (Massey 646). For example, the language most spoken by immigrants in the classic era (Italian) were confined to one country (Massey 646), and assimilationist processes buried the language after several generations. In contrast, Spanish is spoken and comprehended by all inhabitants of Spanish-speaking countries, even speakers (with some exceptions) of indigenous languages (Zapotec, Mixtec, Mayan), for whom Spanish is a second language. The subject-author of chapter 5, the Zapotec Mexican Ramón "Tianguis" Pérez, is one example.[7] This means that while Europeans had no choice but to learn the common language, Spanish-speaking immigrants and the generations to follow have opportunities to create a second viable language and a bilingual society (Massey 646). Although Spanish undergoes changes with each new generation, the newer influxes of first-generation immigrants have added new infusions of Spanish into the country, especially since 1970.

Second, the immigration from Spanish-speaking countries has not yet undergone a "hiatus period," or the forty-year "breathing space" of low levels of immigration that European immigration had from 1930 to 1970 (Massey 633). It has been ongoing, continuous, and pervasive since its beginnings until 2000 (See López, "What is the Future"). This movement also tends to be concentrated linguistically and geographically. Speakers of Spanish are not scattered throughout the country as were European groups. By 1990, the three most important metropolitan centers receiving the immigrants were New York, Chicago, and Los Angeles, which were then and are today the most important centers of communication and mass media in the country. This intensity of concentration guarantees that Spanish-speaking immigrants and the language will be visible and heard, not only in the cosmopolitan centers of the East, Midwest, and West, but in the country at large (Massey 647).

THE RISE OF SPANISH: FROM REGIONAL TO NATIONAL

Up until the IRCA (Immigration Reform and Control Act of 1987), when 3 million Latinx immigrants were made legal residents, and NAFTA (the North American Free Trade Agreement of 1993) almost thirty years ago, Spanish was defined as a regional language, limited to the U.S. southwestern region, to the usual suspects of Texas, New Mexico, and California and to smaller language communities in Chicago and Florida and New York on the East Coast. Up until the 1980s, it had sustained enough presence in public use to have threatened the California senator S. I. Hayakawa enough to break a two-century silence on the national tongue (Crawford, *Language* 1). Indeed, in 1981, he attempted what no one else had, since the time of the framers of the constitution—to legislate at the national level language policy. Though unsuccessful, he prepared the way for a State English Language Amendment to the California Constitution (Proposition 63) which passed overwhelmingly in the most populist state in 1986. The country has been debating the language issue ever since, but Spanish has been resilient and grown exponentially (Romero 2017). It is not only heard and spoken in the Southwest and smaller communities on the East coast; it is not only limited to Spain and the Spanish Americas. The multiple variants of Spanish, of the different Latinx groups (from Latin, Caribbean, and Central America) can be heard from the 1990s onward in Illinois, Iowa, Kansas, Virginia, Washington, Georgia, Louisiana, and other states in the Southern United States. It has become a defacto second national language, a majority–minority language.

In the late nineteenth century, the Cuban-born José Martí, journalist, essayist, poet, translator, and diplomat—an exile living and writing in New York City who wrote and translated English into Spanish for audiences inside and out the United States, from within the Anglophone metropolis[8]—imagined two different Americas. Speaking for Latin Americans, he developed the concept of "Nuestra América" (Our America) in his well-known essay of this title (Martí), and referred to it in his writings, implying "the América that speaks Spanish." The English-speaking Anglo-American United States was by derivation "the other America," the "América that is not ours" (Lomas 292, note

80), the America that does not speak Spanish. The basis of his hemispheric partition was language. Though he did not totally bifurcate his vision into North and South, English and Spanish, the geographical and linguistic spaces of a U.S. expansive empire and the rest of the continental body emerged in his writing. The lines are more blurry now. Spanish in the United States is eminently more pervasive and visible than when Martí resided in New York City (1881–1895) and articulated his linguistic vision, more pervasive and visible even when a sizable number of translations of Spanish American literature appeared in the 1960s. Martí's "other America" is now more saliently a part of "Nuestra América." The United States, more than ever, is part of the Spanish-speaking Américas.

THE TWO BOOMS:

Though other variables can be used to compare the Latin American and Latinx boom, I highlight national and transnational features between them to mark the change in the status of the Spanish language. First, the 1960s through the 1970s, a swath of time that encompasses the writing and translation of the Latin American boom, was the period of international translation when the borders of nation-states held more firmly. The writings of Gabriel García-Márquez, Carlos Fuentes, Julio Cortázar, and Manuel Puig originated outside the United States; the translation of their books into English originated inside a dominant English-language country. The marketing phenomenon of their translation, which transformed them into canonical print commodities, took place under the paradigm of the nation-state, across recognized national Spanish-language borders into the national English-language borders of sovereign states. Spanish American authors catapulted into the international literary space, beyond Spain and Latin America, into parts of Europe, most notably Paris. Up until then, they had been on the periphery of the world's literary space. English translation enabled them to expand their readership into the powerful cultural centers of the United States, Canada, France, and Britain and also into the less visible English-language countries along the global periphery (West Africa, the Caribbean, Australia, and India). Linguistic and geographical borders operated primarily as elements of disconnection and separation (the nation-state model) during the Latin American boom; by contrast, the linguistic and geographical borders operated as elements of interconnection during the Latinx boom in the ever-widening transnational and global world of the 1990s. Both the original English texts and translated Spanish texts of the Latinx boom writers originated inside U.S. borders.

Second, the Latin American boom was confined to the literary domain and to male writers, primarily. The Latinx boom, by contrast, broke new ground:

it included women in general, as well as men and women of different sexual orientations and social classes, and it took in both literary and popular verbal and nonverbal mediums (for example dance, music, and visual art), cross-genres of electronic (television and radio) and print (newspapers, magazines, books) media, new media platforms, advertising, and Web-based Internet media. In Diana Taylor's frame of cultural analysis, this event amplified the cultural expressive sphere from the exclusively discursive dimension of the Latin American boom—written texts and narratives—to embodied performances: from the "archive to the repertoire" (Taylor 18–22). Its products were local (national), global (transnational), importable, and exportable, due to transformational, transnational and global forces. Products and information in Spanish and its dialects were part of this transnational Latinx phenomenon.

Third, the U.S. cultural, philanthropic, and university presses initiated translation and publication of Latin American literature from a foreign (*their* Spanish) language into the national language (*our* English) of the audience for whom the translation was done. Works in Spanish were "foreign" and published elsewhere—they belonged to Spain, Mexico, and Spanish-language countries in the Global South—not here. "They" read and wrote in Spanish, "we" read and wrote in English. Spanish, the most spoken of inter-American languages in the western hemisphere, remained "over there." If translation of the Latin American boom writers brought Spanish closer to U.S. audiences, it, nonetheless, remained "out there" and "foreign." The Latinx boom, on the other hand, belongs to an era when the "foreignness" of Spanish is subject to question. It arguably challenges the one nation–one language model because foreign texts (those from Latin America) were launched untranslated into the U.S. marketplace, as though they were native products; Latinx texts, the native products, in contrast, were translated, treated like foreign material, if seen through the prism of the Latin American boom model. Yet, paradoxically, they were newly affirmed as native material in Spanish. If Spanish is still alien to some after the Latinx boom, it is "strange" from *within*, rather than from outside, the United States.

COMMUNICATIONS MEDIA:

I now focus on the third transnational and global force. Even more powerful than Spanish in the context of the two booms, perhaps, is the persistent presence of Spanish in U.S. communications media—electronic and print—and in public spaces of human communication. Its widespread presence in Spanish-language newspapers, radio, television programming and stations (Univisión, Telemundo), mainstream advertising, popular music and film, and everyday life is symptomatic of what could be seen as the narrowing margin between

Spanish, the most major of minor U.S. languages, and English, the common language and primary tool of communication.[9]

New communication technologies, and eventually social media, caused a heightened awareness of Spanish in everyday U.S. society, not only for migrant populations emitting and receiving messages from home, for example the *remeses* (remittances),[10] and those involved in the processes of conducting these communications but also for the world absorbing the power of the changes. The new high-speed communication technologies, new media, and electronic communications that became available in the 1990s and grew in the first ten years of the twenty-first century made it easier for migrant, exile, and refugee populations to retain economic, familial, and linguistic ties with the home countries.[11] These communication technologies heightened the visual, auditory, and verbal power of Spanish, in all its linguistic and cultural manifestations, in popular and expressive culture: music (the hit songs of Ricky Martin's "*Livin' la vida loca,*" Enrique Iglesias's "*Bailando,*" and Luis Fonsi's and Daddy Yankee's most watched song and YouTube video ever "*Despacito*"; almost entirely in Spanish with 3 billion viewers by August 4, 2017, according to the *NY Times* [see Velazquez-Manoff]); literature, theatre, and film, for example Alejandro González Iñárritu's *Babel*. Iñárritu's *Babel* depicts various languagescapes across several economic borders in what Gramling calls "fragile linguistic ecologies" (353). The previously sequestered sounds and voices of barrio locales, once below the radar of mainstream media and audiences, began to sneak into mainstream domains: FM radio, music videos, TV commercials, and Zumba classes in athletic clubs, featuring salsa, merengue, and *bachata* mixed with rock and pop, with lyrics in Spanish. Let us also include in this communication scenario those networks of ordinary day-to-day life, the public urban spaces with sizeable Latinx populations, where Spanish is heard and spoken in human face-to-face activities: in the streets, the shopping malls, public parks, doctors' offices, hospitals, and courts of law. Spanish and its bilingual and multilingual strains of Spanglish (or *espanglés*), *pochismos*, *caló*, popular vernaculars, etc.[12] entered dominant forms of U.S. media like never before.

Since before and after the Mexican–American War (1846–1848) in the Southwestern region—the "cradle of U.S. Spanish-language broadcasting and Hispanic audience" (Rodríguez 357)—and beginning in the late nineteenth century on the East Coast, especially Florida and New York, Spanish-language print media has promoted linguistic solidarity and group identity among Spanish-speaking U.S. indigenous and (im)migrant populations.[13] Spanish-language audiences became an increasingly important target base for Spanish print media from the late nineteenth century and for conventional forms of Spanish-language electronic media (especially radio and television) throughout the twentieth century and from the 1990s through today. The language has been a factor of engagement for populations in U.S. rural and urban spaces, an integral and constant component of a phenomenon known today as the "Hispanic marketing and advertising industry" (Davila 2–3), an umbrella designation for the Spanish- and English-language marketing and advertising industry that aims to reach Latinx consumers at national and transnational levels through print and electronic communication systems.

The 1970s census created the abstraction "Hispanic" to encompass all people from Spanish-speaking countries—Mexico, the Caribbean, and Central and South America—living in the United States. The emergence of this category, basically an invented English term (formerly an adjective but henceforth turned into a noun) by federal agencies to refer to an allegedly racially and linguistically unified group, began to give this population credence and to bring them into a national discourse. By the 1980s, when the population registered 18 million, the television conglomerates Univisión and Telemundo became dependable and steady bases for independent brokers and advertising agencies to place advertisements in the networks' continuous programming. At first, their audience was primarily a population whose first language was Spanish. By the turn into the twenty-first century, with the growth and visibility of Univisión that became the fifth largest network in a prime time audience in 2011 (Guskin and Mitchell), and the Latinx population, tilting toward U.S. born and registering at over 50 million by 2010—their audience included English and bilingual Latinx viewers (Guskin and Mitchell).[14] By the final decades of the twentieth century, and most specifically the 1990s, Univisión and Telemundo had laid the basis for the conceptualization and projection of a Spanish-language and also a bilingual Latinx population (Davila 25). They not only created a Latina audience; they also helped to consolidate, shape, and define it as a group of viewers and a consumer market.

Between 1980 and 2002, this audience showed a remarkable growth rate of 1000% (Albarran 13): "Spanish-language stations began to leap to the top of the rankings in large Hispanic markets" in Los Angeles, San Antonio, and Miami (Albarran 13). No longer did only Spanish-named corporations want in on this influential market, but mainstream corporations—among them Coca-Cola, McDonalds, Burger King, JCPenny, Toyota, and AT&T—also realized the economic benefits of broadcasting to first-language Spanish-speaking and bilingual audiences (Albarran 14). The high ratings of some stations in Los Angeles, San Antonio, and Miami, growing markets in Chicago and Houston, and the buying power of a population that continued to increase significantly, meant that large mainstream corporations were willing to invest in Spanish radio as advertisers. In 2002, Univision acquired the Hispanic Broadcasting Corporation (HBC) to become the largest owner of Spanish-language radio stations in the United States—a Spanish-language media giant (Albarran 16). This was a longshot from the early period of Spanish radio when station owners could only dream of a Spanish-speaking audience as a product to be mimed and sold to advertisers for profit.

For example, in Paul Espinosa's documentary *Ballad of an Unsung Hero*, about the life of Pedro Jota González, a charismatic musician and performing artist of the late 1920s, who produced a popular local radio show, *Los madrugadores* (The Early Risers) for the Anglo-owned radio station KELW in Burbank (twelve miles from downtown Los Angeles), says that he personally went in search of advertising sponsors and obtained them from Folgers Coffee and Chesterfield Cigarettes (*Ballad*). The station owners allowed him dead air time at dawn's break (4:00 a.m. to 6:00 a.m.) every day to entertain a Los Angeles Spanish-speaking audience. Jota González filled the time the station deemed disposable with live performances by Mexican musicians. The station's gesture suggests the lack of political presence and currency the Mexican community then held as an audience, but it also points to González's political acumen to take advantage of mainstream resources and make his own uses of them.

In the 1980s, listeners of Spanish-language media may have included the most recent Latin American immigrants. But by the 1990s, there were also bilingual and English-speaking Latinos and Latinas who listened to Spanish-language radio and Spanish-language TV. The potential paradigm shift for the future, of which we have now begun to see some emerging signs, is the contact of English and Spanish in mainstream communications media. This conglomerate industry begins to use Spanish to sell products and goods in English-language print and electronic communications (for example, network and cable TV and the internet). In the past ten years or so, we saw TV bilingual commercials aimed at a modern Latinx audience (Casillas 10)—For example, in 2007, Toyota aired its first-time bilingual, diversity Super Bowl commercial that linked the hybrid Camry's usage of both gas and electricity to the driver's choice of speaking English and Spanish to his son—both "for the future" (Toyota). "In the 30-second ad, a Hispanic father is driving his young son in their new hybrid Toyota Camry. When the father explains how the hybrid car switches between gas and electric power, the son compares it to the way his father can switch between English and Spanish." There is the Cox Cable commercial about the monolingual (probably) Mexican grandmother and her bilingual granddaughter; the child seeks to find the Spanish counterpart for a word ("screen") in Spanish to communicate with her grandmother,

but the Cox operator knows the exact word (*pantalla*). Does this suggest that
the operator—not noticeably "Latina-looking" as are the grandmother and
child—is also a Spanish-speaker? For several months, Fashion Valley Mall in
San Diego promoted the monolingual T-Mobile commercial in one of its bill-
boards, advertising unlimited telephone calls to and from Mexico: "Llamadas
Ilimitadas a México y desde México!" More often than in the 1980s, we encounter magazines like *Latina* and *People en Español* in medical offices and
hear about CNN's channel *Español en Vivo* and Gerber's first Latina baby on
advertisements of baby food. In print ads of magazines and billboard advertisements, we see daily the iconic images and verbal texts in Spanish invoking
a Latino presence, from Taco Bell's simple two-word slogan *Live Más* to the
more obscure "El sabor auténtico de los altos de Jalisco" of beer commercials.
Today a "Hispanic marketing and advertising industry" is a robust business, a
multibillion-dollar industry spread nationwide, in the most Latinx populous
metropolitan centers. "Over eighty Hispanic advertising agencies and branches of transnational advertising conglomerates spread across cities with sizable
Hispanic populations now sell consumer products by shaping and projecting
images of and for Latinos" (Davila 2).

THE SECOND U.S. NATIONAL LANGUAGE

Should Spanish be called a "foreign" language? The changed status of Spanish at the national level has led some scholars in the past ten years (Alonso;
Mignolo; McKee and Szurmuk, Pratt ["What's Foreign" 1283]) to propose
that Spanish might well qualify as the second U.S. national language. I whole-
heartedly agree, I too, underline its status as a second national language. In
1995, Mary Louise Pratt, the 2004 President of the Modern Language Association (MLA) and professor of comparative literature at NYU, proposed
that comparatists expunge "*foreign* to refer to languages other than English.
Nothing is more repugnant to someone working in Spanish in this country
than to hear it referred to as a 'foreign' language."[15] To see it as "foreign" is
to see it as an alien language: one that does not belong here. Addressing the
issue of "foreign" languages in a transnational world and within the corporate university, Walter Mignolo, professor of Spanish at Duke University, says
that after five centuries Spanish has become "a minority national language in
the United States" (Mignolo 1239). In 2006, Carlos Alonso added his voice to
a discussion about the prevailing and erroneous perception of Spanish as a
"foreign" language, despite the boom in Spanish in language departments at
that time and the substantial rise in the U.S. Spanish-speaking and Hispanic-
identified population. Like Mignolo, Alonso, professor of Spanish at Columbia University, captures the paradoxical status of Spanish in the title of his

essay, "Spanish: The Foreign National Language." After noting the expected but still "stunning announcement" in 2003 by the Bureau of the Census that "Hispanics had overtaken blacks as the largest racial-ethnic minority in the United States"(Alonso 16) and suggesting that scholars working in and on Spanish "undertake an institutional rethinking and reshaping of the place occupied by Spanish language and culture in the United States academic world" (Alonso 17), he boldly argues that "Spanish is. . . no longer a foreign language in the United States" (Alonso 17); it is rather, he says, a language possessing the status of a second national language: "the evidence of it is everywhere" (Alonso 17). This goes beyond, for example, federally required election ballots in non-English languages. "The omnipresent bilingual English-Spanish signs, the ubiquitous automated telephone option "Para español, oprima el número dos," the direct mailings of advertisements in Spanish, the targeted telephone solicitations in that language, the wide availability of dubbed versions of films, the snippets of conversations in Spanish that we hear with increasing frequency from couples or groups passing by on the street, and so on" are evident of this switch (Alonso 17). In a *New York Times'* op-ed piece (2017) titled "Trump, the Wall, and the Spanish Language," professor Ilan Stavans of Amherst put Spanish in the United States as the fifth largest among the world's Spanish-speaking communities, with only Mexico, Colombia, Spain, and Argentina ahead. "Such is its ubiquity that calling it foreign no longer seems logical."[16] The Spanish-born writer and New York resident, Eduardo Lago, said that English and Spanish in the United States are not separate worlds: "We should not consider our language a foreign language in the United States. It has never been and today, one needn't say it, it is much less foreign" (No hay que considerar a nuestro idioma como una lengua extranjera en los Estados Unidos. No lo ha sido nunca y ahora, no hace falta decirlo, lo es mucho menos; Ruiz-Mantilla, trans. mine). Need more be said?

The increasingly constant presence of Spanish in popular culture and everyday human communication make it possible—at least for those of us interested in going beyond either the celebratory holler "Latinos are in!" or the opposing stance against the exotified and commoditized identities that corporate sponsors and commercial advertising industries produce about Latinos and Latinas—to reimagine the United States as connected to, not separate from, Spanish-speaking countries, especially those in the Américas. It encourages us to rethink the equation between the white, monolingual, English-speaking Anglo-American individual and the American national self, and to go beyond the idea of a single nation-state with one national language and literature. Further, the widespread use of Spanish, in all its bilingualism and multi-dialectical varieties, realigns the way the historical origins

of the United States have been constructed and imagined: not solely an English-language, East Coast *geographical* orientation, but also one that includes
a Spanish-language (and Native American-languages), West Coast *chronological* grounding (Arteaga 25).[17]

However strong Spanish has become in the United States, its place within
a U.S. society that upholds English supremacy is highly unstable. In a literal
and associative-historical sense, its status in the United States lies precari-
ously balanced between the foreign (it is *not* English) and non-foreign (the
language was *here*, in U.S. territory, before English, and still is here). In the
classic psychological sense, it is unhomey (*umheimlich*, foreign from home,
unfamiliar) and homey (*heimlich* at home, familiar, yet hidden). Governmen-
tal and educational institutions designate Spanish, like other non-English
languages, as "foreign," and this contributes to distancing it as coming from
"elsewhere," alien to the home nation. Yet, transnational and domestic historical events have made its presence, formerly "below surface," more visible and
prominent in the last thirty years. The numerous English-to-Spanish translations by mainstream presses and the Spanish publication of *Diario*, a book
that existed for twelve years before it was translated to English, suggest that
what was, one might say, hidden (strange) has stepped into the forefront. The
translations and publications in the original Spanish are U.S. literature and
intended for Spanish-reading audiences inside and also outside the United
States. The distinction between domestic and foreign, familiar and unfamiliar, once clear has blurred: "the familiar and unfamiliar slide disturbingly
into each other and disable the comforting distinction between them" (Yildiz
53). While Spanish fits into the classification of "Languages Other Than English" (LOTE), it also functions as a reference point for the organization of
"Languages Other Than Spanish" (LOTS),[18] by which non-Spanish languages
(except English) are measured. Spanish has given the United States its longest
and most robust, if unacknowledged, positive benefit: a bilingual history. Its
place in the United States as a familiar language turns the standard idea of literary translation as the familiarization of the "foreign" on its head because if it
is true that translation makes the foreign familiar, how can it do so if Spanish
is not fully a foreign language?

A comparison to the Turkish population and language inside Germany
is instructive. Turkish and Latinx cultures are "minor" cultures inside larger
national cultures; both Turkish and Spanish are low-prestige immigrant languages; both Turkish in Germany and Spanish in the United States are the
second-most spoken home languages; and both Turkish and Spanish challenge the supposed homogeneity of German and U.S. English in their own
national zones. Among these similarities are two major differences that un-

derscore the unique but perhaps more threatening place Spanish holds in the United States. While German and Turkish have "mingled together [only] for the last fifty years" (Yildiz 2–3),[19] the longevity of Spanish predates English, not only in what is now the United States but in the Western Hemisphere. The second difference relates to something perhaps more important because it makes Spanish more threatening: the principle of *jus soli* (right of the soil). While Turks born in Germany are not automatic citizens,[20] the majority of the Spanish-language origin population in the United States has birthright citizenship.

Because of its unique place in U.S. society, its extensiveness, its ubiquity, a portion of a mainstream population has become (at best) ambivalent, (at worst) resentful and belligerent against speakers of Spanish. If thought of as outside U.S. national borders, Spanish is simply a "foreign" language, belonging "out there," but inside the United States, where it arrived before English and has remained among Spanish-language origin communities that claim it as a home language, it is linked to vulnerable communities, vulnerable to criminalization, deportation, discrimination, the questioning of citizenship, harassment, and stigmatization. It can evoke an unwelcoming and at times hostile reaction, when it is heard by "the listening ear," a term J.L. Stoever has coined for "dominant listening practices" ("The Noise").[21] In other words, reactions are not only to visual differences (involving the racialized body) of what is *perceived* as "foreign," but also to "sounds" of language and music *heard* as "foreign." Ana Celia Zentella explains that Spanish functions as a social indicator for a Latinx population similarly to the way that skin color functions for Black Americans. Latinos and Latinas who look "Mexican" or "Puerto Rican" are expected to speak Spanish (in this case, the visual is superimposed on an aural plane) and those who speak English with a stereotyped Spanish accent are presumed to be non-white (in this case, the aural is superimposed on a visual plane). Jonathan Rosa puts it this way: people of this ethnic group "look like a language and sound like a race" (11). Language operates at both levels of sound and physical appearance to racialize this population. What comes across as unfamiliar sounds are sonic excuses for discrimination (Stoever "Noise"), and are deemed more threatening, precisely because, I think, Spanish is (too) familiar—a threat, ironically, in its familiarity. Auditory sounds of language, Spanish and accented English in this case, as much as visual cues (dress, haircuts, skin color) can signal to authorities and the general population who "belongs," who "counts," who "fits in" (Stoever "Noise"). Hearing Spanish, to some, is "noise" or "sound out of place": where and at what time it is heard. For example, hearing Latinx musical sounds, such as *mariachi*, *salsa*, *Tejano*, or *cumbias* in a white middle or upper-class neighborhood can be felt as upsetting, as trespassing upon a neighbor's space; in contrast, if heard in a brunch setting at a Mexican restaurant in an upper-class neighborhood, it will be heard as acceptable (Stoever "Noise").

BILINGUALISM OR MONOLINGUALISM?

The Welsh ecologist David Crystal, an English Language Studies expert, and a world authority on language, states in *The Language Revolution* that the 1990s was a "highly significant period in the history of language" (4). The last decade of the previous century, he goes on, "fundamentally altered the world's linguistic ecology" (4). One trend of this altered linguistic ecology was the emergence of English as a "genuine world language" (Crystal 6). The complementary rise of Spanish as the second national language of the United States, and as a major world language,[22] also occurred in the 1990s, when political, economic, and cultural forces consolidated the status of English as the world's primary global language. But on a local national level, this latter turn of Spanish conflicts with the ideology of "one language, one country, and one place," an ideology that promotes the United States as enclosed by not only geographical and political borders but also by monolingual borders. Meanwhile, the world becomes more and more bilingual and multilingual—not monolingual.

Hindi and Chinese are the most spoken native languages, but English is the world's *lingua franca*, the interlanguage of commerce, of worldwide print and digital communication, and of computer technology, business, and commerce. English is the language with the most perceived and actual market value in the global economy. Among global languages, according to Rebecca Walkowitz, author of *Born Translated*, English is "dispersed like no other: it is the first, second, or third language used in the largest number of countries" (20). This includes English as a spoken language by world speakers but also as a read and understood language, a diffusion that makes English *the* dominant global language. Pascale Casanova's definition of a "dominant" language is helpful. "A language is dominant if (and only if) it is a second language used by bilinguals or polyglots around the world" ("What is a Dominant Language" 380). Dominance, she argues, is determined not by the number of "native" speakers (otherwise, she notes, "Mandarin would be the dominant language" 380) but by the number of speakers who choose to learn and use it as a second or a third language.[23]

Spanish today, like English, is a global, transnational language, the national language of Spain and the most spoken language in all the Western Hemisphere. Like English and French, Spanish is a mediating language. Walkowitz discusses that mediating languages can provide world writers in smaller languages a translational path into wider publication and readerships in national markets (11). For example, a writer of German translated to Spanish will have a larger potential audience than if left only to exist in German. Such a form of exchange would afford writers writing in minor languages a greater chance at global transmission, not only because their texts then have greater dissemination through translation into major languages, the lingua francas of the world, but because from these languages they are in a stronger position to reach translation to English—the language, Allen reminds us, of the largest book market in the world ("Translation" 21).

Yet, unlike English, Spanish is not the world's first lingua franca. It is on a local U.S. national level where its newly felt energy in the last thirty-five years has resituated English and created a larger U.S. cultural and linguistic sphere. Beyond the indisputable fact that English is the most powerful global language and this country's defacto national language, Spanish has become, on a domestic level, a battleground and a symptom of deeper conflicts and displaced xenophobic anxieties about immigration status, national origin, race, and ethnicity, on the part of the Anglo-oriented, white, middle-class society. Numerous state legislative measures (to date there are thirty-one) were proposed between 1980 and 2010 to codify the United States as an official English-only country. The first occurred in 1986 in California, the most populous, the most economically developed, and the then-becoming most diverse state; the most recent measure passed in Oklahoma in 2010.[24] The intent of these propositions was not for all school children to master and learn the nuances of the English language, or to become truly fluent and literate in English, or to care for and about—to nourish—the English language. The assumption and intent was to frame Spanish as a problem, not as a resource, driven by fear and anxiety about the economic and cultural insecurity that the "others" represent for "us." Restrictions on language were "not only *for* English, but *against* bilingualism" (Crawford, *Language* 1) and multilinguality.

The first effort of the late twentieth century to push to codify English as the United States' official language began in 1981—a time when immigration from Latin America and Asia had become intense. The late Japanese-American S.I. Hayakawa, a semanticist and then a Republican California state senator, proposed a constitutional amendment to make English the official language of the United States.[25] Unsuccessful at the national level, he started a right-of-center subnational movement that linked national identity to the English language (Crawford *Language* 1), reversing the accommodating provisions of the Civil Rights era for linguistic minorities.[26] Since then, restrictive legislative policies have been aimed at counterbalancing the presumed threat that Spanish and other languages of minority communities allegedly pose to English. The Presidential candidate Rick Santorum in March 2012, publicly told Puerto Ricans in their own majority Spanish-language home territory that they should make English their primary official language if they wanted to obtain Statehood ("Santorum to Puerto Rico")[27]

In the post 9/11 moment, especially in the aftermath of Arizona's influential, anti-immigrant political turn (SB 1070 of 2010), and the dismantling of Mexican American ethnic studies, Arizona's Department of Education mandated that teachers with "foreign" sounding accents ("heavily accented English"), an action affecting primarily Spanish-sounding accents, be removed from classes for students learning English,[28] despite the fact that these were veteran experienced teachers who already had met the English-proficiency criteria to teach students learning English. This recalls Rosa's creative adage "look like a language and sound like a race" since by sounding "foreign" non-native English speakers are easily racialized, identified as "other." Anti-Latinx xenophobic political measures—English-only ballot propositions in several states, including California in 1986—were a testament, paradoxically, to the growth and amplitude of Spanish, interpreted as a threat to the power, rights, and privileges of the majority language. These militant measures, racialized attacks on a community and its language, prompted national news media to turn the spotlight on the Spanish-language community, ironically making it more visible for racialized motives and bringing it to the forefront of a national discourse on citizenship, immigration, and language.

Many U.S. institutions support the politics and policies of English-only communication. Consider the New York Police department's 2013 workplace policy that prohibits bilingual officers to speak a non-English language (Spanish, Farsi, and Nigeria's Igbo) *at any time* while on the job (Fermino). This occurs in a highly diverse city—the "quintessential [East Coast] city of migrants" (Gikandi 868)[29] in the second largest Spanish-speaking country in the world, second only to Mexico. Legislative acts to reaffirm English as a national, "official" language and workplace policies to bar employee's native languages are continual attempts to prevent individuals from speaking in their native tongues and to codify the United States as an English-speaking monolingual country, which goes against the global trend of bilingualism. These political measures aimed at speaking English essentially mean speaking *only* English, speaking *no other* language.

When politically expedient, every now and then, in the case of political candidates, for example, seeking the "Latino vote," the largest ethnic minority group of potential voters in the nation, it "speaks" Spanish. Even non-speaking, non-comprehending Presidential aspirants make their way into Spanish-language settings. In 2008, both Hillary Clinton and Barack Obama went on Spanish radio to cultivate the support of a Spanish-radio listenership. Genuine moments of Spanish occur, as when Senator Tim Kaine became the first senator to deliver an entire speech in Spanish during the immigration debate in 2013 in the U.S. Senate[30] and then on the 2016 campaign trail. Or when in the Presidential Democratic campaign of 2016, on CNN, a few participants more comfortable in Spanish directed questions in Spanish to Hillary Clinton and Senator Bernie Sanders that were translated on the spot by the Univision moderator. Hearing questions posed in Spanish during a presidential election campaign was an event before unseen on national television. Yet, at other times, in popular settings and mass media for example, whether trivial or mockingly and aggressively pejorative, it may be spoken mostly in hyper-anglicized racist discourse to obtain dramatic and jocular effects, that work to reproduce negative stereotypes (e.g., "no problemo," "adios cucaracha," or Trump's "bad hombres") to diminish the unauthorized population but also implicitly the Latinx population overall. (Hill 119–57).

Though the United States is in sync at ground level with world plurilingualism because today the world is more multilingual than monolingual and more languages are spoken in the United States than in any other one country, we insist upon matching one language to one national zone.[31] We insist on a kind of xenophobic monolingualism. Embedded into a U.S. national imagination is, to our cultural and moral detriment, monolingualism as a self-evident fact, a desired goal rather than the limitation it is.[32] We extend our imagined unilingualism to other areas of the world as inheritors of a dominant language. We are too comfortable in assuming that others beyond our national borders will understand and even speak English. A brave student once spoke up in a class discussion on this topic: I paraphrase: "Why bother with learning a language(s); everyone speaks English." Was she right? "Today, the speaker of English has a better chance of being understood in more places across the globe than the speaker of any other language." (Allen, "Translation"13). But even as we profit from our position as English speakers, there is something wrong if we simply ignore whoever does not speak English or whatever is not in English. Isabelle de Courtivron puts it this way: the opposition to bilingualism "has sometimes been bolstered by the regrettable smug assurance that one need only speak one language to be a citizen of the world, as long as that language is English" (7).

In countries like Ghana and Liberia in Africa, Jamaica and Barbados in the Caribbean (to name but two places in each of these regions), English is the sole official language, though its inhabitants speak their mother tongues too (Finegan). Elsewhere, English shares official status with one or more languages: the Philippines, Pakistan, and India (Finegan). In 2004, Crystal estimated first-language English speakers to be about 400 million and second-language English speakers with conversational ability to be also 400 million (8). In 2004, he concluded that there are as many second-language speakers of English in the world as there are "native" speakers of English (Crystal 8). Almost fifteen years later, it is probably safe to say that there are more people using English as a second language. Crystal explains that twentieth-century linguists demonstrated the human brain's extraordinary capacity for language which led to the observation that "bilingualism, multilingualism is the *normal* human condition. Well over half of the people in the world, perhaps two-thirds, are bilingual" (Crystal 38), speaking their native language and English or another language. The world's countries are bilingual and multilingual, meaning that several languages are read, understood, or spoken in varying degrees of proficiency.

Literary multilingualism often involves language combinations involving English, as is evidenced by the various portmanteaus in various parts of the world, for example Brazil. Pratt contends that as English spreads, it behaves as any lingua franca does. "It breaks apart into local hybrids, sometimes unintelligible to one another, like Taglish in the Philippines and Singlish in Singapore" ("What's Foreign" 1287). These mixed forms are examples of shifting and discontinuous linguistic phenomena, distinct strands of two languages, whatever the languages, that acclimate to the specific regions and needs of a given population. Like speakers of Spanish in different national and cultural domains, speakers of English in distinct parts of the non-English world will speak it differently than speakers in the traditional centers of English, such as Britain and the United States. And though English may be "a vacuum cleaner of a language, readily sucking in words from whichever other languages it meets" (Crystal 27), it does not just change the languages it comes into contact; it is also changed by less powerful languages, or the "little" languages Joshua Fishman defends (cited in Ruiz 8). There are already many varieties of spoken English—the "New Englishes"—as their populations in multilingual countries experience a pull toward difference (to develop an English of their own) and a pull toward sameness (a need to communicate on a world scale).

In the next three chapters I analyze specific pairs of texts, originals, and their translations. I visualize the two languages, English and Spanish, not as straight parallel lines going from point A to point B, as demarcated entities closed off from one another. Languages are social and contextual, defined by people who speak them; they are irregular, discontinuous and shifting phenomena—mutable and fluid—that lead to language contact, intersections, and mixing. Languages are not isolated units, even more evident since the 1990s; not pinned down to one geographical location; they move, change, coevolve. They meet one another, in the same country, community, neighborhood, or, as in my own case, in the same family.

CHAPTER 3

POCHO EN ESPAÑOL

The Anti-*Pocho Pocho*

The first of the three hybridized cultural figures I discuss is the *pocho*. This figure populates the pages of José A. Villarreal's classic Chicanx novel. He is part of a long and storied tradition in Mexican and Mexican-American culture. In chapter nine, toward the end of the English-language novel, Richard Rubio, the Mexican-American pocho, protagonist, and subject, speaks to a young woman from Puebla Mexico visiting California. "I am a Pocho" (165) ("Yo soy un pocho," 238),[1] he says. The most important word in the book is pocho, yet Richard's explanation is the first and only time it is uttered and written in the book. It is significant when Richard describes to Pillar what a pocho is by highlighting the linguistic dimension of the identity: "we make Castilian words out of English words" (Villarreal 165). It is ironic that this pocho would use "Castilian" in place of the more commonly used "Spanish." The term "Castilian" is rarely used in an English- or Spanish-language Mexican American context as a substitute for "Spanish"; one reason is that it evokes the Spanish empire's mother tongue. But in this passage, Villarreal, the author, performs his signature literal translation. The word "Castilian" is a literal translation of *castellano*, a term familiar to the bicultural, biliterate Villarreal. If the pocho can make English words out of Spanish words, isolated lexical items, what happens when the entire book is translated from English to Spanish? The word *Español* in the title of Roberto Cantú's translation, *Pocho en Español*, refers to the standard linguistic register of Mexican national culture that rejects the pocho. The national language helps to structure the idea of nation and is usually the standard register of that language, the national norm (sanctioned by the state), its educational institutions, and academic disciplines as the "correct" way to speak and write it. Working toward a better understanding of vernaculars, R. Ruiz in "Orientation in Language Planning" says it is the "world standard languages which one is expected to learn in school for personal enrichment or international understanding or foreign service, not the inferior vernaculars spoken by ethnic groups" (16). The national register is not the languages Fishman refers to, ironically, as the languages spoken by "all those wild little people" ("Positive Bilingualism" 45).

In this chapter, I focus on what Latinx studies tends to overlook, namely language and its multilingual aspects. Nowhere do the contradictions around the phenomenon of the pocho stand out more starkly than when we hold the language of *Pocho en Español*, the translation text, up against the text translated, *Pocho*. I will discuss *Pocho* and *Pocho en español* in tandem to show how the translator's translation creates the "anti-pocho pocho," an odd spectacle: the pocho who speaks a high-level diction of Spanish. The translator translates *Pocho*'s narration and dialogue into a cultivated mode of Spanish, thus making it seem that Villarreal's pocho is either not a pocho, or a pocho who speaks "perfect" Spanish. No matter how we take him, Cantu's pocho is a blatant contradiction, a good example of cognitive dissonance! Importantly, the illusion of flawless Spanish that pervades the book collapses, as I will show later in the chapter, in a key scene when Richard adopts not only pocho but also *pachuco* slang (*caló*) expressions. This is one of those moments characteristic of all three translation texts, moments that jar or rupture the smoothness that the translation texts seem to want to achieve by covering up the act of translation and, in this case, the pocho's dialect. Small and insignificant as this unexpected turn may seem, it is important because we are able to glimpse the "foreign"—a moment of linguistic diversity. The translator's unexpected maneuver shows that Cantú's anti-pocho pocho has a productive multilingual side.

Pocho was first published by Doubleday in 1959 for a US mainstream audience. Villarreal (1924–2010) was a US-born, fluent Spanish- and English-speaking World War II veteran. He is primarily known for this landmark novel, which predates by at least a decade the height of the Chicanx Civil Rights

movement (1968–1975), when a post-World War II Mexican-American generation (U.S. citizens of Mexican descent) achieved political self-consciousness
and claimed their full rights and citizenship. Thirty-five years after its first
appearance in 1959, almost twenty years after the second edition (1970), and
five years after the third English edition (1989), Doubleday, the publisher of
the 1959 *Pocho*, released *Pocho en Español* (1994), the Spanish-language translation by Roberto Cantú, a Professor of Mexican-American Studies at California State University, Los Angeles.

Though linguistic complexity at the level of two languages may be achieved
in actual everyday speech in multilingual societies of the Americas (and beyond—in India, Africa, Asia), it is not fully realized in Cantú's translation.
The linguistic complexity Cantú achieves mostly occurs at an elevated level
of Spanish diction that includes regionalisms from northern Mexico absent
in the English text. The translation text is multilingual within one language
only.[2] The hallmark feature of Villarreal's writing is literal translation—linguistic forms imported from elsewhere (Yildiz 144): in this case, Spanish buried in English syntax that conveys to Anglophone readers Richard's Spanish-
monolingual immigrant parents speaking Spanish and Richard's bilingual
speech. Rather than show a constitutive bilingualism of Chicanx culture inside the same nation-state, Cantú's translation seems poised to move "across
different national languages and borders," emphasizing the idea of "distinct
and narrow lines drawn upon a map between two nations" (Gentzler *Translation and Identity* 143) instead of in "multiple directions, across numerous
borders" within the same nation-state, not just between different nations
(Gentzler "What is Different" 8).[3] He prioritizes the separation dimension of
borders over the connection aspect of borders: nation-state over transnation.
Cantú translates into standard Spanish and misses the linguistic opportunity
to capture the specificity of the pocho for readers of the Spanish translation.
He misses the opportunity to show that the pocho is a hybrid, transnational figure and that *Pocho* is a multilingual text situated at the nexus of two
languages.

It is not that we should expect Cantú to establish exact linguistic equiva-
lencies between his translation and Villarreal's text. This is not the point. The
point is more an issue of limits. Just how far should a translator go to translate
(or not go, and leave untranslated) the novel's dialect—the superimposition
of English and Spanish—to honor the pocho's voice? Here I want to appropriate the words of Elliot Weinberger, translator of Octavio Paz's poetry, for
my purposes: the objective of translation is not to render Cantú's voice in the
translation or language. It is to allow the pocho "*to be heard* in the translation
language, *ideally in many of the same ways it is heard in the original language*"

(emphasis added).[4] Lost is Villarreal's own attempt to pay homage to the bilingual pocho. The translation's elegant "correct" Spanish betrays the pocho to tell his own story in his diction. Cantú thoroughly domesticates him, meaning he assimilates the pocho into the standard national norms of the translation language; he silences the pocho's "phonetic signifying truth" (Berman 291).

Rainier Grutman, the renowned Canadian translator-theorist who has published on the translation of multilingual texts, singles out some translators for their ideas on strategies to translate dialect in "Refraction and Recognition." One of these is Antoine Berman (1942–1991), an accomplished translator -critic of Latin American literature into French and one of France's most astute theorists of translation. Berman strongly believed, says Grutman, that dialect "clings tightly to its soil" and completely resists any direct translating, even into another vernacular (21). The Belgium-born André Lefevere, also a highly regarded theorist of translation, agreed with Berman about leaving dialect untranslated; he suggested that some kind of translation be appended in brackets or given somewhere in the text a bit later (Grutman 20). In his seminal essay, "Translation and the Trials of the Foreign," Berman offered "twelve deformation tendencies" for translators to try to attenuate. One tendency to shun is "ennoblement" (282–83)[5] or the practice of "producing 'elegant' sentences, while utilizing the source text, so to speak as raw material" (282). This tendency, he argued, involved ridding the translation of the source text's "original clumsiness" (282). As Grutman puts it in "Refraction," this practice tries "to put order in a text's perceived chaos by correcting the original in the (false) hope of improving upon it" (21). This "deformation tendency" fits Cantú's approach to translating the pocho, whose "iconic physicality" (Berman 283) he erases. Yet, strangely and unexpectedly, there is the turn I referred to earlier. The pocho's substandard multilingual vocabulary surfaces suddenly in the text when the protagonist performs the role of the *pachuco* (chapter 14), the streetwise urban youth of El Paso and Los Angeles in the 1940s, a cultural first-cousin of the pocho. The discrepancy between the sustained Spanish monolingualism and the unexpected multilingual linguistic elements is so strong and the distance between them so large that the familiar, monolingual literary landscape of the text figuratively explodes. It is a kind of "crack" in the novel's form, as if the narrator's voice snaps under the effort to maintain high literacy in Spanish. This is Cantú's success, unwittingly though it may be. The pocho's "foreign roughness" (Robinson, Rev 472) remains. All in all, *Pocho en Español* is a productive failure.

The translation of *Pocho* raises a difficult problem in multilingual literature. Just how does one, should one translate *Pocho*, a text with bilingual features, when the language necessitated by its translation belongs to the culture the pocho defies and resists? Cantú's translation favors the medium of expression (the national standard of Spanish) of the Mexican culture that has represented the pocho as its false replica, as a sign of "betrayal." In the following, I explore the intriguing paradox of the anti-pocho pocho posed by Cantú's translation at levels of both language and production for the marketplace. But first: the term pocho.

THE TERM POCHO AND ITS MEANINGS

The term pocho is important in my discussion, so allow me to explain its meaning and applicability to Villarreal's novel. The key point is perspective. Historically, from a Mexican dominant national perspective, pochos are *mexicanos norteamericanizados*, Americanized Mexicans, those who adopt U.S. manners and customs, and they fall primarily into two categories: 1) Mexican nationals living in the United States, regardless of how well they may speak Spanish; and 2) U.S.-born "Americans" of Mexican parentage who speak no Spanish or speak it brokenly, "badly." For defenders of "correct" Spanish, Mexicans in the United States and U.S.-born ethnic Mexicans ought to speak standard Spanish, with no interference from English, as though Mexican Spanish and English, so close to one another in geographical space and historical usage, had been impenetrable to the linguistic and cultural influences of each other. Though the inclusion–exclusion axis of what pocho means is coded primarily linguistically, its reference range usually extends to behavioral habits and attitudes, style of dress, national identification (U.S. rather than Mexican), low educational levels, and working-class status. Ironically, the word comes from nonstandard Spanish, not nonstandard English. *Pocho en Español* returns the word and its referent to the previous cultural context of usage in Spanish. Translation, a process that takes the "original" into a foreign locale, is in this case returning the "foreign" (pocho in English) to its "original" linguistic setting (pocho in Spanish). A cognitive misfit? Yes, but only if we assume unsurpassable boundaries between English and Spanish, only if we assume that the translation text and the source text stand at opposite sides of a language divide. In truth, the boundary is porous: the word and its referent belong to the networks of both languages and cultures.

Etymologically, pocho refers to something "cut" from its source (Sobarzo 258–59).[6] Though the term circulates less commonly today in Mexican society (probably with more prevalence in regions closer to the United States), the act of migration to the United States and exposure to English in the first half of the twentieth century exemplified a symbolic "cutting," a loss of "authenticity" and value from an imagined linguistic unity and way of being: in other words, the "betrayal" of a nation. The term also suggests "rotten" (*podrido/a*) "unhealthy" (*dañado/a*; *DEA*) and "discolored." English and exposure to the broader U.S. culture contaminated, "dirtied" if you will, one's speaking of Spanish and the "Mexican" self. The term has no counterpart in English, and unlike English, Spanish easily signals the word's gender usage: *el pocho, la pocha*. Whether in masculine or feminine form, the designation pocho in mainstream Mexican society implied a fraud ("not a *real* Mexican"), infidelity to an "autochthonous" Mexican national identity and language.

In his introduction to the translation, ("Sobre la traducción"), Cantú (1994) credits the Mexican writers Agustín Yáñez (*Al filo del agua* [The Edge of the Storm]) and Martín Luis Guzmán (*El aguila y la serpiente* [The Eagle and the Serpent] and *La sombra del caudillo* [The Shadow of the Strongman]), exiles of the Mexican Revolution who wrote and published in the United States, for inspiring him in the translation (9). In the first half of the twentieth century, Mexican author-intellectuals, including Yáñez (1947), Guzmán, and, of course, José Vasconcelos (probably the figure who most influenced post-Revolutionary Mexican culture in his role as Mexico's Secretary of Education during the 1920s) expressed disapproving views of those in the United States, usually ethnic Mexicans and/or Mexican nationals, who spoke an Anglicized Spanish. In "Asoma el pochismo," an essay in *Ulises criollo* (1937), an autobiographical account of his travels in northern Mexico and Texas, Vasconcelos used the word pocho (probably the first Mexican author-intellectual to use it in writing) and its variants disparagingly, commenting on this North Americanized Mexican with irony and sarcasm. He chides the Mexican friend traveling with him for admiring U.S. culture. He says the United States wants only to destroy Mexico's ancestral Hispanic culture ("la destrucción de la cultura latino [*sic*] española de nuestros padres" [the destruction of our ancestors' Spanish Latino culture]) and replace it with "el primitivismo norteamericano" (Vasconcelos 77), a way of life that is inculcated into los pochos (Vasconcelos 77) from childhood. Responding to the power differential between the United States and Mexico, his concern, like that of other influential thinkers who shaped the Mexican master narrative of the time, was the damage done to Spanish by English. How one spoke Spanish was the paramount concern. To be a pocho or a pocha was to be tainted by U.S. culture.

In *Pocho*, Villarreal wrote the classic coming-of-age story of the pocho. This realist novel entered the U.S. English-language canon in the 1980s, twenty years after its initial publication in 1959. As the first novel of the modern period of Mexican American literature, it thematized the contact of cultures, a minor tongue in a dominant language. Richard Rubio, the title's pocho, is the son of Mexicans who immigrated after the Mexican Revolution. Brown-skinned, indigenous-looking, he is (like Villarreal) born and raised in 1930s

Santa Clara, California, when most of its inhabitants were English-speaking Anglo Americans. Richard hears and speaks his heritage language at home with his working-class parents, who speak no English, while he is simultaneously educated in English-language schools. He eventually becomes a fluent English speaker with little use for Spanish; he challenges Anglo stereotypes of Mexicans that see him as being solely capable of certain occupational roles (gardener, auto mechanic, and boxer), and experiences the breakdown of his family's traditions due to the pressures of assimilation. All his young life, he struggles to "translate" himself into an individual, a writer, an "American."

Doubleday's attempt to reach a mainstream English-reading audience with the first edition in 1959 misfired, in part because this audience had no access to the meaning of the book's linguistically and culturally untranslatable title and contents. As the 1950s ended, the book's audience had not yet been formed. The novel went without an audience until the Chicano Civil Rights movement prepared for it an appropriate audience by creating a bicultural readership that understood its title and reinterpreted the pocho's social and symbolic identification. To meet this audience's demands for material suitable to Mexican American culture, Doubleday published the second 1970 edition. For a Chicano/a readership of the 1970s, Villarreal's pocho was neither a distorted copy of "authentic" Mexican culture, as once predicated by the Mexican master narrative, nor the Cantuían pocho ("Adán moderno"). Cantú attributed to Villarreal's protagonist in his 1994 introduction (5) a universal point of origin, a young man in search of total freedom from traditional influences and social conventions. Rather, the Chicanx audience of the 1970's "culturally reconverted" (García-Canclini 30)[7] the pocho's function and meaning as a translational figure with a hybrid, in-between identity and situational history. The book appeared during the assimilationist *vision du monde* of the 1950s, but the Chicanx audience of the 1970s, even though professing an ideology resistant to the assimilationist one espoused in the novel, saw itself, its history and culture (migration, bilingualism, cultural stereotypes, generational conflict) narrativized in the book. In summary, it is the 1970 Chicanx audience's cultural reconversion of the pocho that Cantú did not capture. Cantú's "modern Adam" is what I call the "anti-pocho pocho."

THE REPATRIATED POCHO

The use of Spanish is a constant reference in Villarreal's plot and sometimes penetrates the semantic territory of his dialogue and narrative voice. *Pocho* is a bilingual and multilingual text. Bilingualism, usually taken to refer to two coexisting languages, with a higher social value assigned to one language over the other, has multilingual aspects. The linguistic complexity of "English" and

"Spanish" refers to a continuum—extending from sparse usage of overt Spanish words and phrases to entire paragraphs; to literal translation (as in Spanish hidden under English), to full-blown interactivity between English and Spanish; to the creative urban slang or argot of *caló* (street language) derived from varieties of Spanish associated with marginalized Mexican and Mexican-American youth. Villarreal wrote at a time before the Chicanx (Alurista and Luis Valdez in California) and mainland-Puerto Rican (Miguel Pinero and Miguel Algarín in New York) writers of the 1960s and 1970s started to overtly mix Spanish and English in their texts—before they and others turned code-switching into a vibrant form of writing, before they rehabilitated *pochismos* (for example, *parquear* becomes "to park"), pocho-Spanish (phrases, sentences, etc.), and caló (for example, *filero* for "knife") into legitimate modes of writing and reversed a tradition of disparagement and humiliation. Writing in 1959, Villarreal does not use single-word pochismos (*marketa* [market], *tengo un deyt* [I have a date], *mapear* [to mop], *shainados* [shined shoes], or *yarda* [yard/patio]), or even longer grammatical units of pocho-Spanish.[8] His protagonist never switches between languages in the same sentence. Villarreal's *Pocho* is at the lower end of the bilingual and multilingual continuum when it comes to explicit mixing of English and Spanish and/or usage of pochismos, but his referent is the multilingual, multicultural lived experience of Mexican immigrant, Spanish-monolingual parents and their U.S.-born children who hear and speak Spanish in the home.

Cantú's translation narrates the paradoxical spectacle of a pocho protagonist whose life is narrated in sophisticated Mexican Spanish and who speaks it, to boot. Cantú has said that his "main concern was how to translate Villarreal's novel in a manner that would best serve its interests in the Spanish-reading world as a novel set in Mexico and the U.S." (email correspondence, February 26, 2010). Whatever his intent, his dominant medium of translation is standard Spanish with multileveled linguistic registers. He is faithful to the architectural blueprint of the source—its story line (scenes, characters, actions), its chapter divisions and section breaks, but his nuanced, versatile Spanish seems out of place when measured against Villarreal's simple, laconic, and direct language. The source text eschews bilingual linguistic complexity: Villarreal does not use differentiated lexical registers in English that might justify those of Cantú's elaborate rendition. For example, in the first chapters dedicated to the development of Juan Rubio (Richard's father and a soldier in Pancho Villa's army) in the *cantina* scene on the Mexican side of the border in Ciudad Juárez, Cantú uses regionalisms particular to northern Mexico: "de pura chiripada" (25) for Villarreal's standard "purely by accident" (10); "no se me achicopale" (18–19), meaning "do not back down on me," with no equivalent expression, standard or otherwise, in Villarreal (6). Later, Cantú's *tan campante* (72) adds a tone of nonchalance to Villarreal's unvarnished description of how Richard's father falls asleep on his mattress, "like nothing was happening" (40). Furthermore, Cantú amplifies Villarreal's language and perspective. In *Pocho*, a police officer apologizes to Rubio for questioning him about a man he killed in the *cantina*: "I am not an ox. I feel deeply the intrusion but, you know, the other died" (4). Here, rather than the colloquial "I'm sorry to bother you," Villarreal uses "I feel deeply the intrusion," his literal translation for the common Spanish expression *siento la molestia* and thus employing a syntax that points to a non-English speaker. Cantú's rendition runs: "*No crea que soy un animal*, siento mucho el haberme entremetido en algo que en otras circunstancias indudablemente no fuera de mi incumbencia, *pero usted ha de saber* que se le arresta por haber cometido un crimen. *Ese hombre falleció*" (16; emphasis added). A back-translation of Cantú's Spanish helps to show the degree to which Cantú has elaborated the source: "Do not think that I am an animal, I feel much having intruded in something that in other circumstances undoubtedly would not have been an incumbency on me, but you must know that you are arrested for having committed a crime. That man died." Cantú more than doubles the word count, employs a more complex sentence structure, turns simple diction into flowery language, and gives the officer a perspective Villarreal did not give him. It seems unlikely, too, that a police officer, whether U.S. or Mexican, would speak with the excessively prim and proper language the translation attributes to him. Cantú says in his introduction that he described Rubio and his surroundings with the "castellano excelente" and "belleza de la palabra" that Martín Luis Guzmán attributed to Pancho Villa (9). But this "excellent Castilian" and "beauty of the word" is far from the plain English Villarreal attributed to the officer talking to Rubio, even if Rubio is a horseman in Villa's celebrated army.

My point here is that Cantú's hermeneutic of translation involves supplementation, improvement and embellishment (Berman's deforming tendency "ennoblement")—regionalisms, complex sentence structures, in addition to development of characters' perspectives–but his multileveled, polyphonic approach does not capture the hallmark feature of Villarreal's text that corresponds to pochismos of his time: the expressions of Spanish vernacular idioms (*dar a luz*, the standard metaphorical expression for childbirth) that he translated literally ("has given light") in the source text. A further example is the important passage toward the novel's end I referred to in the opening paragraph of this chapter where Richard explains his "pochoness"—his otherness—to Pilar Ramirez, his Mexican monolingual female interlocutor. Perceiving she laughs at his spoken Spanish, Richard explains, presumably in Spanish: "I am a Pocho, he said, and we speak like this because here in California we make Castilian words out of English words. But I can read and write *in the Spanish*, and I taught myself from the time *I had but eight years*" (165; emphasis added). Ironically, Villarreal's choice to write in English and to repeatedly encase English in Spanish syntax ("in the Spanish"; "I had but eight years") prevents Richard from practicing what he preaches. Villarreal's choice of English requires Richard to make English words out of Spanish, not Spanish words out of English words, as Richard states in the fiction of the novel to Pila. Cantú translates: "Yo soy un pocho—dijo Ricardo, como si se presentara de nuevo–, y así hablamos porque aquí en California incorporamos en nuestra manera de hablar español palabras tomadas del inglés. Pero sé leer y escribir en español, y yo mismo me enseñé desde que tenía ocho años" (238).

This central passage captures the paradox of the anti-pocho pocho. Cantú normalizes Villarreal's "in the Spanish" and "I had but eight years" into standard "normal" Spanish ("en español" and "desde que tenía ocho años") resisted in Villarreal's literal translations. Or, to put it in a slightly different manner, Cantú *covers up* Villarreal's resistance to standard Spanish—the non-pocho language prescribed by the master Mexican narrative of Guzmán and Vasconcelos. The pocho in this master narrative is a derivative work, a copy, as understood in the traditional representation of translation, of the "real" Mexican, presumably in this context Pilar. In some instances, Villarreal already gives literal English translations of the Spanish; in turn; a back-translation of Cantú's phrases in these passages only leads *back* to the standard Spanish that Villarreal's literally translated phrases already distorted. The back translation of Cantú's translation follows: "I am a pocho—said Richard, as though he presented himself anew–, and we speak like this because here in California we incorporate in our own style of speaking Spanish words taken from the English. But I know how to read and write in Spanish, and I taught myself ever since I was eight years old" (trans. mine). Villarreal's "originals" are already translations, reminding us that textuality presupposes previous productions. He lays bare Richard's Spanish by explicitly translating the Spanish lurking underneath the English, in order to communicate to his English-reading audience that Richard's experience is partially lived in Spanish and that translation is necessarily implicated in his historical identity and situation. He thus makes readers aware of the complexities of living between two languages, of a doubling consciousness, of the conflictive experiences of what it means to be Mexican American. Cantú's translation, to my mind, would have to lay itself bare as a translation, or better still would have to *re-translate* Villarreal's "pochismos," his English that is already a translation. To produce the effect of Richard's "pochoness," a translator would have to listen to how Villarreal sets up echoes, or reverberations, of Spanish in English; he would have to acknowledge Villarreal's deliberate mistranslations in English by marking Spanish with English effects—some unexpected, non-standard usage to create an analogous discomfort in readers of Spanish that Villarreal created for his readers of English and that will alert them to Richard's difference.

In narrating this same incident, Villarreal makes a factual error; he says that Cholula is in the state of Mexico (165) rather than its actual location in the state of Puebla. Cantú corrects the error (237) but adds no *sic*, footnote or explanation in his introduction or elsewhere. The fact that Cantú chooses to correct the "fiction" of the source without making his decision transparent, here and in the examples of Villarreal's deliberate mistranslations already noted, suggests to me that Cantú's translational approach is to pass off, unwittingly I assume, his translated material as real and natural, as if his translated words were analogous equivalents of what is there in the source text. The result of this choice is to cancel Villarreal's productive mistranslations. For me, this factual mistake is productive because it reveals Villarreal's own distance from Mexico, his own pochoness.

Though it may not be Cantú's intent, one effect of his translation strategy is to validate the Mexican national narrative that saw the pocho "cut off" from his alleged national origin, a sign of betrayal of national identity and culture. This national narrative, at least with respect to the pocho, necessitates a kind of translation that annuls syntactical influences of Spanish in the English source—that is, Villarreal's pochismos—as though English and Spanish had no deep history of interactive activity in the United States. *Pocho en español* forbids the pocho a voice in the translation language; it is a metaphoric repatriation of the pocho, the anti-pocho pocho. Cantú's introduction would seem to validate this suspicion:

> Sospecho que la traducción de *Pocho* abrirá posibilidades de revelación al lector latinoamericano o español, llevándole a reflexionar sobre el nivel de "americanización" en que se encuentran los países de habla hispana. A una civilización que está atravesando una etapa de *pochificación*, la novela de José Antonio Villarreal indudablemente servirá de espejo y alternativa (Cantú 1994, 9).

> I believe that the translation of *Pocho* will open possibilities for new vistas to Latin American and Spanish readers, leading them to reflect upon the extent of "Americanization" in which Spanish-language countries find themselves. For a civilization that is going through a stage of *pochification*, José Antonio Villarreal's novel undoubtedly will serve as an alternative (trans. mine).

FROM THREE LANGUAGES TO TWO

The next scene I analyze occurs in chapter 14. The scene in the original *Pocho* involves three languages (English, Spanish, and Portuguese); the translation, *Pocho en Español* reduces them to two (Spanish and Portuguese). In the original, Richard meets João Pedro Manõel Alves, a Portuguese immigrant, who initiates communication with him by speaking broken English (79–87): he asks Richard, "You spik da Portagee?" Detecting their different competencies in English, Richard and João Pedro make a pact: Richard will speak Spanish and João Pedro Manõel will speak Portuguese. The idea is that a Spanish and Portuguese speaker can understand each other; they enjoy the intercomprehensibility of languages. What's more, in the illusion of the scene's language, such communication allows them to bypass obstacles posed by English. However, they make and enact the agreement in English, the language of the text. Spanish and Portuguese, we are to imagine, lie under the novel's English surface. Therefore, English is the language used to represent a representation of the "translation" of an "imagined" conversation in Spanish and Portuguese between João Pedro and Richard. In other words, two different languages are translated in English. This arrangement heightens English as a multilingual bridge language in the assimilative process represented in the novel.

Now, what happens in the actual translation (125–130)? How does Cantú manage this three-language scene? Since the base language of *Pocho en Español* is Spanish, Richard and João, like all other English-speaking characters in this translation, have to communicate in Spanish. This is unavoidable. In the original novel, we are reading—in our mind's eye—Richard and João speaking Spanish and Portuguese underneath English; English mediates Spanish and Portuguese for the novel's audience. But in the translation, one of these "subterranean" languages—Spanish—no longer has to operate to surmount English, since it is now the majoritarian language. The scene enacts and validates the idea that Mexican culture has no room for the pocho because it removes English from the equation of language contact. In other words, it excludes the pocho.

Pocho en Español replaces English rather than defacing or refracting it so that some form of English would still be felt to imply a marred retention of English. André Lefevere talks about translated texts as refractions, as new forms of unique and untouchable classics, but still linked to them—a comic version, a plot summary, a film of a Shakespearean play, for example, popular with readers who may never read the classic of the Shakespearean play. "Refraction occurs when a text is produced to replace an original text for a given audience" ("On the Refraction" 219).[9] These are the multiple rewritings, according to Lefevere, of a classic for promoting ideological values or profit. *Pocho en Español* is linked to the original, to the text Doubleday printed in 1959, and a classic of Chicanx literature by the 1980s. Strictly speaking in Lefevere's terms, *Pocho en Español* is itself a refraction, but as this scene makes abundantly clear, it eschews its relationship to English, a language absolutely necessary to the make-up of the pocho.

Even though Spanish is the main language of the translation, it should not replace English altogether, if its purpose is to be a representation of the life of a pocho in the United States, which I believe is what it wants to be. Both languages have to be present to create Villarreal's pocho. The scandal—the outrageous, the notorious element—is that Cantú erases English. In the original, English is the language of assimilation, so it is the language causing João problems in communication. His English is marked: "Unnastand? Goot!" "You talka da Spañol." But João's Spanish is unmarked: 'Usted habla en español y yo en portugués." The translation loses the effect of a speaker trying to speak the dominant language because João is represented as a competent Spanish speaker. In the translation, only literate Spanish is allowed. Two languages, one actual, the other imagined operate, not three.

Here is the scene that illustrates my point:

Villarreal	Cantú
"You spik da Portagee?"	¿You falar da Portagee? de esta manera
(no added description)	preguntándole a Ricardo si acaso hablaba portugués
"I can understand it if you go slow:	Lo entiendo si usted lo habla despacio—
said Richard.	contestó Ricardo.
"Unnastand? Goot!" . . ."You talka	¿Entiende? ¡Bom!—dijo el hombre—.
Spañol, I talka da Portagee,	Usted habla en español y yo en
Hokay?—	Portugués. ¿Hokay?—
And the arrangement was satisfactory	Y el acuerdo les fue a ambos
to both. (81)	satisfactorio. (128)
—	—
"Tell me of your father," said the boy.	Hábleme de su papá—sugirió Ricardo
I will tell you, Richard Rubio.	Com sua licença, Ricardo Rubio.
My father is a stapud.	Mi padre es un estúpido.

Cantú employs decorative foreignisms (*falar, bom,* and *Com sua licença*) to indicate that João Pedro speaks in Portuguese. No such foreignisms appear in the original text. He does keep "You" and "da Portagee" which function as traces of an authentic sound in English to simulate broken English. He regularizes João's broken English, "spik," "unnastand," "goot," "talka," and "stapud" with corresponding correct words in Portuguese and Spanish, but he keeps "Hokay" even though no *H* is necessary in Spanish or Portuguese. On the whole, Cantú is interested in correcting "flaws," not in finding a word in broken Spanish analogous to "stapud" in broken English, just as he is not interested in making Spanish function as an assimilative language in a *pocho* experience. English is completely removed, except for the initial "you." There is no longer a language to convey a U.S. assimilative experience, which in Cantú would have to take place in a Spanish marked by English. What we get, rather, is literate Spanish—a single language—mediating a dialogue between two speakers speaking two different romance languages, one of which is the language of the translation. Since the two characters communicate in literate Spanish, Cantú thereby destroys the idea of the original text where two characters need a mediating language that is not the dominant one. The reality of an assimilative process mediating between Spanish and Portuguese into English is lost. Again, the point in a nutshell is that while Villarreal allows Spanish to mix with English, Cantú refuses to allow English to mix with Spanish to simulate the dialogue of a pocho. Cantú demonstrates a bond between Portuguese and Spanish, but he avoids the problematic inclusion of English, even though his translation keeps the setting (principally) in the United States. The linguistic border between the two romance languages is fluid, but the one between English and Spanish seems impermeable.

AN UNEXPECTED SWERVE

Cantú's dominant mode is to remove the mixture of English-Spanish linguistic elements of a common working-class and popular language. But in chapter 9, he makes an unexpected swerve worth noting. He beefs up Villarreal's scene where the pocho meets the *pachucos*[10] of his neighborhood and performs the role of a pachuco (Villarreal 153–157; Cantú 223–227). Speaking pocho is a more familiar dialect to English readers, a less radical dialect than the *caló* more commonly used by pachucos. Villarreal does not even use pochismos in the original parallel scene; much less would he have used the caló that Cantú inserts to beef up Villarreal's dialogue in his translation. Villarreal's Richard decides to participate in a gang fight with his pachuco friends, not because he has become a pachuco, or wants to be one, but because he is curious about what it would mean to perform like one. Where Villarreal used plain English, "car" and "man" (Villarreal 153–7), Cantú uses *ranfla* (226) and *vatos* (227), examples of *caló* for the same, and throws in a pochismo (*noqueó* for Villarreal's standard "knocked" 227). These registers of Spanish startlingly depart not only from Villarreal's text, but more importantly, from his own translation where he established very correct Spanish since the beginning of the novel.

In light of the invisibility/visibility dichotomy of translation, I see Cantú using both modes of translation. He has domesticated Villarreal's English to a high register of Mexican Spanish, but he now departs from it by using substandard forms (pochismos and caló) associated with Chicano culture. He gives the pocho a highly elevated diction, both at levels of narration and dialogue (invisibility), but he also rebels against his own anti-pocho pocho, as if he himself cannot sustain the mode of high Spanish (visibility). The fluent Cantú punctures the surface of his translation, the level of Spanish he has controlled all along. The breakdown makes him visible as translator; this visibility reveals his identification with substandard language and figures. Cantú's target level of language—literate Mexican Spanish—is intersected and altered by substandard language. He allows us to glimpse the collapse of at least two unwarranted hierarchies: the superiority of the author (the original, primary creator) over the translator (the derivative, secondary imitator) and the superiority of the national linguistic standard over the substandard dialect. When he uses the high mode of Spanish, he makes himself as translator invisible, as if to say that this mode is the natural, normalized mode of Spanish. When he enters the world of the pocho and pachuco, he breaks with the "natural" mode and reveals himself as a translator. Cantú subverts his own stylistic purism and dares to tread in a multilingual realm where the literary constraints of the time discouraged Villarreal and other ethnic minority writers. The textual crack jolts readers and pulls them out of an acceptance of the translator's role as a self-effacing instrument beholden to the normative translation mode of the translator's invisibility. Readers glimpse and feel the blindness of his translation. The translator pulls aside the curtain and allows us to see the kernel of multilingual forms of speech. The swerve involves only one passage, but an important, symbolic one.

POCHISMOS AND JOUAL

One form Spanglish can take is pochismos, a language variant bearing the marks of orality and popular language, that closely resembles *joual* in a historical and linguistic context ("la langue québécoise"). Joual is the working-class speech of French-speaking Canadians, characterized by linguistic doubling through English loanwords and syntactic patterns, whose status moved from a marginal dialect to a literary style during the Québécois movement of the late 1960s and early 1970s. In *Mapping Literature*, Homel and Simon say it paved "the way . . . for a whole new literary identity of Quebec" (56). The word joual is a distorted translation of *cheval*, the French word meaning "horse" (56); it had always been considered "an inferior dialect, a sub-language, a stigma of a people going nowhere" (56). Sherry Simon, a theorist of translation, a translator, and a major contributor to the study of intranational translation and specifically of the French-writing authors of Quebec into Canadian English, says of joual: "For the purists adopting Parisian written French as their model, joual was an impure and degraded form of speech, its pronunciation vulgar, its grammar incorrect, its rampant anglicisms an affront ("The Language of Cultural Difference" 170). In the introduction to *Culture in Transit*, she offers two examples of joual, or what she calls "English sounds in strange-looking strings of French syllables: *cuiquelounche* for 'quick lunch' and *farowest* for 'Far West'" ("Introduction" 11). Homel and Simon offer this example: "Il s'est assis sur le tchesteurfilde" (He sat down on the [chesterfield] sofa) (*Mapping* 57–58). A *joualisant*, or a person who speaks in joual, is analogous to a pocho or pocha who uses pochismos in their speech/writing. The historical evolution and interlingual nature of joual shares some features with the mixing of Spanish and English in Chicanx and other Latinx speech and literature. Homel and Simon themselves make an explicit connection between joual and pocho speech. "*Joual* is a language against itself. In that contradiction is contained the paradox of *joual*, and, indeed, that of similar dialects, like *el pocho*, spoken along the Mexican-American border" (*Mapping* 58). In an aside, they add: "[p]*ocho*, interestingly enough, means "faded" in Mexican Spanish, as if speakers of this English-flavoured dialect have lost their original colour" (58).

As is true of Latinx narratives translated to English and Spanish in the United States, Simon uses "intranational" to describe the translation of Quebec literature into English in Canada: "Unlike most literary translation which is international, Canadian translation has historically been an intranational affair ("Introduction" 8)." (170). But unlike the intranational translation of Latinx literature, Quebec's translations involve Canada's two official *national* languages, albeit ones asymmetrical in their power relations: French, the minor Canadian language, and English, the major Canadian language. My own examples, *Pocho en Español* and *Cuando era,* are texts whose source language is the de facto official national language of the United States translated to Spanish, the unofficial minority-national language of the same country, and at the same time a global transnational language.

EN ESPAÑOL?

From what *Cantú* says in the passage from his introduction (9) which I already quoted and his practices of translation, his primary audience seems to include a Latin American, Spanish peninsular, and a Spanish-language literary U.S. audience. His standardization of Villarreal's language certainly points to an international audience, primarily in Mexico, given the proximity of the experience narrated. But it is crucial to remember that *Pocho en Español* is a translation of a bilingual source text, that it is commissioned and published by a U.S. publisher, and that it is translated by a biliterate Mexican American. Though one must allow for an audience in Mexico, one must also extend the translation's readership to the borders of the U.S. nation-state. The book's peritextual information in fact points to an audience inside the United States.

Peritextual markers relate to the text's production and consumption in the marketplace. They include those elements that relate to how it is put together, a product to be consumed as a commodity rather than an object of aesthetic value. Examples are a book's cover design, copyright and publishing details, quotations from authenticating powers that can help sell the book, its title and subtitle, and in some cases an author's (or translator's) introduction addressed to its audience. All these factors are part and parcel of the package that circulates in the global book market (Genette 2–5). One important peritextual marker in the case of this translation is the tag *"en español"* immediately below the one-word title on the cover. This tag and other markers point to an intranational U.S. audience.

To explain what I mean, I would like to return to the passage already quoted in which Richard explains his pocho identity to Pilar, the young Mexican from Cholula visiting California. At the level of the characters, the passage represents the intersection between a Mexican-American, working-class pocho, and (probably) an unschooled non-pocha of a peripheral Mexican city of the 1950s. The Spanish Richard speaks to Pilar is submerged in the language of the novel, English. Just as that passage inside the text represents the linguistic complexity of the pocho's identity–the voice of one language woven into the voice of another language–so the peritextual markers in the translation lay bare the intersection of its two audiences: inside and outside the United States. Other signs stated on the copyright page show that this book, its producer-publisher, and its place of publication are situated in the United States:

> Traducción española copyright © 1994 por Doubleday, una división de
> Bantam Doubleday Dell Publishing Group, Inc.
> Todos los Derechos Reservados
> Impreso en los Estados Unidos de América
> Primera Edición de Anchor Books: Junio 1994

These markers are comparable to Villarreal's literal translations of Spanish idiomatic expressions hidden in the novel's English language. They constitute the "Made in the USA" label that tells its audience—inside or out of the United States—that this book is a U.S. translation of a U.S. source product, commissioned and published by a U.S. press. Just as Richard in the passage already cited speaks to Pilar without being able to hide his pochoness to her and to readers of *Pocho*, so likewise this product cannot point to a Mexican or Latin American audience without revealing its intranational origins through the peritextual signs of "Made in the USA." The Spanish that tainted the English of Villarreal's text now reemerges as English tainting the Spanish of Cantú's translation in the text's production. In other words, the peritextual markers at the level of the text's production and preparation for the marketplace replicate the intersection established between Richard and Pilar at the level of the text's fiction.

Both the publisher and translator tell us that the 1994 *Pocho* is a translation, therefore the reader has to take this into account. The phrase "traducción de Roberto Cantú" appears on the reverse side of the title page as opposed to the translator's name receiving first billing with the author's name on the book's cover, a placement far easier for a reader to notice. The same phrase is camouflaged with other front piece information on the copyright page. This out-of-sight, out-of-mind positioning of the translator's name by the publisher reinforces the tradition of translation that encourages the invisibility of translators. Furthermore, Cantú explicitly identifies his work as a translation in the introduction he writes, making several references to Villarreal's *Pocho*, gesturing allegiance to the original. Hence, the publisher and translator see themselves co-implicated in the act of translation. Both invite us to collude with them and read the book as a translation.

But why does Doubleday display "*en Español*" on the cover? The tag is certainly not a label one would see in Mexico as an announcement for the language of any print or telecommunications product. A Mexican publisher would not put it on one of its domestic literary products or even on an international product it commissioned for translation. This kind of tag emphasizes that this text is available to a U.S. audience in Spanish. It signals a kind of translation practice distinct from the "international" translation that operates across different languages of separate nation-states. It stresses the connection between the dominant national languages and cultures of source text and translation, and is initiated by a press in the country for which the translation is done. In international translation, the translating language, whatever the language, whatever the country, is a taken for granted; it goes without saying. If any tag is used to designate the source language, it is usually something like "translated from the English" or "*traduit en français*," for example. There would be no need to add "*en Español*," since pocho is already a Spanish word, probably known to more readers in 1994 than in 1959 when the English text was first published. Doubleday, a U.S. national publisher, is doing intranational translation: it is publishing a translation into a major–minor language of a text already in English, the dominant language of the receptor culture. These paratextual signals reinforce the statements by New York presses, I discussed in chapter 1, such as Random House and Harper Collins, who saw themselves marketing the translations to Spanish reading audience elsewhere but primarily to a domestic U.S. audience.

The tag on the book cover intimates that this translation is *something more* than standard international translation. What is this *something more* and for whom is it intended? The "something more"—that which cannot be absorbed into the international grid—is the intranation, yet also the transnation. The fact that *"en Español"* is apparently necessary leads me to speculate that the press may intend[11] the translation for a Spanish-language audience both in and outside the United States. It especially rings bells to an inside biliterate English- and Spanish-reading audience in the United States, for whom the special indicator forewarning that this *Pocho* is in Spanish would be somewhat meaningful, though perhaps a bit odd.[12] A Chicanx-Latinx audience, especially, knows the meaning of surplus, of needing to state openly and directly the language of translation, even if it constitutes excess, of constantly needing to translate, of double audiences, of the perils and joys of living in a society where unequal cultural exchange takes place between the hegemonic language and its minor languages. These readers would know that the 1959 English-language text and its 1970 and 1989 reprints had no marker announcing the book's language, although it would have made logical sense, though awkward, to have added *In English* to these prior editions. Such information would have assured uninformed English readers that this book with a Spanish word for its title was indeed in English. But since the previous English editions carried no such tag, these words had to appear, I assume, below the main title of the 1994 translation because the publisher and its primary audience knew there was a tangible text already in the public domain against which the translation could or would be measured. The publisher found it necessary to insert *"en Español"* to differentiate the translation from the extant 1989 edition.

The case of this U.S. text is different since its language of translation is a majority–minority language in the United States, the second language of the country, a language major enough for a mainstream publisher to risk a translation into it and to afford the book a special marketing label, lest it lose one of its audiences. This translation underscores a major press's shift from translation between specific nations—one language for one nation, another for a different nation—to translation within the same country, to tap a national market of biliterate consumers. This is an intranational but also a transnational translation because it is aimed at Spanish-reading audiences elsewhere.

The audience contenders outside the U.S. market are Spanish readers in Latin and Central America, and Spain, but especially Mexico. True, Mexican Spanish readers also would assess the marker as constituting excess because they would assume, rightly, that under ordinary circumstances, the language of translation would be their own, and they need not be informed that the book is in Spanish. Instead of alerting them to the source language the work has been translated from (such as, "Translated from the English"), the tag-phrase *"en Español"* informs Mexican readers that the receptor language is their own. This information should tip off a Mexican audience that something is slightly off-kilter. However, the book's title, its setting (the Mexican Revolution), its subject matter, and its erudite Spanish (at times pedantic) all point to an imagined community of Mexican readers. This translation is dually aimed: at an internal audience yet it also implies a Mexican audience, at least from the standpoint of its production, if not from its actual reception. *Pocho en Español* exceeds the limits of the international model of translation, which cannot absorb the surplus, the *something more*. The "something more" is the remainder (Neate 17–18), the overflow that exceeds the scale of the binary national/international model.

INTRANATIONAL TRANSLATION

I return to the question posed in my introduction. Just how does one, should one translate a text like *Pocho* when its medium of expression, along with its content and title, imply resistance to the Mexican master narrative and to the standard Spanish that narrative upholds? To subvert the notion of the pocho's "betrayal" to national origins, a translator would need to respect and capture the pocho's cultural difference erased in the Mexican master narrative of the first half of the twentieth century. A translator would need to reformulate the function and meaning of the relationships that once defined the pocho in debilitating terms to insert him into new affirmative contexts of reception—in short, a translator would have to find the appropriate idiom in Spanish to approximate something close to García-Canclini's "cultural reconversion" (30). Instead, Cantú primarily has altered Villarreal's unexpected syntactical constructions from English into standard Spanish and reinforced the notion of the pocho as a betrayal of nation. The one exception to the novel's form is the unexpected swerve into a pocho and pachuco dialect.

Pocho en Español, only one of the many English-to-Spanish translations published in the United States, underscores two important, related shifts in the publication of translation by major U.S. presses: 1) a shift from a country's dominant source language into the country's major–minor receptor language, thus defying the convention that translation moves from one national language into another national language, and 2) a shift from translation between different countries (one national border to another) to translation within the same nation-state, in order to reach an intranational market of consumers. To be sure, intranational translation does not replace international translation, but it does highlight local, domestic changes which are directly linked to a transnational and global market. In the United States, translators doing intranational translations must recognize that the signs of different languages—in this case English and Spanish in Chicanx and Latinx literatures—constantly interact, and they are always at work on each other, neither language "foreign" to the other but interdependent in the social and political context of their cultures. Intranational translation underscores the uncontainability of Spanish, its dialects and its various cultures, to the usual Spanish-speaking nations of the world. The United States today is part of the Spanish-speaking global world.

CHAPTER 4

UNFORGETTING THE FORGETTING

The Sonics of the *Jíbara* Dialect in Esmeralda Santiago's *Cuando era puertorriqueña*

I am struck by a particular passage in the textual pair *When I Was* (*Cuando era*) where Esmerelda Santiago's protagonist and alter ego Negi (short for Esmeralda) explains how much as a child living on the island she enjoyed drawing maps. Impressed by her skills, her father tells her that she should grow up to be a cartographer. Miss Jimenez, on the other hand, her third-grade teacher, tells her she is more of a topographer "because cartographers' maps were flat, while mine had the bumps and dips of mountain ranges and valleys" (149). I take Santiago's images of cartography-topography, nonverbal forms of "writing," as a springboard into my analysis of her writing-translation practices. The image of cartography-topography provides me with an entry point into the broad outlines of two common approaches to the translation practices she charts in her original and translation texts.

Much like a cartographer draws political borders around regions, delimiting and defining territories, states, or nations, segmenting one from another, the first approach to translation imagines languages as basic units, as self-contained, discrete systems with potential to be isolated from, and juxtaposed to, one another. This is reminiscent of Sakai's reproach of theories of languages as unified wholes.[1] Yet, in translation practice and theory, this approach implies movement from one language to a different language, otherwise translation would be not only unnecessary but impossible. In a sense, it invites the kind of translation that involves semantic equivalence, or interchangeability: a word in one language has its equivalent, or closest approximation, in a different language—no mountain ranges, no valleys. Rebecca Walkowitz, author of *Born Translated*, finds this approach to encourage works to enter the sameness and fluency of "the pipeline of multinational publishing" (31). Broadly speaking, it would correspond to the "flatness" of cartographers' maps in Santiago's quote. In contrast, the image of topography adds a third dimension that complicates the cartographic two-dimensional first approach. Rather than sanctioning easy equivalence between languages, the second approach privileges opacity, posing some obstacles to the target audience's understanding. This translation practice eschews fluency, easy access; it resists the idea that the translation ought to read to the target audience as smoothly as the original does to its "native" audience. It allows room for experimentation, seeing value in local heterogeneity rather than in the intertranslatability of the global market. This approach aligns more closely with the "bumps and dips" of topography in Santiago's quote.

How best to register the tension between these two approaches in Santiago's self-translation? My approach is to read original and translation texts as one ensemble, not as separate entities. Each one is incomplete without the other. In the original text, she conducts external multilingualism, movement between Spanish and English, as in "*Muñequita*" (little doll, 13) and "*La Colorá*" (the red girl, 13), which is necessary to translate Spanish Puerto Rican local idioms to two of her three main audiences: a monolingual English and a non-Puerto Rican bilingual audience. One might call this approach "translation-friendly" in a market sense. Her third audience is the island and mainland bilingual Puerto Rican audience for whom no translation is necessary. She also conducts internal multilingualism or varieties within English and within Spanish (Walkowitz 41). In the original, she offers a transliterative form of English to capture the mangled sounds of English uttered by Spanish-speaking, second-language English users. The translation text performs a kind of meta-play on the source text because the transliteration is different: she renders the English sounds made by the same Spanish-speaking characters to a Spanish-dominant Puerto Rican audience. The book's central local idiom is the speech of a *jíbaro/a* (meaning, for now, a "mountain peasant," a hillbilly). Her translation text, ironically, bears the hidden traces of "originality"—the jíbaro/a dialect—that source texts are assumed to bear, if we accept reigning translation paradigms of "origin and target texts" that suppose source texts are "more original" than their corresponding translation texts. *When I Was*, however, attempts to suppress the sounds of a jíbaro/a vernacular that instead surface in *Cuando era*. In her intranational self-translation, Santiago incorporates in *Cuando era* key phrases from a jíbaro/a Puerto Rican vernacular she heard as a child growing up on the island: for example, the spoken language "yo no soy zángana" (28). In *When I Was*, she renders them into English-sounding standard form: I'm not stupid" (24). The popular exclamatory expression "¡Ay no qué chavienda!" conveying disgust in *Cuando era* (71) is absent in *When I Was*. Therefore, in the original text we find examples of conversions into written language of the more "original" spoken dialect in the translation text. Although the spoken dialect (the human voice) is part of a written literary text, the act of translation can be a medium of "origin" and not just an "after-life," as proposed by Walter Benjamin (71, 73). It is not just something that comes after the original work but may indeed precede it.

The two text worlds of *When I Was Puerto Rican* and *Cuando era puertorriqueña*, original and translation, constitute a chronological narrative of remembrance in which Esmeralda Santiago reframes an experience already lived. Like all other fictional autobiographies, the "I" sees herself from the distance of a "now," a "now" implicit in the verb tenses of her English and Spanish titles (*When I Was*; *Cuando era*). The focus is on an effort to remember a "then," to make the past actual. The adult English-speaking "I" narrates from a place on the New York mainland the "I" of the young girl who arrived from Santurce to Macún, a fictional name for a small town in Toa Baja, a region in the northern coast of Puerto Rico, in 1952, the same year the constitution of the Estado Libre Asociado, the modern commonwealth of Puerto Rico, is signed. Growing up on the island, moving back and forth between city and country, she leaves the island permanently with her mother at age twelve for New York in the early 1960s. A span of more than thirty years separates her island and mainland identities. A significantly smaller period of time—indeed almost simultaneous publication—separates the original and translation texts. What interests me here is the relationship between Santiago's English-speaking "I" and her Spanish self-translating "I." The Spanish self-translating "I" corrects the misreadings of the English speaking "I" in the original text. To put it another way, the Spanish self-translating "I" *unforgets the forgetting* of the English speaking "I."

Cuando era is different from the two other transnational translations I discuss in this book in the sense that it is a self-translation, meaning that Santiago (and her editor) produced the writing of both the original work and the translation. Yet *Cuando era* carries no attribution of a translator, either on the physical exterior of the book, namely its cover, or the interior initial pages of copyright information. The book's interior framing device that identifies the translator is the introduction Santiago writes to *Cuando era*, probably at the request of her editor. She mentions Robin Desser, her editor, and credits her with the suggestion to translate *When I Was*. This is an ironic request since Santiago tells us in the introduction—in Spanish—that she is primarily a speaker of English: "El idioma que más hablo es el inglés" (*Cuando era* xv).[2] She says in the introduction that in the intervening years, between island and mainland, her relationship to Spanish changed and then changed again when she relearned it to translate her book. On attempting the translation, she became aware of "cuánto español se me había olvidado" (*Cuando* xvi).[3] Does the editor's request to translate the book presuppose that if a child's "mother tongue" is Spanish, the language of her parents and childhood, she will maintain it into adulthood, even to the point of being able to translate a book? Between the writing of *When I Was* and its translation into *Cuando era*, Santiago had to *unforget the forgetting* of her Spanish. She feels forced to re-remember it, to relearn it; again in the introduction, she says "me forzó a aprender de nuevo el idioma de mi niñez" (*Cuando* xvi).[4]

The introduction functions both as a bridge between source and translation texts and a metacommentary about her rewriting (self-translating). Santiago composed no introduction for the English original. In the thirty-plus years after the migration, English had become her taken-for-granted language, her default literary language, the language that needs no explanation, no interrogation. Hence, there is no paratextual indicator of any kind—no introduction, for example—to alert us that *When I Was* began somewhere else, that her actual life in Spanish preceded her textual English one. Even though the translation narrative itself bears no easily perceived signs of the source text's multilingual features, her Spanish-reading audience upon reading the introduction to *Cuando era* will know the circumstances of how the writing of this book began in another language, culture, and history. The variable she highlights of her Puerto Rican identity is not gender or class, two important social variables of her identity in her books, but "that most intimate of sites—language" (de Courtivron 2). In self-translating, Santiago is "rewriting" a text she knows not just well enough, but too well (Pérez-Firmat 106–107). She has an intimate relationship to the text she herself wrote in a different language and that she now renders into another. The personal, subjective element of self-translation foregrounds the desire "to tinker, to amend, to get it right or righter the second time around" (Pérez-Firmat 107). Her stress on language in the prologue suggests to me that the act of translating into Spanish made Santiago self-conscious of her loss. Perhaps, she had never felt a need to think about the loss of her mother tongue before accepting to translate her book professionally.

DISCOVERY OF SPANGLISH, THE "PECULIAR DIALECT"

Santiago's life-path in Spanish and English did not move along the smooth, solid lines of cartography, with each language demarcated clearly from each other. Her life, like that of other Latinx writers, was not associated with a single tongue or a single geographical space. It resembled more the "bumps and dips" of topography, taking a rougher road through uneven terrain. Let me elaborate. She writes *When I Was*, a book she can only write in English about a life she lived as a jíbara in Spanish on the island. She says in the introduction to *Cuando era* "la vida relatada en este libro fue vivida en español, pero fue inicialmente escrita en inglés" (Cuando xv).[5] She learned to speak English through phonetic presentations of songs and rhymes her Spanish-speaking island teachers used to teach students English: "and we learned all our songs phonetically, having no idea of what the words meant. She tried to teach us 'America the Beautiful' but had to give up when we stumbled on 'or spacious skies' and 'amber waves of grain'" (77). The two languages collide in the children's heads to produce a hodgepodge of inchoate sounds: "4 espé chosk ¡Ay!" and "am burr gueys oh gren." These disfigured words appear in *When I Was* and evoke the historical importance and agency of colonized populations (77). Once in New York, she attends a mainstream English-language school (today she would potentially be assigned to an "English as a second-language" class). Accents of Spanish continue to mark her spoken English, to the point that she is unable to recite the lines in an American play like a "native speaker" in her audition toward the book's end to the Performing Arts School in Manhattan, and thereby gain the opportunity to "get out of Brooklyn" (266). However, with time she becomes a proficient speaker in sound and sense, the adult fluent writer of *When I Was*, a graduate of Sara Lawrence College (Prosper Sánchez 134) and Harvard's MFA program to boot. English by now has become so deeply part of her being that Spanish is no longer her primary language.

Santiago's gain of one language and loss of the other language was something educational, something that happened to her *at school*, just as it did to the two other writers included in this book—and to so many other Latinos and Latinas, and writers of other worldwide colonized cultures.[6] In Santiago's case, however, just one year after writing *When I Was*, she is asked to translate it. She decides to relearn Spanish, now the silenced language, in order to convert the book about a life lived in Spanish and recaptured already in English into the idiom of standard monolingual Spanish to satisfy the expectations of her editor, the press, and her primary island Puerto Rican audience (and readers of Spanish elsewhere). The act of translation takes her back to a memory of her life in Spanish on the island, represented on the textual surface of the original text by the scattered words and expressions in Spanish, sometimes in dialogue, as when Negi asks her father, "Papi, what's a *jamona*?. . . . It is a woman who has never married" (89). In translating, then, she is no longer writing about a life lived in Spanish; she is rewriting/translating into Spanish a written text in English about a life lived in Spanish on the island, about coming-of-age experiences in a bilingual New York setting, and about her struggle to master English.

In the introduction to *Cuando era*, she says the act of translation ("el proceso de traducir del inglés al español," xvi) leads her to realize ("me ha demonstrado," xvi):

> . . . el idioma que ahora hablo, el cual yo pensaba que era el español, es realmente el espanglés, ese dialecto forjado del español y el inglés que toma palabras de los dos idiomas, las añade a las expresiones familiares puertorriqueñas y cambia la manera en que se escriben hasta crear palabras nuevas (*Cuando* xvi).
> . . . The language I speak now, the *one I thought was* Spanish, is really Spanglish, that dialect of Spanish and English that takes words from both languages, adds them to familiar Puerto Rican expressions and changes the way they are written so as to even create new words (trans. mine, emphasis added).

She offers examples of *espanglés*: "mop" in English is not *trapeador* in standard Spanish but *mapo*; market in English is not *mercado* but *marketa*; "ticket" in English is not *boleto* but *tique*; and "busy" in English is not *ocupado* in Spanish but *busi*.[7] With this discovery she realizes her mistake: what she thought to have been Spanish was really espanglés. This mistaking of Spanish for espanglés, a recognition that only the translation allows to emerge, implies a doubling of self between the monolingual Spanish she uses in *Cuando era* to satisfy her editor, the press, and to speak to her island audience, and the Spanglish she now sees as her own. In short, she needs both the demarcated boundaries that separate Spanish from English, and English from Spanish (cartography), the standard norm of conventional translation and called for by international translation, and the promiscuity of English and Spanish (ups and downs) that produces Spanglish (topography). Santiago's relation to her two languages is a bumpy ride: from Spanish to English back again to Spanish but this time with the twist of Spanglish.

WAS AND ERA: FINALITY AND CONTINUITY

This tension between univocality and multivocality is caught in the verb tenses of the English and Spanish titles. Santiago's best choice for an English title is *When I Was* (as opposed to "When I used to be"). The "was" expresses the simple past of the first-person singular and usually conveys a condition in the past that no longer exists, though the ambiguity of its duration never can be fully removed. In Spanish, her best choice is *Cuando era* (as opposed to *Cuando fui*). According to the logic of Spanish grammar, "era" even more emphatically than the English "was," or for that matter "used to be," conveys that the condition in the past continues into the present. The connotation of "was" to signal a definite past in the English title led some Puerto Rican critics to "misread" her meaning.[8] Efraín Barradas ("Esmeralda" 41), for example, thought that Santiago was stating that she was no longer Puerto Rican (gone forever). The title of his book review says as much: "Esmeralda Santiago o cómo *dejar de ser* puertorriqueño" ("Esmeralda Santiago or how to *stop being* Puerto Rican" trans. mine, emphasis added). He asks: "qué era lo que profetizaba éste [el libro] que gritaba desde la portada que la autora ya no era puertorriqueña" ("Esmeralda Santiago" 199).[9] He continues: "[p]ero más que la portada, me atrajo el "Was" del título. Aquí la autora declara que no es puertorriqueña. ¿Y por qué no lo es? ¿Qué es ahora? ¿Por qué dejó de serlo?" (199).[10]

Barradas's misreading is certainly plausible, especially after one reads the text. Santiago transferred Negi's sense of loss of her Puerto Ricanness inside the text into the "was" of the English title. In the end, Barradas argues, I think correctly, that the migration created the division that led Negi to suppose she was no longer Puerto Rican since she had felt, before the migration, that to be Puerto Rican was to be a jíbara. The migration, she feels, erases her jíbara identity. This intense loss of Puerto Ricanness is due to Negi's misreading that to be Puerto Rican is to be a jíbara, a misinterpretation captured in the English title. Although Barradas might be toying with the title to use as a tease into his review, I doubt that this bilingual, biliterate Puerto Rican critic would have suggested Santiago's disavowal of her Puerto Ricanness had he reviewed the Spanish text. My point here is that the Spanish title provides the three-dimensional correction, the continuity of *era*, to the two-dimensional message, the finality of "was," in the English title.

THE TERM JÍBARA/O

Who is the jíbaro, the jíbara[11] that Negi so ardently desires to become and that she misrecognizes for the true Puerto Rican? The following are some broad outlines of the long-standing discourse on this word and what it signifies. An overdetermined term, with multiple associations, identifications, and connections, it has characterized Puerto Rican history, literature, and culture across classes and cultures at least since the mid-nineteenth century on the island and, in the twentieth century, among the diaspora into the barrios of New

York. At no time, though, did it have as wide a popular and symbolic currency as in the late 1940s to the 1960s, the period of Santiago's/Negi's youth on the island. During this time, a predominant ideology was jíbarismo, a cultural elite's idealization of the jíbaro. The jíbaro, to them, was a provocative presence, a source of evocative pleasure. They longed for what they saw as the original jíbaro's harmonious pastoral past, a past whose relevance was diminished, yielding to the disappointments of urban modernity.

Santiago tells us in the introduction that the word is a *puertorriqueñismo* (xvi), meaning it is *netamente* (uniquely) Puerto Rican, "untranslatable," with no comparable English equivalent in meaning and emotional affect. In this sense, it is comparable to the identity terms *pocho* in the previous chapter and *mojado* in the next chapter. As a historical construct, however, it functions most comparably to the image-text of *indio* in Mexico because, unlike the other two terms, both *indio* and jíbaro served ideological projects and populist movements of the political and cultural elite in Mexico and Puerto Rico in the twentieth century. Both figures represented marginalized social groups, transformed into keystones of a Mexican and Puerto Rican national ethos, iconic of a proximity to land, of a longing for authentic Mexicanness and Puerto-Ricanness, points of origin and embodiments of nation.

Denotatively, jíbaro refers to the first mountain-dwelling peasants of Puerto Rico, reputedly descendants of Spanish colonizers. José Luis González, the Puerto Rican Marxist intellectual—essayist, university professor, and journalist—wrote about the coexistence of social classes and cultures in Puerto Rico in his 1980's seminal essay "El país de cuatro pisos" (Guinnes Puerto Rico: The Four-Storeyed Country"). He refers to *jíbaros* as the *campesinado blanco*; *un campesinado pobre* (González, J.L. 21) ("white campesinos;" "a poor peasantry" Guinness 10).[12] These campesinos (or "field workers") were coded "white" and male through the years; their physiognomy, dress, and accoutrements became the symbolic image and heart of a twentieth-century cultural elite's construction of a Puerto Rican national identity. The twentieth-century version of the discussion on the jíbaro started on the island before Santiago was born and continued through her adult years. Notably, the cultural elite did not use their critical powers to construct the African or mulatto populations of the coastal areas as the symbolic habitus of a national culture, a highly ironic position since it was the Afro-Antillean peoples, González argues, that were the first puertorriqueños, the foundational "storey" of the Puerto Rican "mansion" or country (20). Jíbaros were economically poor, isolated, illiterate, and rustic in manners; they often went barefoot. An agricultural sector that worked the island's hinterland during preindustrial, premodern Puerto Rico, throughout the nineteenth and twentieth centuries, jíbaros and jíbaras had formed part of Puerto Rican folklore and literature in drawings, paintings, and poetry. Prior to the 1930s, a prevailing view portrayed them as uncouth, a "wretched sickly, aloof, and morally suspect" (Córdova 173), part of the population, with no political or cultural agency. They were objects of ridicule and shame not only among *gente de buenos modales* (well-mannered people) but also other social classes too. Negi's mother and Sra. Leona, her math teacher, express vestiges of this pejorative view, showing that the term's negative residue lingered among the populace in the era of the height of jíbarismo:

For Negi's mother, jíbaros/as are born in the country; for her, they are *of* the country, meaning illiterate and crude. Negi cannot be a jíbara, or so the mother argues, because she was born in Santurce, the city. The family moves to Macún where Negi is impressed positively by the country people. The mother warns Negi never to call those she loves and respects jíbaros/as. The girl is confused because she sees no observable differences between her family and the older generation of jíbaros (Doña Zeño, Doña Lola) she comes to know in Macún: the poor who live close to nature and seem intractable in their ways; above all, those rooted in a proud nationalism, and happy, presumably, in their poverty. Ironically, Negi is forced to experience cultural duplicity: when she is in Santurce, the city, she is seen as a jíbara and is mocked for it; when living in Macún, her mother says she cannot be a jíbara because she was born in the city. The mother scolds: "¡No seas tan jíbara!"[13] and Sra. Leona laments: "tanto jíbaro ignorante en este país (151).[14]

In 1935, Antonio Pedreira (1899–1939), one of Puerto Rico's foremost man of letters, wrote "La actualidad del jíbaro" (The *Jíbaro* Today), an important essay of the major recovery project then under way by writers, poets, and artists of *La Generación del Treinta* (The 30s Generation), who aimed to define Puerto Rico's national identity. They turned inward to glorify the peasant figure in the remote past of their Spanish colonial history. Pedreira's generation came from well-to-do families, some of them children of the former landowning elite displaced economically, socially, and politically by North American imperialism (Guerra 29). Although invested in, and benefiting from, the policies of North American imperialism, they resented it. They became intensely focused on searching for a definition of who they were: "la necesidad de buscarnos a nosotros mismos: de definirnos, de saber lo que somos y cómo somos." (Pedreira 12).[15] This famous *jíbarista* outlined the jíbaro trope's historical evolution through literature, contrasted its significance for his generation with that of nineteenth-century intellectuals, and reinterpreted its previously maligned legendary image to imbue it with positive meaning. He noted: "Lo que ayer era un mote despectivo hoy es un título, blasonado de criolla estirpe, que todos quisiéramos tener" (Pedreira 14).[16] Concluding that no figure more than the jíbaro held the key to Puerto Rican national identity, Pedreira and others, like Luis Lloréns Torres (1876–1944) whose poetry Santiago cites in her book, used it to project a vision of the nation they envisioned (Guerra 68).[17] They, the non-jíbaros, invoked a sense of longing for the jíbaro; the image or abstraction was more real to them than any manifestation of a flesh-and-blood jíbaro could be. By making the jíbaro the cornerstone of their search, they emphasized the rural past and their Spanish "white" lineage,[18] obfuscating alternative realities—non-white, Afro-Mestizo, proletarian, feminist—of Puerto Rican identities and cultures.

No one, perhaps, did more to popularize the term in the mid-twentieth century than the charismatic Luis Muñoz Marín (1898–1980) and his *Partido Popular Democrático* (PPD) established in 1938. Muñoz Marín, the son of a famous Puerto Rican statesman, was educated in the United States. He became the island's first democratically elected governor (1948–1965) and the architect of Puerto Rico's constitution, the basis of the Commonwealth (1952), and of *Operación manos a la obra* (Operation Bootstrap), a model of economic development that brought significant progress to the island, yet made it permanently dependent on "the capital, goods, and government transfer payments provided by the United States" (Guerra 266). Prior to committing himself to a political managerial career, he had been a writer, poet, and journalist.

In 1898, the U.S. American Edwin Markham wrote "The Man with a Hoe," a poetic depiction of the American laborer. In 1919, twenty-one-year-old Muñoz Marín translated the poem into "El hombre de la azada," seeing in Markham's laborer an analogue to the Puerto Rican jíbaro.[19] Interestingly, Muñoz Marín was born the same year Markham wrote the poem that inspired him to appropriate Puerto Rico's jíbaro for his own political use at home. This year also saw the end of home rule with the U.S. invasion of the isle in the Spanish American war. Interested in the jíbaros, and the working poor, Muñoz Marín did actually meet with jíbaros, by then semi-rural peasants; he traveled throughout the island speaking with politically disenfranchised groups and mobilizing them to political action. He and his party made the image of the jíbaro its pictorial emblem and rallying cry during his senatorial campaign in 1940, a prelude to his 1948 election of governor. The rustic jíbaro's profile and his *pava* (hat) became the key element of the emblem and always inscribed below the image was the text *Pan, Tierra, y Libertad* (Bread, Land, and Liberty). "The field laborer's hat was part and parcel of the depictions of the *jíbaro* since early in the nineteenth century. . . . Hence, the *pava* facilitated identification, and made the emblem instantly recognizable as an image of a *jíbaro*, enhancing the audience's ability to 'read' the emblem" (Córdova 175–76). Muñoz Marín and the PPD (*el partido de la pava* [the party of the pava] Córdova 175) effectively tapped the jíbaro's evocative force and rhetorical power and converted it into an icon of Puerto Rican nationalism and identity.

JÍBARA: MIGRATION AS METAPHOR OF TRANSLATION

Given that Santiago's Negi's grew up on the island in the 1950s era of *muñocismo*, Muñoz Marín's governorship, during the political and cultural excitement over the jíbaro and jíbarismo, it is understandable that Negi "misrecognize" the jíbara as the essence of an authentic Puerto Rican identity. Poems and stories about the jíbaro were required reading in school; Negi hears the traditional music of rural Puerto Ricans on the radio, and she hears her father recite celebratory poetry on the jíbaro. Her father, *un . . . jíbaro ilustrado* (Barradas 41)[20] refuses to migrate and, to Negi's chagrin, does nothing to impede her migration. Her favorite patriotic song is Noel Estrada's *En mi viejo San Juan* "In Old San Juan," a classic bolero in the jíbaro tradition that expresses the immigrant's typical yearning for home. All this inculcates in Negi positive beliefs about, and a desire to be, a jíbara. The migration, however, changes things. Santiago's writing of the migration is a pivotal scene, a primal splitting between the jíbara Negi desires to be and the adolescent and adult she will become. The scene divides the book into two major sections: from island to mainland, from jíbara to *norteamericana*, from the working-class Spanish Negi speaks to literate English. Santiago presents Negi feeling cut off, fearing she has lost what she had gained of a jíbara identity. Since the vitality of Negi's jíbara image measures her Puerto Ricanness, its diminution measures the extent she feels disconnected from it. Here is the scene of the traumatism, of the leave-taking.

> For me, the person I was becoming when we left *was erased*,
> and another one was created. The *Puerto Rican jíbara* [read "purity"]
> who longed for the green quiet of a tropical afternoon was to become
> a hybrid [read "mixture"] who would never forgive the uprooting
> (*When I Was* 209).

> Para mí, la persona en que me iba convirtiendo cuando nos fuimos
> *fue borrada*, y otra fue creada en su lugar. La jíbara puertorriqueña
> [o "pureza"] quien soñaba con la verdez silenciosa de una tarde tropical se
> convertiría en una *híbrida* [o "mezcla"] quien nunca perdonaría el desarraigo
> (*Cuando era* 227).

Santiago pointedly writes the migration as a decision taken by her mother against her will. In the introduction, she tells us: "Pero muchas veces siento el dolor de haber dejado a mi islita, mi gente, mi idioma. Y a veces ese dolor se convierte en rabia, en resentimiento, porque yo no seleccioné venir a los Estados Unidos. A mí me trajeron" (*Cuando* xviii).[21] Her involuntary departure from the island is a violent occurrence, a life-threatening experience. The English word she gives is "uprooting" (209); the Spanish word is *desarraigo* (227); both connote a yanking from her jíbara roots, from the deep material of her self. She feels the migration is a wiping-out, an erasure of the movement toward the formation of the Puerto Rican jíbara she so desired to become: "the person I was becoming . . . was erased" (la persona en que me iba convirtiendo . . . fue borrada, 227). It seems especially violent because something was in movement when yanked—not just lying immobile but in process of becoming. Migration brutally interrupts the process of becoming: a cut, a precipitation of the loss of her childhood, a tearing away from the homeland.

We are to believe that there is a sharp rupture, a gulf, nothing to hold onto, between the "old" identity (was erased; *fue borrada*) being lost and the "new" identity being created (and another one was created; *y otra fue creada*). It is as if now she has to start everything over again; she has to undo everything she has done up until now. She is losing a constitutive part of herself. A wall-like boundary seems to form, to efface the folds of continuity and to simulate the sharp lines of physical flat maps. But we know that the absolutely new—a singular point of origin, an "authenticity"—is impossible; something cannot come from nothing. The sequence of temporality cannot be thrown out of the continuity of the temporal order. There must be a prior context; something of the jíbara must remain to form the basis of the "new" identity. Negi's "mistake" is to misread— to equate—jíbara with a supposed totality of what it means to be Puerto Rican. But in the final lines of the above quote, she belies the wall-like boundary she only just claimed because the act of migrating provides continuity, a sentiment echoed by the word *era* in the Spanish title. She corrects her misreading, and also, by implication, the cultural elite's misreading of the jíbaro as the origin of Puerto Rican culture, because she says she was "to become a hybrid" ("se convertiría en una híbrida"). She puts herself together again in a different form. As in topographical maps, wall-like boundaries become insubstantial. I cannot resist remarking on the rhyme in Spanish. While English blocks it, Spanish connects *híbrida* and jíbara. Is she a jíbara or a híbrida? The neat rhyme connects the two identities. Her jíbara and linguistic identities are not objects, pieces of property she can take with her—they have been socially mediated, politically engineered. They can be ruptured by historical circumstances. Yet, she does not lose them altogether—she takes something of them with her in the migration.

Migration and translation have things in common. Translator Elliot Weinberger tells us the "etymological origin of the very word 'translation' is 'move-

ment,' which means 'change.' Translation is movement, the twin of metaphor,"
he says, which means "to move from one place to another" (7). The anthropologist Talal Asad says that translation in medieval ecclesiastical usage meant
the "removal of a saint's remains, or his relics, from an original site to another.
. . . the narratives relating such events were called *translationes*" ("A Comment" 325). I bring together the two phenomena—migration and translation.
In this scene, migration is a metaphoric representation of translation.

Negi misreads, albeit momentarily, the process of migration, thinking
it needs to erase her identity of jíbara before she can become another self.
Similarly, we might suppose, erroneously, that a translation needs to erase
the source text to become its own new text. However, just as the migration
can never fully erase the jíbara of Negi's youth, so translation can never fully "wipe-out" the original book. Here I use "erase" in the sense of a translation sounding fluent, with no noticeable traces of the original language in
the translation-language. The Anglo American tradition and practice of eval-
uating translations places high value on fluency: the more fluent, the more
effortlessly it reads to the target audience, the better the translation (Venuti, *Translator's Invisibility* 1–6). Translations are to sound original, yet they
are, paradoxically, also thought of in common practice as derivatives, fakes,
second-order performances; only the original text deserves top billing. I
would argue that both are codependent, not separate entities. Indeed, translations ought *not* to be fluent. Something of the original should show through;
the mark of cultural difference should be visible in the translation.

The word *hybrid* makes explicit a prior context. What was there before
the migration? So too, the act of translation, I believe, ought to make visible (felt) its prior context, or the original text. Rather than prioritize fluency,
the illusion of authenticity and originality, as jíbarismo was wont to do on a
sociopolitical-cultural level, I would prioritize opacity, posing a challenge to
readers in the target culture. Keijirō Suga, commenting on Yōko Tawada, the
contemporary poet of Japanese origin who writes in her adopted German language, says he takes sides with opacity, not transparency (Suga 23). I agree.
There are irreducible differences, unsolvable conflicts that a translation can
never, indeed ought not, to overcome because exact equivalence, what Weinberger calls an "Utopian dream" (7), is impossible. Words in each language
carry their own sets of referents. Rather than fully domesticate the original
text to the norms and values of the target culture, a foreignizing translation
calls for some elements to remain visible to the reader of the translating culture. Echoing Walter Benjamin's "The Task of the Translator," Weinberger
notes in the citation I modified in chapter 3: "[T]he purpose of, say, a poetry
translation is not, as is usually said, to give the foreign poet a voice in the

translation-language. It is to allow the poem *to be heard* in the translation language, ideally in many of the same ways it is heard in the original language" (8).

SANTIAGO'S SELF TRANSLATION

Just as there is a doubling of self in Santiago's discovery that she had mistaken Spanish for espanglés, there is a doubling of self at the plot level. When in the city, Negi is desirous of being *like* the other city (non-jíbara) girls she meets in Santurce, wishing to send her jíbara-self home. But as soon as she returns home, she reaffirms her desire to be a jíbara, different from the city girls. Likewise, the doubling that occurs at the level of plot is mirrored by the doubling of her self-translation voice. She translates overtly, appositives in Spanish to English, making her accessible to her broad audience, but she also shows resistance to translation and maintains the specificity of her jíbara voice.

In standard translation, what I am calling international translation, the original text is proposed as foreign to the target audience. The idea is that the translation text makes the strange—the taken-for-granted in its local habitat—familiar. In Santiago's case, *When I Was* is a bilingual text and the bilingualism of this original text—not the translation text—makes the foreign familiar. The bilingualism of *When I Was* consists of different *linguascapes*, various types of bilingual writing practices. One linguascape is overt translation: words and phrases in Spanish are translated by appositives in English to make them intelligible for the English-language reader. The act of translation draws solid lines between Spanish and English, keeps them contained in their separate places. It enacts their interchangeability, from language A to language B. Translation moves from one word in one language to another word in another language, in parallel form, but it does not bring them together— they do not touch. A few examples are *sinvergüenzas* immediately followed by "had no shame" (29), *Muñequita* by "little doll" (13), *pasita* by "raisened" (13), and *bohíos*, a word probably familiar only to a Puerto Rican audience, by "the kind of house *jíbaros* lived in" (12). In this sense, Santiago's translations in the original—her misreadings—are more transparent than opaque, closer to the linear human-made political boundaries of the cartographer than to the uneven geographical divisions of the topographer. She opts primarily for fluency, aiming to naturalize, to reproduce sameness, to minimize obstacles for her audience. Her narrating "I" voice in the English original occupies a translator's position in relation to her primary audience. Her text, like so many other multilingual Latinx texts, has a built-in component of translation. She translates words and phrases into a standard version of the English language, assimilating Spanish into English, replicating the social process that imposed

English on her in Brooklyn as a young girl. She uses the Spanish words to mark her Puerto Rican identity, but she makes them accessible to her monolingual audience by translating them to English. They are meant to specify her Puerto Rican narrator's voice; they belong to her; they are not meant for readers to learn and make them theirs, only to grasp their definition in English.

Santiago uniformly italicizes all Spanish words and phrases, the standard gesture in print to signal the "foreign." Italics is one of the typographical conventions, argues Brian Lennon in *In Babel's Shadow*, of the "authorial-editorial translation of foreign words in books published in U.S. English today" (3). Such conventions, he says, construct "reader 'markets,'" and they are intentional and substantive features of an editorial discipline (3). Santiago also translates these words and idiomatic expressions in the extratextual apparatus of the glossary in the book's final pages, as if to insure doubly their intelligibility. This is surplus translation—inside the text and then again outside in the glossary. But then again, this excessive translation, this overly naming of Puerto Rican things, might suggest the inadequacy of translation, precisely because it is repeated so many times. Again, there is residue of tension between "was" and "era," an uneasy oscillation between final definition and continuous ambiguity, transparency and opacity, cartography and topography. In this way, Santiago may be performing both translation and untranslatability, inviting and impeding translation, embracing and eschewing the multinational marketplace.

Santiago's topographer side in the original text lies in the untranslatable words—a second type of linguascape—that mark the point of resistance to translation. She knows some things are untranslatable. This returns us again to the introduction where she reflected on the self of *When I Was* who felt the difficulty of communicating irreducible differences. "Cómo puedo explicar lo que es un jíbaro? ¿Cuál palabra norteamericana tiene el mismo sentido que nuestro puertorriqueñismo, 'cocotazo?'" (*Cuando era* xvi).[22] However, if she was to be intelligible to her English readers, she had no choice but to "misname"—to translate—these words, to find the equivalent in English the first time she used them to keep her English readers reading; jíbaro becomes "country dweller" with "unsophisticated customs and peculiar dialect" (12). From then on, she remains true to its untranslatability: it is simply jíbaro or jíbara, an objective category to her Anglophone, and even to some Hispanophone listeners, but having so much more meaning to her Puerto Rican audience. A *cocotazo* (from "coco," slang for "head," and "azo," a suffix to indicate something huge, as in Bogotazo, a coup d'etat in Bogota) is a "rapping" of Negi's mother's "knuckles on [Negi's] head." The first time she uses it, it appears in translated form. ("Mami swatted the side of my head" 8). From then on, she uses the colloquialism in Spanish but with enough context to assure understanding. Mami's fingers "knuckled my head in *cocotazos* that echoed inside my brain" (80). These words, and also *fogón* (cooking fire), *quinqué* (kerosene lamp), and *morivivi* (sensitive plant)[23] are left untranslated in the narrative and give the uninitiated a sense of an inability to fully capture Puerto Rican culture in the reading experience. The definitions in the glossary mislead us into thinking that we know the meanings of Puerto Rican culture.

Santiago's translating "I" voice operates differently in Spanish. The difference is captured perfectly in the way she presents, in the original and translation texts, the classic children's Puerto Rican verse rhyme, "Pollito, chicken," that Negi and her peers are taught to sing in school. Below, I face Santiago's English "I" to her Spanish "I."

Pollito, chicken	Pollito, *chi-ken*
Gallina, hen	Gallina, *jen*
Lápiz, pencil	Lápiz, *pén-sil*
y *Pluma*, pen	y Pluma, *pen*
Ventana, window	Ventana, *güín-do*
Puerta, door	Puerta, *do-ar*
Maestra, teacher	Maestra, *tí-cher*
y *Piso*, floor.	y Piso, *flo-a*.

The first column is the verse in *When I Was*, a series of matching *en face* italicized Spanish words alternate with their dictionary equivalents in English, presented in standard form. This is one-on-one translation. The second column taken from *Cuando era* shows her Spanish translating "I" voice doing more than translating. She is also transliterating English—a third type of linguascape—replicating the way she herself learned English in island schools, by emphasizing pronunciation. The italics approximate the way she was once heard—when sound was more important than sense. The nursery rhyme in the original text is Santiago the writer, the now native fluent English-speaker," translating to her audience, assisting them to understand the meaning of the Spanish words. In the glossary, she provides not only a definition but also a phonetic rendition of words in Spanish, reversing what was done to her on the island, now teaching her English readers to pronounce the words: *vaguadas* (heavy rains), *dignidad* (dignity).[24] The nursery rhyme in *Cuando era* is Santiago's voice before the migration, struggling to reproduce the English sounds of "native" speakers. This English is triply marked: it is italicized, broken into syllables, and accented, as though imitating a non-native English speaker working hard to reproduce the "native" sounds of English. In transliterating these words, Santiago aims to fulfill a sound—not a meaning—requirement. The important point of this transliteration is that she wants to be heard differently by each audience. The English audience sees Spanish as "foreign," outside of itself; for convenience, they might even skip the Spanish words. The Puerto Rican audience, in contrast, is to learn English, to assimilate and make the sound, if not the meaning, part of itself.

The above are one-word examples of transliteration. The following examples are transliterations of whole sentences. Negi is to play Christina, a young married woman confronting her monster mother-in-law in a scene from the American playwright's Sidney Howard *The Silver Cord* (1926). "I learned the monologue phonetically from Mr. Gatti [her teacher]" (261). The script that Negi's monolingual-English teachers give her to read for her audition to the Performing Arts School follows: "You belong to a type that's very common in this country, Mrs. Phelps—a type of self-centered, self-pitying, son-devouring tigress, with unmentionable proclivities suppressed on the side" (261). Her teachers want her to "pronounce every word correctly"—never mind understanding them. The novel invites the English-language audience to replicate the shape of Negi's awkward sound and tone, to move their mouths and lips to accommodate the visual script on the page. They too stumble on the script the Performing Arts Teachers use to vet Negi as a "native" speaker. English is now for them too an unfamiliar, contorted language: "Ju bee lonh 2 a type dats berry cómo in dis kuntree, Meessees Felps. A type off selfcent red self pee tee in sun de boring tie gress wid on men shon ah ball pro klee bee tees on de side" (264).[25] The fact that Negi's Brooklyn teachers emphasize pronunciation rather than meaning would seem to indicate the acceptance of a globalized English rather than global Englishes. Emily Brown Coolidge Toker, a second-language acquisition instructor, differentiates between these two kinds of Englishes. The first is a standardized "ideal" English belonging to historically First World Anglophone countries (the United States and Britain, for example) and "toward which individuals. . . are expected to strive" (113). The second accepts multiple and fluid "(but mutually intelligible) dialects or strands of English" (113) spoken by specific populations worldwide, for example Ireland, India, New Zealand, and Nigeria. Negi's teachers would like her to erase all traces of her Spanish Puerto Rican accent—errors in pronunciation—in her English.

In the Spanish translation, the same Negi reads the same Christina enacting the same script in the same setting speaking to the same characters. The only difference is that now a Spanish-language audience imitates her sounds. Santiago's transliteration shapes most phonemes to accommodate the way Spanish speakers hear Negi pronounce English. "Llu bilón tú é tayp dats beri cómo in dis contri Missis Felps. É tayp of selfcente red self pí tí in són de baurin taygrés huid on menshonabol proclibétis on de sayd" (289). In both cases, the point is not language as a communicative tool but the distortion of language to make its corresponding audiences feel the materiality of the words Negi reads aloud. Santiago's transliterative linguascapes require she be heard differently by English and Spanish speakers.

The transliteration in the original English captures the way Negi's "native" English speakers hear her without having any knowledge of Spanish. In the Spanish translation, the Puerto Rican audience hears the "anglogibberish" they imagine her "native" English-language audience hears. The transliterations simulate Negi's foreign-soundingness by capturing the phonologies of each language—the kinds of sounds they make—without Negi being able to pronounce English well at all. Both audiences are familiar with what English spoken by a Spanish speaker sounds like. This is the paradox of "foreign-soundingness" David Bellos discusses in *Is That a Fish in Your Ear?*: "[T]he 'foreign-soundingness' of a translation seeking to give the reader a glimpse of the authentic quality of the source can only reproduce and reinforce what the receiving culture already imagines the foreign to be" (50).[26] This imagining of the foreign is made possible by the long established relationship between U.S. English and Spanish. In other words, the foreign can only sound foreign if it is already somewhat familiar to an audience.

Yet another linguascape of Santiago's multilingual literary writing practice is the espanglés she claimed to speak in the introduction to *Cuando era*. This vernacular of a mixture of English and Spanish presents a challenge to the monolingual paradigm, that is the idea that English and Spanish are closed language systems: words in each language system are unable or should not move into the other. Hybrid words unexpectedly emerge in *Cuando era* in the section of her teenage years in Brooklyn. I say "unexpectedly " because given their monolingual versions in the source text, we do not expect them: for example, *breiks* (269) replaces "breaks" (as in coffee breaks), *rocanrol* (260) replaces "rock and roll" (240), *asémbli* (251, 257) replaces "assembly" (232), *welfear* (271) instead of "welfare" (248), *le daban leyof* (271) instead of "laid her off" (249), *bloque* (275) instead of "block" (252 as in neighborhood), *séconjanstor* (250) becomes "second-hand store" (232), *sóchelwerker* (273) becomes "social worker" (250), *sóbuey* (275) becomes "subway" (252), *cerró el ziper* (261) becomes "zipped himself up" (240), *terf* (276) becomes "turf" (253), and *dáim* (254) becomes "dime" (234). Santiago uses Spanish to multilingualize English in pronunciation and appearance, sound and spelling on the page. In *When I Was*, external multilingualism takes the presence of foreign words (some examples: *fogón, puta, ¡Ay bendito!, bohío, sancocho*). In general discourse, we need think only of *voilá, bon vivant, de rigueur,* and *Schadenfreude.* The foreign-derived words amateur, portmanteau, adobe, lasso, wanderlust, and kindergarten might be more a kind of internal multilingualism. Internal multilingualism can also take the form of one-word neologisms of Spanglish that result from the merger of two languages. In Spanglish, the copartnership is not equivalent. Spanish pronunciation distorts English, not the English pronunciation of Spanish. When foreign words enter from Spanish into English, they remain intact and unchanged (just think of food items like tortilla, guacamole, taco, enchilada, burrito, and chimichanga, or musical genres like cumbia, chachachá, merengue, cha cha, bachata, and bolero). Spanglish assimilates English and alters it in sound and spelling: *garaje* for "garage," *deyt* for "date," *raité* for "ride," *yarda* for "yard," (patio), *dona* for "doughnut," *carro* for "car," *mapear* for "to mop," *puchar* for "push." English and Spanish are not separate languages; they are not closed off from one another. Spanglish does not enact translation. Translation emphasizes movement from one language to another. Spanglish does more than this. It takes on a form of simultaneous presence. The words and expressions mix, touch one another, become one. They do not get translated into separate entities.

Her espanglés does something similar to what Homel and Simon in *Mapping Literature* define as the "working-class French dialect of Canada's East End Montreal" (56) and that I already discussed in chapter 3.[27] Just as *joual* accepts English words into its French lexicon and "distorts them once they are inside, in a kind of sabotage action against a linguistic occupying force" (Homel and Simon 56), so similarly Santiago's utterances in espanglés (as do analogues of it in the works of other Latinx writers) instantiate an acceptance of Spanish expressions in these instances to alter or—more boldly—disfigure English. Santiago's experimental voice, like joual, engages in a dialect that represents both the submission and revolt of her experience (Homel and Simon 56).

The "break-outs" in the Spanish text, I suggest, express Santiago's consciousness about her "new" place in relation to Spanish, a chance to be heard as herself in front of her Spanish-dominant island audience, a speaker not of Spanish but of esplanglés. It is instructive to note that Santiago has been removed twice from the island; in neither case did she choose it. The first removal was a literal one—the migration. The second was spiritual, when she returned to Puerto Rico in 1976, twenty-three years after first leaving the island. She anticipated her family would be so proud of her but discovered they did not consider her Puerto Rican enough because she had lived in the United States for so long, did not speak Spanish as they did, and was so Americanized. "Yo vine a vivir con mi familia que tenía en Bayamón y pensaba que todos iban a estar muy orgullosos de mí. Pero encontré que ya nadie me consideraba lo suficiente puertorriqueña; me consideraban americanizada" (Torres-Robles, "Esmeralda" 212–213).[28] She was, so to speak, misrecognized by her Puerto Rican family. Her departure not only detached her socially and culturally from traditional Puerto Rican society, but it also unsettled her linguistic grounding in the monolingual "mother-tongue." More broadly, this change suggests that access to a mother-tongue is not guaranteed; it is neither internal nor innate; neither forever attached to geographical territory (Puerto Rico in her case) nor to person. Recall Santiago's editor who implied that after years of disconnection from Spanish she could translate *When I Was*. On the other hand, access to Spanish is not foreclosed to her either, because she relearned it to translate her book. This might explain why Santiago chose the past tense in her English title, one that disturbed her audience. No matter what, she knows she is no longer "Puerto Rican" in the same way she would have been had she never left for New York. She does not speak Spanish as her island family did, since she received little or no oral and literate training in Spanish. But she can make her way with Spanglish/espanglés and still be Puerto Rican.[29]

The only espanglés that characterizes *When I Was* are the italicized variations of New York (*Nueva Yores*, *Nueva Yor*, or *Nueva York*) and the three-line dialogue of external multilingualism (258) between Negi and her Spanish-dominant school friend in Brooklyn (258). This external multilingualism is not translation. Neither does it take the form of Spanglish as simultaneous presence. Here, Spanish shifts into English and back again within the same sentence. The Spanish words are italicized, visually set apart in an English-language context. Negi asks her friend:

> *Te preguntó el* Mr. Barone, you know, *lo que querías hacer* when you grow up? . . . .
> *Si, pero,* I didn't know. *¿Y tú?*
> *Yo tampoco.* He said, *que* I like to help people. Pero, you know, *a mí no me gusta mucho la gente* (258).

Instead of changing the Spanish in *When I Was* to English and the English to Spanish in *Cuando era* (this would be one option), she transliterates the English and presents the transliterated words with no italics.

> *¿Te preguntó el Mister Barone, llu no, lo que querías hacer juén llu gro op:*
> *Sí, pero, ay dint no. ¿Y tú?*
> *Yo tampoco sé. Ji sed que ay laik tu jelp pipel. Pero, llu no, a mí no me gusta mucho la gente* (283).

Why not the following?

> ¿Did Mr. Barone ask you, *tú sabes*, what you wanted to do cuando crezcas? Le
> pregunté.
> Yes, but, *no supe. And you?*
> Me either. *Dijo that me gusta la gente.* But, *tú sabes*, I don't like people very much
> (283).

The translation forbids the use of English; it prefers distorted English.

TRANSLATION AS MEDIUM OF "ORIGIN"

I said earlier that translation can be a medium of "origin" and not just of "afterlife." To illustrate this dynamic requires we understand that the linguistic
hybrids (like *breiks, lanlord,* and *rocanrol*) were uttered first in spoken language by Negi in Brooklyn. Upon writing *When I Was,* Santiago replaced (or
translated) them with their standard literate versions ("breaks" and "land-
lord"). Then, in writing *Cuando era* (the derived text), she retranslated them
and returned them to their "original" form. The same goes for the colloquial
jíbaro dialect that appears in *Cuando era.* Santiago replaced (or translated)
the *jíbaro* dialect of her unschooled family—for example, "yo no soy zángana" (28) in spoken language—into the standard "I'm not stupid" in *When I
Was* (24). She then retranslated it back into the orally-based jíbaro dialect for
Cuando era. To put it another way, Santiago retranslated for *Cuando era* the
spoken espanglés and jíbaro expressions she had first translated for *When I
Was.*

  Cuando era gives the false impression that Santiago (Negi) had never suf-
fered the interruption of the migration and had never had to remember the
"forgotten" Spanish to become a dominant English speaker. Some will no
doubt argue that the monolingualized Spanish is necessary because the text
is aimed at a Spanish-language island Puerto Rican audience. So why bother
translating, as the thinking goes? Why mark the text with English at all? Is
external multilingualism (from one language to another inside the same text,
or Spanish-to-English for English-language readers) necessary to mark the
source text as multilingual but unnecessary to mark the target text as multilingual? Surely, island Puerto Ricans need no translation of Santiago's Spanish. But the English language is familiar to island Puerto Ricans in a way it is
not to the inhabitants of other countries of Spanish America: Puerto Ricans
are no strangers to English. It is a matter of historical record that after more
than half a century the island remains a commonwealth of the United States.
As Zentella asserts, the "roots of bilingual style are located not in New York

but in the colonial policies that the US imposed in Puerto Rico after occupy-ing the island in 1890" ("Growing Up" 3).

The conventions of the Anglophone trade publishing industry, argues Bri-an Lennon in *In Babel's Shadow*, discourages the effects of "plurilingualism," that is, the presence of words and phrases in a different language (10). San-tiago's translated text, like many other Latino translations, is published by U.S. presses. The translations from Spanish into English in the original text are inconvenient blocks to cartographic fluency of Spanish monolingualism. Is there a way to mark a two-language original in its translation text? Allow me to recite a question posed by Sylvia Molloy. How "do you translate bilin-gualism, how do you convert the switching so that the effect of two languages working on each other, against each other, remains?" (292). It is no small challenge.

Santiago remains faithful to the route she herself charted in the original text; her translation replicates the descriptions, the plot, the character mo-tivations, and chronology of events. But she also chooses at times to beat a different path with respect to what appear to be translations "hidden" in the original text: where literate English covers up a Puerto Rican oral dialect. The only way to detect the "hidden" translations, to access the bilinguality, is to juxtapose translation and original texts, a practice that presupposes a bilin-gual readership. This readership partners with the linguistically monolingual audience on each side of the Atlantic (or facetiously a *charco* [a puddle] to Puerto Ricans) that is shut off from this aesthetic strategy—in the sense that it forms part of these audiences—but it also goes beyond them. For example, in *When I Was,* she presents her mother's colloquial Spanish in fluent English. "I'm not the kind of person to sit around doing nothing" (115), fulfilling how the mother *should* sound to an English-language audience, or the demand of a monolingual paradigm for native competency. But in *Cuando era* she decides on a different route.

We learn what her Spanish-speaking mother actually might have said in her colloquial jíbaro Spanish. One example is "yo no soy zángana," which has been already quoted. A second example, "Yo no sirvo pa' estar sentá haciendo ná" (125) corresponds to the naturalized English of the original: "I'm not the kind of person to sit around doing nothing" (115). She did not translate it into a literate Spanish the mother probably never spoke. Yet a third example occurs in the chapter "The American Invasion of Macún" (61-83)[30] that describes the Americanization of her home village in the 1950s, during the beginning years of Luis Muñoz Marín's *Estado libre asociado*. A representative from the States provides lessons in nutrition, recommending foreign "imperialist" food, ac-cording to Negi, like peanut butter and canned fruit instead of the local fresh plants and fruit. A jíbara neighbor reacts to the representative's instructions on dental hygiene: "If I have to spend that much time on my teeth, I won't get anything done around the house" (65). In *Cuando era*, Santiago captures the emotional and exclamatory force of a dialect, complete with the appropriate punctuation marks missing in English, that approximates more closely what the unschooled neighbor probably said: "¡Ay no, qué chavienda! ¡Se me va el dia lavándome los dientes!" (*Cuando era* 71).[31]

The third example emphasizes how crucial it is to factor the translation into a reading of the original text to obtain bilingual effects apparently lost in the translation. This example involves heteronyms, or words that are spelled and look alike but are not the same because they have different pronunciations and different meanings. Negi asks her mother how she came to be called "Negi," when her name is "Esmeralda." The mother explains: "[B]ecause when you were little you were so black, my mother said you were a *negrita*. And we all called you *Negrita*, and it got shortened to Negi" (13). The mother's linking of negrita with "black" is a mistranslation, and it might give English readers a false sense of security that negrita means "black" in racial terms. Negi's response reinforces this false assurance: "So Negi means I'm black?" (13). Why "black"? Why not "dark" or "brown"? The simple answer is Santiago wants to help the English reader with negrita, a word she absolutely needs to explain her name "Negi." It is easy to gloss negrita (short e) and the U.S. English "Nēgro" (long e) given their similar surface structure, and then to jump from "Nēgro" to "black." The translation is laced with more nuances. In *Cuando*, Santiago replaces "black" with *trigueña*, a common term in the Caribbean for someone who is dark-complexioned: "Porque cuando tú naciste, eras tan trigueña que mi mamá dijo que eras una negrita. Y te llamábamos Negrita, y lo cortamos a Negi" (16). Negi now equates *trigueña* with *negra* (short e): "Entonces, ¿Negi quiere decir que soy negra?" (17).[32] In this instance, her association between negrita and negra makes sense because in Spanish negra is one of many terms possible to designate a person's skin tone (others are *prieta* or *morena*). It does not compute into "Nēgro" or "Nēgress" in English. In Spanish negra is a false cognate for the racial terms "Nēgro" or "Nēgress" or "black," which in the United States designate race and racial identity (African American); no such term exists in the Caribbean to mark race or racial identity.[33] My point is that, like the previous examples, the mother actually used Caribbean Spanish: she said trigueña, and Santiago translated it to "black" in the original text to accommodate her English readers. Santiago returns in the translation to rewrite the naturalized English of the original text into a more colloquial jíbaro-sounding Spanish. She is translating the writer who herself is translating.

The next chapter takes us into a discussion of the third and final cultural hybridized figure—the *mojado*, or as translated by Reavis, the "wetback." The pair, *Diary* and *Diario*, is an act of translation in two senses: a metaphorical shuttling between two languages and an actual physical shuttling by the translator of his subject from one geographical border to another.

CHAPTER 5

I MAY SAY "WETBACK" BUT I REALLY MEAN *MOJADO*

Migration and Translation in Ramón "Tianguis" Pérez's *Diary of an Undocumented Immigrant*

About one fourth of the way into *The Diary of an Undocumented Immigrant* (1991), a translation by Dick Reavis of Ramón "Tianguis" Pérez's *Diario de un mojado* (2003),[1] the protagonist, an undocumented person (a *mojado*) from Mexico makes his way through Houston. Stumbling upon a Spanish-language newspaper with "most of its space . . . devoted to photographs" (*Diary* 56–57), he focuses on a three-panel cartoon by the Mexican artist Antonio Eduardo Licón, whose comic strips appeared weekly in Houston's *El Mundo* during the second-half of the twentieth century.[2] He sees a "shoeless and ragged" (*Diary* 57) Zopilote (buzzard) and Mr. Migra, a border patrol agent. Zopilote's incessant objective is to outsmart Mr. Migra, a "typical *gringo*-looking guy" (*Diary* 57) and to pass undetected to the other side. For this purpose, he must appear to seem what he is not. Wily Zopilote makes a "cow's head" (*Diary* 57) to camouflage himself with the cattle in the truck that are about to cross the border. Inspecting the cattle, Mr. Migra looks toward the bottom of the truck and sees "a cow with no hoofs" (*Diary* 57). The "wetback" (mojado) Zopilote is unable to conceal his anthropomorphized illegality. In other words, intending to look "authentic," like the "real thing," he appears foreign and strange. The tell-tale detail is that he has no hoofs. The border cameras, the eye of power, have fixed laserlike on Zopilote.

Zopilote's chances of crossing the international border would have been higher had he, somehow, been able to perfect the subterfuge and given himself hoofs. In the early twentieth century, Rachel St. John tells us in *Line in the Sand*, when national distinctions were unclear and border people (especially those whose businesses straddled both sides) resisted inconvenient crossing requirements and expensive custom duties, local and federal officials "willing to bend the rules" (100) adjusted enforcement laws to keep from derailing transborder trade, for example the crossing of goods and animals, particularly ranchers crossing cattle who were "more likely to simply drive their stock across the line at the nearest point" (99). Transborder business aside, Licón's caricature is meant to represent a human being, and both Zopilote and Mr. Migra know that each one of them belongs to one or the other side of the international border. Attempting, implicitly, to violate the sharp delineation of the modern nation-state, the division between native and foreign, and to pass for a U.S. original, Zopilote is exposed as a fraud: a "wetback" to Mr. Migra. This strict division in the nation-state model emphasizes the dividing function rather than the parallel dependence and connecting purposes of borders and conceals the continuities in a long history of migration that implicate the two countries.

Neat boundaries of nation-states are analogous to the neat divisions of the international translation I have outlined in the introduction and ensuing chapters. The neat divisions also typify a dominant tradition that has shaped the interpretation of translation, especially in Anglo American and Western European culture. According to this long-standing tradition, there can be only one original act of writing, usually in the author's mother-tongue, usually equivalent to the national language of the country from which the author writes.[3] The act of translation, usually in a language foreign to the one of the home nation of the original text,[4] is, therefore, derivative of the creative act in the original language. One implication of this position is to privilege individual authorship (and hence the national language) and to relegate the translator (and hence the foreign language) to a secondary status serving the author, "creator" and origin of meaning.[5] A second, and somewhat contradictory, implication of this servile relationship, is fluency, a value already confronted in the previous chapters; that is, if translations are to register approval and legitimacy, they should sound as fluent in the translation language as the original does in its own language. Translators must erase themselves as translators— remove all noticeable vestiges of their translating voice.

Like the strict international geographical division of nation-states, the discursive boundary (author-translator) in mainstream thinking, doing, and reception of translation also conceals the continuities and parallel processes that characterize an original text and its translation. Both types of border crossings, geographical and discursive, create acute divisions of identity: not only for the individual who migrates (especially the ones with no documents) but also (as in the case of *Diario* and *Diary*) for the translated literary text. *Diary* and *Diario* enact an undocumented identity resulting from different modalities of movement—migration and translation—across national borders. *Diario*'s national and literary identity is tenuous because it is a text translocated to a foreign nation without ever enjoying a connection as a published original in its native homeland—it was never published (or read to a wide extent) in Mexico. To which national space does the text belong? Published twelve years before the original, *Diary*, the translation, stood-in for the original because it was read first, thus prioritizing reading over writing and inserting doubt about *Diario* as an "original" text. *Diary*'s identity is similarly indefinite because it is a translation of an original text published in the same national space as its translation. These texts belong to more than one language within the same nation. Both original and translation were published by the Latinx press Arte Público in Houston, Texas.

Diary challenges the discursive divide between invisibility and visibility because it makes, as I argue in what follows, the translator visible. Although Reavis strives for the fluency (invisibility) advocated by mainstream theorists and practitioners of translation, he presents us with what I consider a primal scene that upsets the either/or logic of fluent translation in a chapter titled "*Mojados.*" The specific scene, I argue, enacts an intersection of Pérez's two main identities captured in the terminology chosen by the author (mojado in *Diario*) and the translator ("wetback" in *Diary*). It is Reavis who changed the mojado of Pérez's manuscript title (*Diario de un mojado*) into the "wetback" of his own manuscript translation (*Diary of a Wetback*) submitted to Arte Público Press. Arte Público, a Latinx publisher, then changed the "wetback" of Reavis's title into the definitive "undocumented immigrant" of its published text (*Diary of an Undocumented Immigrant*),[6] though Pérez was not strictly speaking an immigrant. Yet, all the while it kept "wetback" in *Diary*'s narrative, perhaps implementing the tested practice that words in the title help to sell a book more than any words inside the narrative. The identities of mojado and "wetback" compete for central importance in the scene that ruptures the translator's invisibility.

At stake is Pérez's identity (and by extension that of undocumented migrants). In choosing to transform him from a mojado into a "wetback," Reavis normalizes him, linguistically incorporating him into the norms of the translating language and culture. Reavis, striving for fluency, makes the translation sound natural to the ordinary English-speaker. But he does so at some cost because he chooses the most offensive term among the liminal status categories in U.S. English for Mexicans who are "outside the normative teleology of immigration" (Ngai 13). For the greater part of *Diary*, the translator usurps Pérez's preferred term of mojado and linguistically substitutes it for "wetback;" that is, he inserts Pérez's identity into the conventions of speech and behavior of an immigrant-hostile U.S. society. Reavis domesticates the narrating voice of *Diario*. We might go further and say that he performs an act of epistemic violence.

The appellatives mojado and "wetback" serve as my entry points into the transborder nexus of migration and translation in *Diary/Diario*. Author and translator, Reavis and Pérez, are constitutive of this nexus. Reavis doesn't only translate Pérez's book. He also literally and physically translocates him across the national border. Reavis orchestrates the author's crossing; he goes down personally to *la frontera* to bring him into a different national space. The crossing is a literal representation of the inextricable connection between linguistic cultural translation and national migration.

I divide the chapter into four sections. Each section foregrounds a different facet of the transborder nexus of migration and translation. In the first section, I provide important details about Pérez's migration, his texts, and the bilingualism of Pérez and Reavis; then I situate *Diary* in a multilingual, multicultural geographical space that upsets the conceptual limits of nation-states and their national literatures. The in-between space marks the transborder nexus at extra-textual dimensions of audience and book-market translational formats. Second, I offer a socio-etymological biography of *mojado* and "wetback" to anchor these terms in historically located practices that occur in a specific transborder, transnational region. Third, I explain the relationship between translator and author to call attention to their mutual collaboration enacted in the "wetback"/mojado pairing. Finally, I take up the analysis of the primal scene to demonstrate how the translation text enacts multilingualism by making both terms simultaneously present. It breaks up the one-to-one correspondence and the divisive boundary between "wetback" and mojado. Their usage in *Diary*'s primal scene thematizes linguistic and cultural difference ("wetback" and mojado are not interchangeable), puts into question textual authority and the either-or logic of author and translator, and, most importantly, stresses multilingualism over simple translation. Who is writing? Who is speaking? Who is telling the story? Is it the author (with his choice of mojado) or the translator (with his choice of "wetback")? The rupture in the scene raises a related question on the issue of naming: who controls the undocumented migrant's identity? Who is authorized to name migrants like Pérez? My interest is to show how Pérez and Reavis reconfigure a transborder, multilingual, and transnational discursive field rooted in migration and translation.

A MULTILINGUAL TRANSBORDER TEXT

Pérez is a Spanish-speaking, Zapotec Indian Mexican from Oaxaca, one of Mexico's lowest-income states with a sizable number of Mixtec and Zapotec migrants in cities and towns of California and Oregon (Stephen 32).[7] He migrated and lived in the U.S. Southwest from 1979 to about 1987. In *Diario*, he tells about his experiences during this eight-year span as an undocumented person. Pérez's years of migration were temporary—he chose to leave the United States rather than seize the opportunity to apply for legal residency under the 1987 Immigration Reform and Control Act (IRCA),[8] even though he would have met the requirements for permanent residency set by this law. If migration offered him a temporary stay, translation gave him a more lasting place in the social, literary map of a U.S. print culture medium. Following Walter Benjamin's thinking about translation's assets, translation offered Pérez and *Diario* an "afterlife" elsewhere (Benjamin [1923], 1969 71).[9]

Reavis also translated Pérez's second book, *The Diary of a Guerrilla* (1999), published eight years after *Diary* and four years before *Diario*, also by Arte Público Press. *Guerrilla*[10] is a translation of a typewritten manuscript about Pérez's activities as a young *guerrillero* in the mountains of Oaxaca in 1978. Although all three texts are called "diaries," Pérez's mode of writing simultaneously lies within and outside the literary genres of "diary" and *testimonio*. While *Guerrilla* alludes to a couple of dates where the events it tells occurred, neither it nor *Diary* are full-fledged diaries; they are not narratives organized around dated entries. For example, no explicit dates are attributed to Pérez's departure from his home village, though *Diary*'s dust jacket tells us he left his Oaxacan village in 1979, one or two years after his clandestine experiences in the Oaxacan jungles and mountains. Rather, it is "diary-like;" a series of vignettes, loosely organized around a single theme that string together in a topical arrangement the macro events of Pérez's life in the United States. It is also "diary-like" in the sense that he and no one else is the writer. Even by today's standards, Pérez is an atypical undocumented Mexican migrant in that he is fully literate. According to Reavis (personal communication, July 19, 2011), Pérez is a "born writer," a veritable storyteller. It is by means of the technology of writing that Pérez moves from a position of a migrating pilgrim—crossing the U.S.–Mexican border, arriving in Houston, moving to San Antonio, then to Oregon and California, and finally returning to Mexico—to the position of a reflective poet who after his return home draws on his cognitive and emotional memory, makes use of knowledge gained from his pilgrimage, and inserts a new informed consciousness into the moment he is describing. He becomes a traveler-migrant who now looks back upon and edits his memories.

To be sure, he wrote his own stories rather than speak them to an interlocutor in the traditional Latin American testimonio style. In the classic Latin American testimonio, someone illiterate in their country's dominant language, especially in writing it (think of the Guatemalan Rigoberta Menchú and the Bolivian Domitila Barrios de Chungara), speaks his or her story to a literate party from a metropolitan culture. The literate party then transcribes and/or translates it and helps to find a publisher in the national language of the speaker's country. An intralingual Zapotec, Pérez speaks both Zapotec and Spanish, but Spanish is the language he writes.[11] He is independent of the collaborative mediation of the testimonio genre; he has his own meaning-making capability to build his narrative. *Diary* is, therefore, "testimonio-like." He has a collaborator in Reavis, and he is an indigenous narrator who tells of lived events in first-person. His writing, however, does not sanction above all else the value of the individual author. He has a consciousness about a larger social unit. In these senses, *Diary* is and is not a Latin American testimonio.

Pérez writes in Spanish only, though Spanish is not his mother-tongue in the sense of the chronologically first language he spoke for the earliest years of his life.[12] Yet Spanish is no more a foreign language to him than English is a foreign language to Villarreal and Santiago. Spanish is for him, as is English for them, the functionally primary language, first in importance in the total life of his experiences. Other than the covert multilingualism (Spanish and English) in the primal scene I discuss in the fourth section of this chapter, a multilingual context of two languages (vocabularies of Spanish and Zapotec or of Spanish and English) is not overtly present inside *Diary/Diario*—he uses one Zapotec word: *estádu* ("es la manera en que se dice 'estado' en Zapoteco, nuestrra lengua autóctona" (*Diario* 7).[13] I situate these texts differently in relation to multilingualism. In addition to my analysis of the primal scene, they are multilingual texts at levels of the texts' reception and production. Pérez has been read in English translation and Spanish in the southwestern United States. His books were commissioned, edited, and produced by a Latinx Press. Thus, what looks like a monolingual text in Spanish has traces of two languages at levels of audience and publication that highlight the effects of multilingualism.

Reavis, a white, U.S. American, Spanish-speaking journalist, is a functional Spanish speaker, but Spanish is not a family language for him, as it became early in life for Pérez. Reavis translates quotidian Spanish to equally quotidian English. Though he is not a code-switcher of Spanish and English, he uses some informal registers of the Spanish language in the translation: for example, he titles *Diary*'s crucial chapter "*Mojados*," breaking from his customary "wetbacks." He also uses colloquial Spanish to title two other chapters: "*La Migra*" (the Border Patrol) and "*La Mota*" (marijuana [Maryjane]). These specific deviations ever so slightly suggest that a single language is not one-dimensional. Reavis does not produce a flat, pancake-like text. But he is enough of an outsider to think that "wetback" is the most appropriate translation for *mojado*. He is an outsider, gone in.

Diary and *Diario* lie more within the general corpus of multilingual, transnational U.S. Latinx translations than in the typical kind of international Mexican Spanish and United States English translations. They belong to an interstitial space between mainstream U.S. and Mexican national literatures, more a part of U.S. Latinx Literature than of U.S. mainstream or Mexican literature, for three reasons. First, the publisher of both translation and original is neither a U.S. mainstream nor a Mexican press, but a U.S. Latinx press with a readership in the United States. Secondly, *Diario* has had no print or digital circulation in Mexico, where Pérez was born and raised. Its only life in print is in the United States. Third, both the Spanish original and the translation had substantial readerships of audiences interested in the issue of Latinx immigration: *Diario* has had three printings and *Diary* five printings.[14] It is truly a Latinx text because it goes both ways across national borders. The texts found their audiences not in an English-only United States, not in a dominantly Spanish-speaking Mexico, but in dual English-and-Spanish social networks of readership in a border region unlimited by national monolingual frames. We might imagine these books as bridge texts connecting a transborder, transnational region where authorized and unauthorized migration of people, languages, and cultures, and also traffic of economic commerce, have flowed, miscegenated, and collided into one another since at least the first half of the nineteenth century.

In the framework of international and transnational translation which I have set up in this book, *Diario* and *Diary* form a bridge-space between these two types of translation, sharing characteristics of each without exemplifying fully either one. More precisely, they are transborder texts. Published in the United States, they intersect with and partially reproduce the classic international translation paradigm. *Diary* moves from one country's national language to a different country's national language, from Spanish to English. But its transnational situation also resists an international mode of translation which reinforces national boundaries because, unlike most Latinx and world literary originals (which are published in their countries of origin), *Diario* has no semantic or cultural anchorage in Mexico, at neither consumption nor production levels. It too was published in the United States. Therefore, I situate these texts between the two categories of translation. They only fit international translation if Spanish is seen as a foreign language. But since Spanish is now the majority–minority language in the United States, its translation cannot be fully international.

A SOCIOETYMOLOGICAL BIOGRAPHY—"WETBACK" AND *MOJADO*

Two popular variants used in Mexico and the United States respectively to refer to people who cross without documents are mojado and "wetback." The semantic lineage in the United States stretches from "wetback" to "illegal," "illegal alien," "undocumented," "undocumented worker," and "undocumented immigrant." The list in Mexico includes *espalda mojada, mojado/a, indocumentado/a, sin papeles* (without papers), and *alambrista* (wire-jumper). Both terms signify the act of unauthorized migration, albeit from different national perspectives and with different connotative emotional charges, and their relationship in *Diary* is defined by translation. They are translational equivalents, a linguistic phenomenon that results from frequent interface and common usage between diverse cultures for a long period of time.

These two linguistic colloquialisms in the English and Spanish lexicons evoke strong images of informal crossers in the discourse of transnational clandestine migration. Each signifier, one in the translation text, the other in the "original" text, represents Pérez's main identification in the journey of transborder migration and translation. Formulated in the 1920s,[15] in the era of immigration restriction, "wetback" had already obtained popular currency before mojado emerged in Mexican Spanish vernacular. Xenophobic terms for the alien "other" are usually initiated first by the more powerful insider group (in this case U.S. Anglo-Texans) who can take its claim to legality for granted, not by the less powerful outsider community (in this case Mexican Americans and Mexican nationals in Texas) whose legality is subject to question, depending upon who judges. The labels originated and developed autonomously of each other, but by the 1950s, they had acquired, and to this day hold, parallel Spanish-to-English, English-to-Spanish dictionary translations. Since the 1920s, the two terms mutually define one another in practical speech. But unlike other Spanish terms for Mexican migrants, *bracero* (contract laborer) for instance, simply integrated unchanged into the English language, mojado began to function as an original translation of "wetback," as "wetback" did of mojado to accommodate the neighbor language.

When used as two separate words, "wet" is an adjective modifying the noun "back," as in the human anatomy, and it means just that—someone's or some thing's back is wet. But when joined together into one word, "wetback" is transformed into a noun, later shortened into another noun, "wet." The referent of "wetback"—usually a person—is reduced to a body part. Since the mid-1920s, these English tags have referred to, most commonly, a Mexican national who has violated the immigration laws of the U.S. nation by swimming the Rio Grande/Rio Bravo. In the mid-1920s the United States began to attribute to itself the right to control space and property as bounded territory with regards to Mexican and European populations, culminating in the establishment of the Border Patrol (1924) in the context of the 1924 Quota Acts. Immigration restrictions were formalized for the first time and as immigration from Asia and Europe came to a near halt, the regulations impacted Mexico's and the United States' contiguous borders and hence Mexican migrants. Douglas Massey, an immigration expert, stated that "wetback" "date[s] to the 1920s. The Border Patrol wasn't founded until 1924, so before then the border was essentially open and there was no need to swim the Rio Grande" (personal communication, July 23, 2011). Curiously, the 1924 restrictions attempted to implement the nation's first comprehensive immigration law, but they also simultaneously created illegal immigration and produced the illegal alien—"a subject barred from citizenship and without rights" (Ngai 4, 7).

The Rio Grande/Rio Bravo is the key feature in the cultural, etymological, and geographical development of "wetback" and "wet" on the U.S. side, and of espalda mojada and mojado in the transnational region of the Lower Rio Grande Valley of South Texas and Northeastern Mexico, and later in all Mexico. Even before it became the international dividing line in 1848, resulting in Mexico's partition, what Gloria Anzaldúa has called *una herida abierta* (an open wound, 3). The river, especially in South Texas and Northeastern Mexico, marked a transnational area for intercultural cooperation among English and Spanish speakers. But in 1848, it became the organic aquatic connector and separator between two nations. Diplomats who redrew the map of North America, on the east side, "chose a well-known geographic feature, the Rio Grande, settling a decade-old debate about Texas' southern border and dividing the communities that had long lived along the river" (St. John 2). Due in large part to the river, according to Américo Paredes, the cowboy and *vaquero* borrowed and negotiated cultural elements, and cattle culture thrived ("Problem of Identity" 20). The South Texas–Northeastern region was "especially suited for smuggling operations" (24). It was a place to flout "custom and immigration laws, not so much as a form of social or ethnic protest but as part of the way of life" (26).

Of course, even prior to 1924, social reality, practically and symbolically, had linked "wet" and "wetback" with smuggling by borderlanders on both sides. Since about the turn of the century, "wet" designated *sub rosa* activity harking back to frontier times of cowboys, *vaqueros*, ranching, and smuggling of animals: "wet stock" stolen and taken across the border, usually "wet cows" to Mexico and "wet horses" to Texas (Samora 34).[16] The linguist William Randle explains, "[t]he extension of *wet* to Mexican migrant labor began with head tax and visa requirements set up in 1924. By 1926, the Border Patrol was using the *wet* designation in listing apprehended illegal entrants" (Randle 78). In other words, illicit passing of objects and animals primarily shifted to the smuggling of humans. A few decades later came the Bracero Program (1942–1964), a "labor and immigration policy . . . a cornerstone in establishing Mexican migrant labor and residency patterns in the United States" (Stephen 96). During this program, families in the Southwest employed "wet maids," likely the wives of braceros and mojados (Ngai 152).

The longer form "wetback" was initially an English-speaking Texan society's verbal folk expression to refer disparagingly to Mexicans, and, from what Massey says, it did not exist widely prior to 1924 when Mexicans would have had no reason to steal across the river.[17] Depending on region and people, some U.S. English-speakers still use it as a slur to slight a population from south of the Mexican–U.S. border, as the term is seldom or never applied to undocumented persons of other ethnic groups entering (or perceived to have entered) the United States. The word in English, although known in Mexico, originated and was limited in usage to the U.S. side.[18]

In standard Mexican Spanish, mojado/a is an adjective which means "soaked" or "drenched." It is a derivative of espalda mojada. At its primary level, like "back" in "wetback," espalda refers to the anatomical back. Therefore, espalda mojada is literally someone's back that is wet. Similarly to "wetback," when the two words are used colloquially to refer to a person (el espalda mojada),[19] or when the adjective is transformed into a noun to produce the clipped mojado, it means someone (male or female) who has entered U.S. territory through a particular non-official entry area. For example, they have swum clandestinely the Rio Grande/Rio Bravo.[20]

Although "wetback" became encoded first in a U.S. national imaginary, historically both pairs of epithets—"wetback" and "wet," espalda mojada and mojado—were unique to the Lower Rio Grande Valley of South Texas and Northeastern Mexico, where much of the undocumented migration occurred in the early twentieth century and where migrants had to swim the Rio Grande/ Rio Bravo. In contrast, on the western side, U.S. and Mexican diplomats "drew a line across a map and conjured up an entirely new space where there had not been one before" (St. John 2). In the Tijuana–San Diego region, another area that would develop a long history of frequent border crossings and where no natural divider separated the two nations, other popular culture terms, like alambrista (a wire jumper), dominated the discourse (Spener 4). In contrast to "wetback," reserved by English speakers for those perceived as inassimilable Mexican "foreigners," ineligible for residency and citizenship, mojado has a wider range of positive and negative registers. Generally speaking, "no disrespect is necessarily implied by Mexican-speakers who use the term" (Spener 5),[21] but it may have a belittling effect when used by those Mexicans who disdain their fellow citizens who migrate illegally.[22] In this instance, Mexican nationals may use it to suggest betrayal of nation since the mojado goes outside the limits of national borders and may be seen, therefore, to "turn his back," literally and spiritually, on the homeland.[23] But it can also be used by the migrants themselves with tinges of self-affirmation (*Me vine de mojado* [I crossed as a mojado]; *Soy un mojado* [I am a mojado]). This redefinition of the term resembles the historical linguistic process in which words formerly derogatory (like queer, *pocho*, or Chicano) are revalued, their illocutionary effects semantically ameliorated. When self-attributed, reformulated into an indigenous Mexican code of speech, the speaker asserts agency and turns the label against itself to suggest someone who dares to defy the odds of both Mexican and U.S. regulatory systems. To some Mexicans, he may represent a trickster figure, wily enough to pass undetected (like Licón's Zopilote in my opening paragraph who never ceases to try). Most importantly, unlike "wetback," the semantic resonance does not extend into illegality or criminality. It does not convey "a dangerous and criminal social pathogen" (Ngai 149).[24]

By the 1950s, both mojado and "wetback" were the most used in the pantheon of terms for the "undocumented." They expanded to include anyone and everyone who entered the United States, by land or water, no matter where in the almost 2,000-mile border. By the late 1940s,[25] mojado had traveled south from the border into the Mexican interior. The Mexican filmmaker Alejandro Galindo presented his feature film Espaldas mojadas to a national audience in 1953. Galindo's film was the first to show *la frontera* on the large screen, thus demonstrating the Mexican government's lack of interest up to that time in its border region, perceived as marginal, uncultured, dangerous, and overly Americanized.[26] One exception was the Mexican journalist-author Luis Spota. Spota lived the life of a mojado, an eyewitness, to prepare to write *Murieron a mitad del rio,* a novel set in the Texan-Mexican border along the River and first published in 1948.[27] His protagonist lives the precise moment of his transformation into a *mojado*, reinforcing the linkage between migration, geography, language and thought. "Ya sus pies, ahora, no se apoyaban en su país . . . Porque ya no estaban en éste sino del otro lado, experimentó un gran pellizco de miedo; supo del riesgo de ser un mojado, un inmigrante ilegal" (Spota 20–21).[28] In the novel, mojados has no insulting connotation when the characters use it to refer to themselves, but when white U.S. Americans use the word to address them, it conveys a sting and stigma. Novel and film were produced well into the period of the Bracero Program. Both sets of terms probably became colloquial usage during the various installations of the Bracero Program, whose attempts to import temporary labor in a legal manner also produced large numbers of undocumented immigrants.[29] Once the legal quota of formerly authorized braceros was met, the agricultural business still wanted more workers. The desired labor surplus was filled by informally authorized mojados. In spite of the transnational legal agreement, social reality created a fluid boundary between braceros and mojados. Like their legal counterparts, mojados were equally employable, and, in fact, even more desirable because they worked for lower wages and were more easily exploited. The folkloric pairing refers to the traffic of migration between nations, not to migration internal to one nation, as is true of "okie" and "snowbird" in the United States and *chilango* in Mexico, a term used by Mexican northern "borderers" for migrants from Mexico City who come to border cities.

The lexical existence of "wetback" is due to a human presence that comes into the U.S. nation unauthorized from Mexico. The term mojado refers to someone gone outside his own nation but is also indigenous to a bilingual, bicultural region to which migrants have come for almost a century. A transnational term, spoken and heard on each side of this particular border, it is, in its origin, usage, and regional distribution, part of a transnational linguistic circuit. In different ways and to different degrees, these lexical signifiers of low-status employment, unlawful social status, and racialized difference underscore an interdependent relation that implies the sending-receiving dimensions of the political, economic, and cultural borders of two nation-states.

COLLABORATION OF TRANSLATOR AND AUTHOR

The third facet of the transborder nexus of migration and translation is the collaboration between translator and author. In no other text among those considered in this book, perhaps in no other Latinx text translated either to English or to Spanish, is the relationship between author and translator more graphically represented than in the production of *Diario* and *Diary*. The power disparity of their partnership is exemplified in the "wetback"—*mojado* dyad. Each term is a reductive identity of the undocumented (im)migrant.

Reavis, deeply involved in the production and publication of all three of Pérez's narratives, plays an enormously significant role in Pérez's migration and the translation of his "diary" about his migratory experience. He takes a gamble in both acts of migration and translation, in hopes that something will come for Pérez: financial betterment and a chance to tell his story in print to an interested audience, albeit a non-Mexican one. It is important to understand that Pérez's urgency to leave his home emerged more out of political than economic circumstances. In *Guerilla*, Pérez tells the story of his involvement in an armed rebellion in Oaxaca against encroachment of indigenous lands (*tierras comunales*) and resources by Mexican large landowners and paper companies. During this period of guerrilla warfare, two years prior to his migration, he met Reavis, a senior staff writer for Houston's *Texas Monthly*, who was assigned to cover the rebellion.[30] The rebellion broke down when Florencio *el güero* (the fair one) Medrano-Mederos, the leader of the *campesino* revolt, was murdered in 1979 by militiamen (*guardias blancas* "white guards" hired by big landowners).[31] Members of Medrano's organization, among them Pérez, were jailed and tortured after his capture and murder. He tells this traumatic episode in the final pages of *Guerrilla*. Therefore, Pérez was a *revolucionario* before becoming a mojado. The armed struggle's failure and the need to escape further pursuit and persecution led Pérez to cross the international border. His friendship with Reavis was an asset in this objective.

On becoming an undocumented person, Pérez has one main identity. When immigration is the topic, a U.S. popular imagination primarily envisions "undesirable alien Mexicans." There is only one identity in the normative narrative of immigration for a dark-skinned, working-class, Spanish-speaker like Pérez. Once in the border area, Pérez is perceived by both Mexican-U.S. border guards and people he encounters in Houston as "Mexican," and hence in the United States linked to illegality, a "wetback." Reavis seems to implement this reductive strategy because in *Diary* he sets aside Pérez's three identities— Zapotec, revolucionario, and "Tianguis"—this last moniker so important in *Guerrilla*, where Medrano connects the village name Pérez is from, Macuiltianguis, to the man.[32] In *Guerrilla*, Medrano makes Pérez aware that *tianguis* means "poor people's market" and bestows the name on him (65).' Medrano's naming act amplifies rather than constricts Pérez's identity. Instead of subsuming his different identities into one singular identity, Medrano's act operates more on a level of contiguity and connection than of substitution or replacement. It relates to Mary Louise Pratt's image of multilingualism, which she sees as a *desdoblamiento*, a multiplying, and not as translation, a substitution ("Translation Studies Forum" 96). Tianguis is a name Pérez holds to this day, between "Ramón" and his surname Pérez. But when it comes to immigration, however, any internal regional distinctions have to disappear; only a Mexican national identity is intelligible. Reavis no doubt thought it best to separate these two experiences—a Zapotec revolucionario renamed "Tianguis" in *Guerrilla* and a Mexican "wetback" in *Diary*.

Between Reavis and Pérez, there is to this day a strong bond of friendship, trust, and support. Both men incurred responsibility by embracing a partnership in migration and translation, but it was Reavis who directed Pérez's actions. Pérez never mentions Reavis by name in *Diario*, but one can safely assume that the "friend" he does refer to in the story is Reavis.[34] "As soon as we're in Nuevo Laredo I go to a phone booth where long distance calls can be made. I talk to my friend and tell him that La Migra has spoiled our attempt" (*Diary* 48).[35]

The friend supports him in the crossing, the details of which Pérez describes in *Diario*. When Pérez is robbed of his coat and wallet while waiting to cross the border, he understandably becomes desperate because he knows he has to pay the *coyotes*. He telephones the one person he trusts to advise him. When his first attempt at crossing fails, he is swept back to Mexico. As I recounted in the introduction, Reavis then goes down into Nuevo Laredo and locates a *patero* (*Diario* 55) literally "duck-man" (*Diary* 49), who will provide the service of ferrying (of bearing across) Pérez across the River. The ferrying successful, Pérez is now a translated man and walks at night through rugged brush South Texas country to meet his friend who awaits at a designated place on the U.S. side, and together they drive a road known to only a few. Pérez entrusts himself to Reavis, and Reavis does not disappoint.

This implied contract of their relationship in migration extends into translation. Reavis motivates Pérez to write his story. He offers Pérez one dollar per page to write *Diario*,[36] and advises him at certain strategic moments in writing the manuscript. He works tirelessly to find a publisher; and he negotiates the details between Arte Público and Pérez. In brief, he functions as Pérez's agent. All the more surprising that Reavis would translate Pérez's mojado into the stereotypically insulting "wetback." He translates less important but no less strange-sounding words upon first usage—patero, "*perreras*, or 'dog wagons'" (*Diary* 46), "*chivos* or 'goats'" (*Diary* 16), "*ficheras* or 'taxi dancers'" (*Diary* 86)—or refrains from translating them—*achiote, mescal* (*Diary* 12). So why not retain mojado? This strategy would convey at minimum the untranslatability of mojado and would suppress the insulting bite of "wetback." For whatever reason—he thinks the book will have newsstand value, he wants to resist the "political correctness" of "undocumented immigrant,"[37] or he believes a translator should adhere closely to the dictionary meaning—Reavis renders mojado into "wetback."

I offer two textual examples to demonstrate the connotative difference and resonance of "wetback" and mojado and to reinforce my suspicion that Reavis's translation of mojado into "wetback" is dependent on the principle of linguistic equivalence. Pérez develops a story of generational migration in *Di-*

ario. In his own voice, he says: "me atrevería a afirmar que somos una comunidad de mojados" (*Diario* 6). Reavis ventriloquizes Pérez's voice: "One could even say that we're a village of wetbacks" (*Diary* 12). He changes the sentence from first to third person but even more important, he makes Pérez attribute "wetback" to himself and to his Zapotec village, a decision which jars the bilingual mind, since no Mexican, I dare say, would assign this label to himself. Pérez is talking about his village's long tradition of migration, noting that his decision to go North was not as painful as the distress he felt knowing that he shared this situation with so many of his fellow villagers who had gone before him: as braceros, as mojados: "[my] townsmen have been crossing the border since the forties, when the rumor of the *bracero* program reached our village, about ten years before the highway came through" (*Diary* 12).[38] Pérez glosses these two distinct categories of marginal labor. What he might mean is that the village mojados continued the same migratory path as its *braceros* until the program officially ended in 1964. Once braceros fled the program and remained in the United States—and many did—the line between bracero and mojado became less clear: the two types sometimes existed within the same family, leading to a comingling of status categories (Ngai 151). The label "wetback" does not convey the sense of shared experience captured in mojado. The first is imposed on a group of people to emphasize "outsiderness;" the second conveys a sense of solidarity with an excluded community.

The second example is emblematic of Reavis's literal translation. Pérez represents an incident that happened to him early in his migration journey. He realizes that in order to find work he needs an authentic-looking social security card. He goes to see a man he is told makes valid-looking (or fluent) imitations. In his real-life experience, unable to read it, Pérez showed the card sold to him to Reavis who translated the language for him. Reavis explained to him that the imitation was a doubly deceitful invention: it explicitly announced its deception and, to boot, warned that it should not be taken for the "real thing." But in *Diario/Diary*, Pérez gives us an alternative explanation of how he came to understand what the card said. In the scene, he represents himself doing a simple correspondence of meaning: "I buy an English-Spanish dictionary. Later I spend more than an hour at a table in a hamburger joint, looking up the meanings, word by word. When I've deciphered them, I'm not as proud as I was at first" (*Diary* 55).[39] This is a tedious, demanding undertaking, especially for a recent arrival unfamiliar with English. Pérez expected a fluent translation; a copy, yes, but a copy that could pass for the "real thing," very similar to Zopilote's intention in Licón's cartoon. He expected it to be credible enough for him to use to find a job. Instead, he receives a card that telegraphs its duplicity, much as Zopilote's "no hoofs" telegraphed his attempted deceit. The difference is that this card intentionally lays itself bare, disavows, and flaunts its deceit. Paradoxically, it is not even an authentic fraud.

The arrangement between translator and author is as bothersome as it is beneficial. Pérez knowingly entrusts himself to Reavis's best judgment and is stained with the pejorative label "wetback," but he also gains something too—a place in U.S. culture and print, a chance to tell his story, I presume, to a sympathetic audience. He obtains a community of readers. In exchange for appearing in print and for access to an audience, Pérez implicitly submits himself to conventional discursive codes of Anglo American language and thought. The contract that the undocumented migrant is willing to take on—to submit himself to danger, humiliation and suspicion—in exchange for the opportunity to work and help his family in Mexico parallels the contract between author and translator because in exchange for a place in the cultural-literary order, albeit a foreign one, he must, implicitly of course, submit to calling himself a "wetback" in the English translation, without fully knowing the word's emotional and pejorative charge. "I'm sure that they know I'm a wetback" (*Diary* 113).[40]

Reavis's experience, his contacts in the United States, his status as an educated Spanish-speaking white male journalist, give him the upper-hand in the relationship, the one who can help steer Pérez clandestinely across the border and into a position of writer. The "wetback"-*mojado* dyad marks the empowering and affirmative but also debilitating relationship between Reavis and Pérez. The translator in this case enjoys the superior position not only because he knows the translated language and the language of translation (true of most other author-translator relationships), not only because he helps to shape the material and is the spokesman to his publisher, but also because the translator is his guide in migration across the border. But Reavis also naturalizes the "foreign" text, linguistically incorporates it into the target culture. He substitutes the mild-sounding, more vowel-driven mojado for the harsher-sounding, more consonant-driven "wetback." Reavis treats "wetback" as the literary equivalent of mojado.

IS IT "WETBACK" OR *MOJADO*?

I'd like now to turn to the primal scene, the more exceptional because it occurs within one ("*Mojados*") of the three chapters ("*La Migra*" and "*La Mota*") with titles in Spanish. These are idiomatic expressions which, if translated, would lose their emotional punch. Why is not the title of this primal-scene chapter "Wetbacks," the word used throughout the narrative? Why break with the precedence set by the text and foreground *Mojados* at this point? The non-translation of the term emphasizes the importance of this chapter. In addition to the peculiar change, what catches my attention is how the scene ruptures the fluency of the textual fabric to create ambiguity in who is speaking: is it the translator or the author? The scene undermines the illusion of fluency in translation. It does this in a multilingual way: instead of doing what translation usually does—moving one language into another—it makes both languages simultaneously present in the translation text. I will explain.

Once he arrives in Houston, Pérez struggles daily to find a job. One man he meets outside a mechanics shop offers him advice. "Why don't you go to the church of the Virgin of Guadalupe? I hear that they help wetbacks find gigs"(*Diary* 70). [41] Pérez refers to this man as "Hispanic," which is Reavis's substitution for Pérez's "Latino" in *Diario*. Both definitions are coded-language for people whom Pérez perceives as ethnic Mexican, or Mexican American. For this particular "Hispanic" man, the relational form of "wetback" lies in *function*. In other words, his message to Pérez primarily is that the Church performs the action of helping "wetbacks."

At the Church, Pérez meets a Cuban man who directs him to a second-story office. The man is specifically identified as "Cuban," a choice which, according to the labeling logic of this scene (Hispanic or Latinx), may suggest that Cubans are excluded from the U.S. Hispanic/Latinx category. This Cuban man is a first-language Spanish-speaker with more time in the States than Pérez. A former pilot in Cuba, this defector from the Castro regime who expects to return one day to Cuba, and who, like Pérez, has sought dry land, is by U.S. immigration law a political refugee, legally entitled to political asylum in the United States. "'Is it true that here they help wetbacks?'" [42] Pérez asks him, only to then utter silently to himself and to his readers, "I use the usual word in Spanish for wetbacks, *mojados*" (*Diary* 70). This is surplus but significant information in the translation text because the narrative focus pulls out from the "wetback" frame and gestures toward the original text where Pérez, of course, used only mojado to identify himself. There is no comparable sentence in *Diario*. Why does Reavis break up the fluency of the translation and add what he surely must intend as nonverbal communication in Pérez's dialogue with the Cuban man? Both ciphers are simultaneously present in the translation text.

Once inside the Church, Pérez meets a "tall woman of about thirty-five in a pale green dress" (*Diary* 72).[43] with "bronze skin" (*piel morena*; [*Diary* 72], *Diario* 88) whom he tells us, again via Reavis, is Hispanic. Common to both Hispanic woman and Cuban man is that they are non-*mojados*, non-"wetbacks." In terms of legality, they are nondeportable subjects. Once again, Pérez asks, this time with Reavis's insertion of "in Spanish" to create a sense of linguistic realism: "'Pardon, I say *in Spanish*, is this the place where you help wetbacks?'" (*Diary* 72, emphasis added).[44] Again, in an immediate aside, Reavis has Pérez add: "'As always I use the word *mojados*'" (*Diary* 72), with no comparable sentence in *Diario*. Reavis, the translator-narrator in these two interruptions, first to the Cuban and then to the woman, breaks the frame that masks his fusion with Pérez: translator-narrator with translated-subject. Reavis, therefore, exposes the mirage of fluency between a translation ("wetback") and an "original" (mojado) by keeping both words before the reader's eye.

In the book's second vignette ("Headed North") and where the words appear for the first time, Reavis establishes the equivalence between "wetback," or "wet," and mojado: "My plan is to go to the United States as a *mojado*, or wetback" (*Diary* 12).[45] But between this first equivalence and the primal scene, Reavis consistently replaces Pérez's *mojado* with "wet." With these asides, of a sudden, he begins to lift the English layer of "wet" to reveal the term (as in a palimpsest) that Pérez has spoken and written all along in *Diario*. Reavis does something here he has not done before or will do again: he shows his allegiance to the translated-subject by stepping aside to expose the act of translation, self-consciously referencing the translation act between himself and Pérez. He allows the translated-subject now to openly use *mojados*, the shadow presence of "wetback" up to this point in the text.[46] He uses it in direct speech to the Hispanic woman, thus opposing fluency, and giving multilingualism a lime-lit visibility. We are privy to both terms at once in the translation text.

We know the Hispanic woman hears *mojado* because she repeats it to herself: "'*Mojados*'? she says to herself. . .[h]er slight smile has vanished and now her lips are tightly shut" (*Diary* 72).[47] Put off, she repeats the word again, this time aloud: "*Mojados*?" She thus confirms Pérez has spoken *mojados* aloud—not "wetbacks." Pérez then reassures her that mojados is the word he uttered: "Yes," Pérez tells her, "somebody told me that here you help *mojados*" (*Diary* 72). The woman's response is telling: "'¡No!'—she says with cold emphasis. "'Here there are no *mojados*'" (*Diary* 72).[48] Had she said, "Here we do not help *mojados*," she would've answered Pérez's question directly and linked the word's signification to function, denying that her church helps mojados. But she is not speaking at the level of function, as the man outside the mechanics shop did. She seems to be familiar with *mojado*: she is not hearing it for the first time. What she emphatically does say is: "Here there are no *mojados*" (*Diary* 72).[49] Is her problem the term itself? Is her response a resistance to the terminology? Confused and, perhaps, feeling conspicuously "other," Pérez makes his way downstairs, only to be enlightened later by his *au courant* Cuban friend that he used the wrong term. "'Undocumented worker is the correct term'" (*Diary* 72).[50] For the Cuban man, the misunderstanding between Pérez and the Hispanic woman lies in terminology.

We are compelled to ask—who is telling the story? Translator or author? Which word did Pérez actually use in the translation text: "wetback" or mojado? In the anthropologist Clifford Geertz's terms, is Pérez "twitching" or "winking" at his audience? (Geertz 6). Or, is it the translator who "winks"? Or, is it both? It is as if Pérez, through Reavis, is saying: "I may say "wetback" to communicate with my audience but I really mean mojado. In other words, Reavis acknowledges that Pérez is not relinquishing his identity-term.

The woman's disavowal of mojado suggests she is neither a Mexican national Spanish-speaker nor is she a U.S. English-speaker. She is a bilingual Hispanic or Latina who understands the meaning of mojado and for whom the term is offensive. Perhaps Reavis chose to use *mojado* here to stress the woman's ethnic status as a Spanish-speaking Hispanic or a Latina, perhaps a Mexican American.[51] Regardless, her words are a blatant denial of the term. Most likely her preference is "undocumented worker." She cannot reject "wetback" because the translator chose to rupture the discourse and privilege mojado. The phrase "undocumented worker" is Reavis's translation of Pérez's *trabajador indocumentado* in *Diario*. But Pérez's rendition (trabajador indocumentado) in *Diario* is the Cuban's translation of "undocumented worker" he has heard in English in his travels in the United States and that he repeats to Pérez. For a fact, he did not hear the term in Cuba. Pérez incorporates the epithet into his Spanish narration, and then Reavis *retranslates* the Cuban's translation (or Pérez's words in *Diario*) into the U.S. term, "undocumented worker." To make it even more complicated, the press then performs another translation act when it titles the translation *Diary of an Undocumented Immigrant*, because, understandably, it disapproves of "wetback." Remember, Reavis's original title for the translation-manuscript he offered to Arte Público was "Diary of a Wetback." In another turn yet, the press decides in favor of *mojado* in its Spanish publication title, *Diario de un mojado*, thus honoring Pérez's choice and suggesting the word in Spanish carries a less harsh pejorative connotation. Ironically, however, "wetback" pervades the translation narrative. The constant back-and-forth movement of these terms reaches a point of not knowing whether the translational tail wags the original dog or the original dog the translational tail.[52]

My discussion has shown the historical and textual interdependency of "wetback" and mojado. This element and the unexpected pattern in publication—the fact that the translation is published before Pérez's original and that his original is never published in his home country but instead by a small press in the destination country—highlight the idiosyncratic signs of translation in a transnational, transborder space. In terms of the translational direction, the books fit a Spanish to English pattern, but in terms of their publication, they chart an English to Spanish direction. Such translation and publication, perhaps also characteristic of other transnational spaces (Algerians in France, Moroccans in Spain, Turks in Germany) says something about the resonance in the destination country, the United States in this case, for the subject matter of Pérez's texts. It may well be that within this transnational space there is a more intense level of interest about the subject of undocumented movement across national borders in the United States than in Mexico.

Of all these terms, it is "wetback" and mojado that open up a history of national and transnational linguistic exchange that has taken place between the United States and Mexico since the first half of the twentieth century. They generate an unfolding or multiplication of selves. The translator-narrator says "wetback," erasing the history of the term mojado, but then he and the translated-subject retrieve this history by choosing to say mojado. The Cuban character translates "undocumented worker" into trabajador indocumentado when he speaks to Pérez; Reavis then retranslates it back into English. Readers/listeners must hear all, especially Pérez's mojado beneath his translator's "wetback." The translator-narrator says "Hispanic" while the translated-subject says "Latino," the term that appears in *Diario*. We know all this only if we read both original and translation texts together. Like Pérez, readers must learn to listen with a transnational linguistic ear, if they expect to assimilate the constellation of nuances in the names that result from the production of a text that crosses not only a U.S.–Mexican geographical border but also the linguistic-cultural borders unique to it. We must learn to live transnationally, albeit temporarily, in more than one national space, in more than one ethnic location, and in more than one language. This does not mean that we cease to exist in national space, only that we must widen our national, cultural, and linguistic identifications to include alternative spaces and formations: one is not enough.

AFTERWORD

As a young child and teenager, I had many experiences translating and interpreting for my Spanish-monolingual maternal grandmother, in relation to her medical, immigration, and other government- and work-related needs. Given her educational and class background, my illiterate grandmother would not be able to read or comprehend the subjects and issues about translation and multilingualism I write about in this book, but she, and others like her, lived the materiality of the need for translation and interpretation in a bilingual society. Today, many children and teenagers, living in communities like Boyle Heights where I grew up in the 1950s and 1960s, are experiencing the centrality of translation and interpretation in their everyday lives when they explain memos, letters, immigration forms, prescription inserts, banking and school notes, legal documents and other business print and electronic material to their parents, and possibly other family members, who cannot negotiate on their own behalf.

Little did I know that service in translating and interpreting everyday mundane matters for my grandmother—negotiating between a home language and a national lingua franca—would become the basis for a strong positive identity and attachment to Spanish and English, to bilingualism and multilingualism in literature. Usually, attitudes toward bilingualism and multilingualism are negative, rendered as attacks on the majority language and associated with poverty, disunity, disorder, interference, a social stigma and a stumbling block, as Joshua Fishman argues, "to progress, peace, and plenty" (42). The thinking is: as the language goes, so goes the nation (Fishman 45). For me, an affirmative identity with bilingualism opened wider paths and goals and eventually connected me to scholarly issues around literature, language, translation, and bilingualism/multilingualism.

My book has been an exploratory attempt to fill a perceived vacuum in Latinx and translation studies since their establishment almost three decades ago. I said before that little attention has been paid to the connections among language study, translation, and bilingualism/multilingualism in the context of Latinx literature. I chose to focus on the publishing activities of U.S. major presses, such as Random House and Harper Collins, that began to publish Latinx literature in English for the first time and then proceeded to commission and publish the translations of many English texts to Spanish during the 1990s. I also focused on one of the more interesting cases of Spanish-to-English publication and translation conducted by Arte Público Press of Houston Texas, probably the most long-lived and successful of the alternative Latinx presses. By focusing on the translation of three cornerstone texts (two from English to Spanish by mainstream presses and one from Spanish to English and back to Spanish via publication by a smaller nontraditional publishing house), I had the opportunity to bring together the disciplines of literature and language, translation studies, and Latinx studies. Much more needs to be done on the relationship of the English and Spanish languages in the United States and their creolization in a context of the transnational translation of bilingual or multilingual literary texts within the nation-state.

One language alone cannot be a center of gravity. English may appear, at present, to be the strongest of the global lingua franca, but it only exists in relationship to other languages. Even in a single language, there is a constant translating activity as we interact with those who may have diverse linguistic experiences. So, English ought not to behave like an invasive species (Allen, "Translation" 19), ready to turn every other language into an image of itself. The United States has been, as Mary Louise Pratt has suggested ("What's Foreign" 1285), a *cementerio de lenguas* (a cemetery of languages), a nation where languages have been killed due to anxious antagonisms in linguistic and cultural differences, to foreignness and foreigners, and to deliberate legislative policies and bans against them. Therefore, we must work to turn around attitudes towards minority languages. English and Spanish in the United States are linked more than any other two languages. No razor-sharp edges or definitive lines separate them. They have been culturally entangled like no other two languages in histories of migration, colonization, empire, and conquest. They can also offer joy and pleasure when we allow ourselves to see and experience their exciting comingling and partnering in communicative situations.

As seen in appendix 1, there is a cadre of almost sixty translations from English to Spanish (about thirteen from Spanish to English translation as shown in appendix 2) published between 1990 and 2010. Some bestselling authors like Junot Díaz and Esmeralda Santiago are still being translated. There is a lot more work to be done. The original texts and their translations must be studied in tandem to develop a typology of how the translations are reframed and refracted in relation to their source texts. These texts can offer a historical and textual testing ground for theories of translation practices in Latinx narratives, be they translated from English to Spanish or Spanish to English, be they published by mainstream or smaller presses. Does my hypothesis and observations that translations of Latinx texts are rendered into monolingual versions of the other language hold, or are there important qualifications to be proposed and examined? Are there translations that preserve the interlingual features of the source texts? If so, what strategies do they propose?

More texts must be examined and connected to the broader context of Latinx literature, language study, and translation and bilingualism-multilingualism to assess whether the translation to Spanish of English texts—the direction of the majority of the Latinx translations—constitutes evidence of a growing multilingual consciousness on the part of U.S. mainstream publishers. Some, like myself, are desirous that we as a country recognize a multilingual U.S. society. Have publishers who commissioned the translation of Latinx fiction to Spanish in the 1990s and first decade of the twenty-first century laid the foundation for a new canon of U.S. American literature in Spanish as well as a U.S. American Spanish-reading audience? At present, I think not—the project remains aspirational. In pulling the nation away from English, they aimed for a global and domestic Spanish monolingual audience, rather than moving toward a multilingual audience that the original texts implied. Still, as commercial media enterprises with strong economic motives, their effort is a sign of a growing consciousness of the readiness of the market to yield financial profit in Spanish publication. Even more important, I believe, is that their endeavors suggest they are sensing the importance of a different kind of audience in the United States and worldwide. My challenge has been to chart the contours of a multilingual reality that is not overtly visible when the original multilingual texts are translated: to make the "foreign" visible, to learn from it, and to respect it.

Rene Alegría, a Mexican American business entrepreneur, a native of Tucson, Arizona and the son of Mexican immigrants, started up the Rayo imprint at HarperCollins in the mid-1990s to reach readers like himself: "young, Latino and having a great deal of purchasing power" (Ojito). In 2015, at Ello, a New York marketing social media site, he reflected back to his ten years at Rayo: "'I got struck by the fact there were no Hispanics in the building,' he said. 'Publishing is a notoriously un-diverse industry. Still is. I thought it was a travesty. Here we are, a large portion of the American population and we're not being represented in books'" (Ambrosio). Alegría hit on the root problem—the need for hiring practices in the publishing industry to make these industries more diverse racially, culturally, and along lines of gender. But unless diversity extends into the hiring of a multilingual work force (editors, translators, readers) who know not only the monolingual standard register but the U.S. population and the manifestations, practices, and interrelationships of its languages, we will keep seeing English and Spanish as entities to be translated (one language passing into a different language) rather than languages in contact. Though they exist in asymmetrical relations of power, they interact and change one another. Crucial too is the need for authors to work collaboratively with translators and with editors on the translation of their books to find new and creative ways to capture the multilingual features of the texts.

My coming into a social consciousness in the 1970s and my involvement with Chicanx and continental Puerto Rican literatures and culture, and with students of these and other backgrounds interested in these subjects, allowed me to see how unusual, how against the grain of things, how counter these translations were in aiming to overturn the linkage between English and the U.S. nation-state. When English-language mainstream presses undertook translations from English to Spanish, I saw something unfamiliar in a very familiar world. Without the vantage point of the 1970s, without having seen and experienced these up-until-then unknown literatures in the academy in the 1970s, only then beginning to be published by small specialized Latinx presses who were barely coming into existence themselves almost simultaneously, I would not have been able to detect the major swerve the publishing and translating of these literary narratives in Spanish within the United States took away from a business-as-usual-model in the publishing world. I lived the unanticipated change. The unexpected translation I have focused on here did not begin in 1990 nor end in 2010: translations of Latinx narratives were done before (mainly from Spanish to English) and will be after, but probably not to the extent, at least for a while, that they were done during this period of unprecedented migratory flows, which in turn brought about a realignment of languages, especially Spanish, in the United States.

I have learned from and been inspired by the work of literary scholars who, all in their own creative ways, have made language a central category of analysis, especially bilingualism and multilingualism, in their research in Latinx, literary, and translation studies. Some I know personally, others I hope to meet some day. These are Mary Louise Pratt, Jésus Rosales, Lauro Flores, Esther Allen, Frederic Aldama, Laura Lomas, Ilan Stavans, and Gustavo Pérez-Firmat. I have learned from scholars interested in languages and education, especially, Ana Celia Zentella and Joshua Fishman, and I have profited from the work of those interested in languages and literature: Werner Sollors, Rainer Grutman, Yasemin Yildiz, Pascale Casanova, Rebecca L. Walkowitz, Stephanie Jed, and others whose thoughts permeate the chapters of this book. It is my hope that this book will make a small contribution to the study of languages, Latinx studies, and literature and translation.

APPENDIX 1: ENGLISH-TO-SPANISH TRANSLATIONS

Author	English	Spanish
Julia Alvarez	*How the García Girls Lost Their Accents (1991)* *In the Time of the Butterflies (1994)*	*De cómo las muchachas García perdieron el acento (2007)* *En el tiempo de las mariposas (1998)*
Rudy Anaya	*Bless Me, Ultima (1972)*	*Bendíceme Última (1994)*
Ron Arias	*The Road to Tamazunchale (1978/1987)*	*El camino a Tamazunchale (2002)*
Norma Cantú	*Canícula: Snapshots of a Girlhood en la Frontera (1995)*	*Canícula: Imagénes de una niñez fronteriza (2001)*
Ana Castillo	*The Mixquiahuala Letters 1986* *Goddess of the Américas: Writings on the Virgen of Guadalupe (1996)* *So far from God (1993)*	*Las cartas de Mixquiahuala (1994)* *La diosa de las Américas: Escritos sobre la Virgen de Guadalupe (2000)* *Tan lejos de Dios (1999)*
Denise Chávez	*Last of the Menu Girls (1986)* *Loving Pedro Infante (2001)*	*La última de las muchachas del menú (2005)* *Por el amor de Pedro Infante (2002)*
Sandra Cisneros	*The House on Mango Street (1983)* *Caramelo or Puro Cuento (2002)* *Woman Hollering Creek (1991)*	*La casa en Mango Street (1991)* *Caramelo o Puro Cuento (2002)* *El arroyo de la llorona (1996)*
Lucha Corpi	*Eulogy for a Brown Angel: A Gloria Damasco Mystery (2002)*	*Loa a un ángel de piel morena (2012)*
Junot Díaz	*Drown (1996)* *The Brief Wonderous Life of Oscar Wao (2007)*	*Negocios (1997)* *La breve y maravillosa vida de Oscar Wao (2008)*
María Amparo Escandón	*Esperanza's Box of Saints (1999)* *González & Daughter Trucking Co. (2005)*	*Santitos (1991)* *González e hija transportes (2005)*
Roberta Fernandez	*Intaglio: A Novel in Six Stories (1990)*	*Fronterizas: Una novela en seís cuentos (2001)*
Cristina García	*Dreaming in Cuban (1992)*	*Soñar en cubano (1993)*
Alicia Gaspar de Alba	*Desert Blood: The Juárez Murders (2005)*	*Sangre en el desierto: Las muertas de Juárez (2008)*

Diane Gonzales Bertrand	*Trino's Choice (1999)* *Trino's Time (2001)*	*El dilema de Trino (2005)* *El momento de Trino (2006)*
Reyna Grande	*Across 100 Mountains (2006)* *The Distance Between Us (2012)*	*A través de cien montañas (2007)* *La distancia entre nosotros (2013)*
Oscar Hijuelos	*The Mambo Kings Play Songs of Love (1989)*	*Los reyes del mambo tocan canciones de amor (1996)*
Graciela Limón	*In Search of Bernabé (1993)* *The Day of the Moon (1999)* *The Song of the Hummingbird (1996)* *The Memories of Ana Calderón (1994)*	*En busca de Bernabé (1997)* *El día de la luna (2004)* *La canción del colibrí (2006)* *Los recuerdos de Ana Calderón (2011)*
Nina Marie Martínez	*¡Caramba! (2005)*	*¡Caramba, una novela! (2006)*
Cherríe Moraga	*This Bridge Called My Back (1981)*	*Esta puente mi espalda (1988)*
Alejandro Morales	*The Brick People (1992)*	*Hombres de ladrillo (2010)*
Yxta Maya Murray	*The Conquest (2002)*	*La conquista (2002)*
Judith Ortiz Cofer	*Silent Dancing: A Partial Remembrance of a Puerto Rican Childhood (1990)* *The Year of Our Revolution (1990)*	*Bailando en silencio: Escenas de una niñez puertorriqueña (1997)* *El año de nuestra revolución: Cuentos y Poemas (2006)*
Américo Paredes	*George Washington Gómez (1990)*	*George Washington Gómez (2013)*
Stella Pope Duarte	*Let Their Spirits Dance (2002)*	*Que bailen sus espiritus (2003)*
Ernesto Quiñonez	*Chango's Fire (2004)* *Bodega Dreams (2000)*	*El fuego de Changó (2004)* *El vendedor de sueños (2004)*
Luis Rodríguez	*Always Running, La Vida Loca, Gang Days in L.A. (1994)*	*La vida loca: el testimonio de un pandillero en Los Angeles (2005)*
Esmeralda Santiago	*When I Was Puerto Rican (1993)* *América's Dream (1996)* *Almost a Woman (1998)* *The Turkish Lover (2004)* *Conquistadora (2011)*	*Cuando era puertorriqueña (1994)* *El sueño de América (1996)* *Casi una mujer (1999)* *El amante Turco (2005)* *Conquistadora (2011)*
Gary Soto	*Baseball in April (1990)*	*Beísbol en abril (1993)*
Piri Thomas	*Down These Mean Streets (1967)*	*Por estas calles bravas (1997)*
Elva Trevino Hart	*Barefoot Heart: Stories of a Migrant Child (1999)*	*Corazón descalzo: Historias de una niña migratoria (2007)*
Luís Alberto Urea	*The Hummingbird's Daughter (2005)* *Into the Beautiful North (2009)*	*La hija de la chuparrosa (2006)* *Rumbo al hermoso norte (2009)*
Alisa Valdes-Rodriguez	*The Dirty Girls Social Club (2003)*	*El club social de las chicas temerarias (2003)*
Richard Vásquez	*Chicano (1970)*	*Chicano (2005)*

José Antonio Villarreal	*Pocho (1959)*	*Pocho: en español (1994)*
Victor Villaseñor	*Macho! (1973)* *Rain of Gold (1991)* *Thirteen Senses: A Memoir (2001)* *Walking Stars (1994)*	*¡Macho! (2004)* *Lluvia de oro (1996)* *Trece sentidos (2001)* *Estrellas peregrinas: Cuentos de magia y poder (2005)*

APPENDIX 2: SPANISH-TO-ENGLISH TRANSLATIONS

Author	Spanish	English
Aristeo Brito	*El diablo en Texas (1976)*	*The Devil in Texas/El diablo en Texas (1990)*
Mario Bencastro	*Odisea del Norte (1999)* *Disparo en la catedral (1997)* *Árbol de la vida: Historias de la Guerra civil (1997)*	*Odyssey to the North (1998)* *A Shot in the Cathedral (1996)* *The Tree of Life: Stories of Civil War (1997)*
Margarita Cota-Cárdenas	*Puppet: a Chicano Novella (1985)*	*Puppet, A Chicano novella Bilingual edition (2000)*
Eduardo González Viaña	*El corrido de Dante (2006)*	*Dante's Ballad (2007)*
Hinojosa-S, Rolando	*Estampas del Valle y otras obras (1973) Bilingual edition* *Klail City y sus alrededores (published in Cuba 1976)*	*Published in bilingual edition as Generaciones y semblanzas (1977)* *Published in bilingual edition as Klail City / Klail City y sus alrededores (2014)*
Miguel Méndez	*Peregrinos de Aztlán (1974)*	*Pilgrims in Aztlán (1992)*
Alejandro Morales	*Caras viejas y vino nueve (1975)* *La verdad sin voz (1979)*	*Old Faces and New Wine (1981)* *Death of an Anglo (1988)*
Gustavo Pérez Firmat	*Next Year in Cuba: A Cubano's Coming-of-Age in America (2005)*	*El año que viene estamos en Cuba (1997)*
Ramón "Tianguis" Pérez*	*Diario de un mojado (2003)*	*Diary of an Undocumented Immigrant (1991)*
Tomás Rivera	*. . .y no se lo tragó la tierra (1971) Bilingual edition*	*. . .y no se lo tragó la tierra / And the Earth Did Not Devour Him (2015) Bilingual edition*
Rosario Sanmiguel	*Under the Bridge: Stories from the Border/Bajo el Puente: Relatos desde la frontera (2008)*	
Luis Valdez	*Zoot Suit (1992)*	*Zoot Suit: A Bilingual Edition (2005)*
Daniel Venegas*	*Las aventuras de don Chipote, o, Cuando los pericos mamen (2000)*	*The Adventures of Don Chipote, or, When Parrots Breastfeed (1998)*

*As indicated by the publication dates, the English translations of Ramón Pérez's and Daniel Vanegas's texts were published before the Spanish originals.

NOTES

INTRODUCTION: SETTING THE STAGE

1. To protect his identity, Dick is left unidentified in the book.

2. Phone interview with Dick Reavis, 2011.

3. Phone interview with Dick Reavis, 2011.

4. Nicolás Kanellos, editor of Arte Público, explained to me that the press did not use Reavis's "wetback" for the published English translation because the word was very pejorative at the time. He published the Spanish original using Pérez's word for himself in his manuscript-original because mojado does not have the same connotation in Spanish as "wetback" in English (email correspondence July 27, 2017). I agree; *mojado* is used among undocumented people today. "Wetback" is, I think, to this day a very insulting term.

5. For the sake of brevity, excepting *Pocho and Pocho En Español*, I abbreviate throughout the titles of the other main texts: *When I Was Puerto Rican* is *When I Was* and *Cuando era puertorriquena* is *Cuando era; Diario de un mojado* is *Diario* and *Diary of an Undocumented Immigrant* is *Diary*.

6. Allen discusses Domingo F. Sarmiento's biography of the Argentinian *caudillo*, Juan Facundo Quiroga, translated with the English title of *Life in the Argentine Repub-*

lic in the Days of the Tyrants; or, Civilization and Barbarism and published by the New York publishing house of Hurd and Houghton in 1868. Another well-known Spanish-to-English title is Mariano Azuela's *Los de abajo* (*The Underdogs*), first translated by Enrique Munguía in 1929, republished in 1962 (See Munguía). Since then there have been four other translations. See Hendricks (1979), Fornoff (1992), Robe (1979), and Pellón's (2006). Pellón offers an introduction to his own translation (vii). On the other hand, because he mainly had Spanish-language audiences in Latin America in mind, José Martí translated from English to Spanish while in exile in New York (1880–1895), although Lomas (2008) notes that he did some Spanish to English translation, most likely in collaboration with others, for a domestic market.

7. Rolando Hinojosa-Smith's *Klail City* and *This Migrant Earth* (1987) are recreations of "original" texts in Spanish: the former of Hinojosa's own *Klail City y sus alrededores*; the latter of Tomás Rivera's *. . .y no se lo tragó la tierra*, with substantial differences between the two language versions. There is no strict definition of translation, and Hinojosa's adaptations may qualify as a subcategory of translation, depending upon one's approach, but his recreations are not translations in the sense that I use the genre in this book. Whereas *This Migrant Earth*, for example, recreates Rivera's already translated text to English, the translation texts I discuss are first-time renditions into Spanish and English, intended to follow their source texts, in terms of plot, characters, and chapter structure. They are also marketed as translations, in the conventionally understood sense of the word, and taken by readers to be Spanish translations of their English source texts. Even *Pocho en Español*, a radical departure from the source text's linguistic register and style, is an intentional rendition of Villarreal's *Pocho*, as suggested by Cantú's introduction (see chapter 3), the book's title and statement on its back cover " . . . la decisión que ha tomado la casa editorial Anchor de verter al español la primera novela de Villarreal en el trigésimimo quinto aniversario de su primera edición en inglés" (the decision taken by its publisher Anchor to translate to Spanish Villarreal's first novel in its thirty-fifth anniversary of publication).

8. Both Villarreal and Santiago learned Spanish prior to English. Villarreal was born in Los Angeles, California. His parents were born and raised as peons on a hacienda in the state of Zacatecas, Mexico (see Vallejos). Santiago explains her loss of Spanish to English in the introductory pages of *Cuando era*.

9. For Jorge Luis Borges, there is no "definitive text"; in his view there are only translations of translations, not only in the sense that there no "originals," only drafts and versions, but also in the sense that one text, say *One Thousand and One Nights*, can have many translations. See Waisman 2005, 43.

10. Clyne, an Australian linguist, notes that "bilingual" is the larger umbrella term because even though many multilingual situations exist in the world, multilinguals are perceived to use no more than two languages habitually ("Multilingualism." 301–

314). On the other hand, Li Wei states: "bilingual" can be taken to refer to people in the world "who have varying degrees of proficiency in, and interchangeably use, three, four, or even more languages" (7). Who is or is not bilingual is the question? Only persons who have equal competence in both languages? Does it include those who speak two languages but not write or read the second language? Or, those who understand a second language but not speak it? See Wei for the many forms two languages can take under the rubric of bilingualism (2000, 5–6). For my purposes, "bilingualism" is a continuum, extending from sparse usage of overt Spanish words, phrases, sentences, paragraphs, and/or English phrasing hidden in Spanish syntax, to a full-blown sustained level of intrasentential interactivity between two languages.

11. Bandia attributes this insight to Venuti, *Scandals* (1998) 11.

12. In chapter 5, I make reference to Luis Spota, the Mexican journalist-author who chose to perform a mojado identity in preparation to write his novel, *Murieron a mitad del río* (1948). This is one of the few times the figure appears in Mexican literature. In contrast, Pérez actually became a mojado. Furthermore, he comes from a Zapotec community in Oaxaca with a long line of men who have left their village to cross the international border, in hopes of sending economic support to their families.

13. The terms *pocho* and *mojado* have their feminine counterparts: *pocha* and *mojada*. I use the male label for the two male protagonists and the feminine or *jíbara* for the female protagonist.

14. The work of Lomas, Pratt, Shell, Sollors, and Stavans has laid a strong foundational basis for my work on the study of multilingualism and translation.

15. The work of Talal Asad in anthropology and Vince Rafael in postcolonial studies are examples.

CHAPTER 1. REVERSE CROSSOVER LATINX NARRATIVES

1. I focus on print literature of Latino communities, but Mexican, Puerto Rican, Dominican, and Central American communities with histories of migration to the United States have long oral traditions, particularly in Levine's sense of "the great unwritten": cultural material (narrative, song, poetry, performance) that has circulated as orature for over a century and a half (Levine 217–219).

2. David William Foster translated Méndez's and Brito's texts. See his comments about translating Méndez's *Peregrinos* to English.

3. Venegas's document was first published in 1928 by *El heraldo de México*, a Spanish-language daily newspaper in Los Angeles. See Kanellos 2000, "Introduction."

4. Carreira is also codirector of the National Heritage Language Resource Center at UCLA, chair of the SAT Spanish Committee, and associate editor of *Hispania*.

5. *Pocho* and *With His Pistol in His Hand* were published in 1959 by mainstream presses. The sole Puerto Rican fictional narrative published prior to 1980 by a main-

stream press was Piri Thomas's *Down These Mean Streets* (1967). It was translated as *Por estas called bravas* in 1998. For the significance of Thomas's narrative within continental Puerto Rican and Latinx Studies, see Sánchez, "La Malinche."

6. Random House Mondadori covers the market in Spain and Latin America. Esmeralda Santiago and Julia Alvarez are two Latinx authors published in Spain.

7. "Latino" and "Hispanic" are used interchangeably in press releases by HarperCollins, Random House, and others to designate the U.S. Spanish-language market. While "Latino" designates more specifically an inside U.S. audience, "Hispanic" may encompass a global Spanish-language market, though it is also commonly used to refer to a U.S. market. Strictly speaking "Hispanic" is an adjective, but in the United States it is used as a noun, as in "She is Hispanic."

8. All comments attributed to Castillo are from an email correspondence on July 12, 2017.

9. Allende's books had been published by Spanish presses and translated by U.S. presses, but in the 1990's U.S. houses began to publish her originals in Spanish. HarperLibros published Allende's *Paula,* a memoir about her daughter in English and Spanish. "Since Allende writes in Spanish, the house doesn't have to worry about translations" (See Oder 31). Octavio Paz and Pablo Neruda were the leading poets published in Spanish in the United States.

10. "Rayo publicará obras que incorporan la diversidad latina en ediciones en español e inglés, conectando así la cultura con el pensamiento, y fortaleciendo la tradición y el espíritu."

11. More often, translation is *from* English rather than *to* English. For specific data about translation from English, see Venuti, *Translator's Invisibility* 11–14; also Allen, "Translation" 24–25. For a glimpse of worldwide translated fiction into English published in the United States between 2000–2006, see Allen, "Translation" 26.

12. In 2015, The Modern Language Association (MLA) reported a drop in foreign language enrollments since 1995, with a 6.7 percent overall decrease since 2009 in major European languages, including Spanish. The translation which is the focus of this study occurred during the years of highest college course enrollment in Spanish.

13. The book has been translated into German, Korean, Danish, French, Italian, and Finnish. See *Index Translationum.*

14. Bearden says that "It was Esquivel . . . who urged Doubleday to publish her book in Spanish" because "so many clients came to her bookstore readings with their own Mexican-published versions of the book" ("Esquivel's Spanish Primer" 40–41).

15. *The House on Mango Street* has been translated into Catalán by Vanesa Coronado (*La casa de Mango Street,* Arola Editors, Barcelona, 2007). It has also been translated into German, French, Persian, Japanese, and Croatian. See *Index Translationum.*

16. Yoko Tawada, for example, is a native-born Japanese author who became a German immigrant and writes in Japanese and German separately. Her German writ-

ings if translated and published in Japan would be an example of international translation. See Yildiz 2012, 110.

17. I develop connections between the international translation of Latin American boom writers and intranational translation of Latinx writers in chapter 2. See pages 000. A word of caution about my use of "international translation" with respect to Latin America—the translation of Latin American literature is international, but it entails going from "Spanishes" of different nation-states into different national languages, such as French, German, etc.

18. Yildiz links the rise of the modern nation state to the rise of the monolingual paradigm (2-3). See note 32, chapter 2.

19. The English sales, as of June 2017, were 9000, and the Spanish sales were 5,400. I am indebted to Nicolás Kanellos of Arte Público for this information.

20. Barradas cites page 196, but the correct page is 197.

21. Díaz says he negotiated with the New Yorker about their "style sheet" and convinced them not to italicize foreign words: "I was opposed to letting them italicize any Spanish that I wrote in my columns. I stood my ground and now, no references to a foreign language are carried in italics in the New Yorker." See "Create."

22. Spanglish, like other terms freely chosen by or imposed on marginalized populations, is a loaded term, often pejorative depending on speakers' perspectives. I use the term neither in its celebratory nor in its damaging connotations. All national versions of Spanish in the Spanish-language Américas have various popular/colloquial forms and usages, but Spanglish is a unique form because of the Spanish language's long-standing intimate relationship to English in the United States. Depending on the specific Latinx population group (Dominican, Puerto Rican, Guatemalan, etc.), Spanglish embodies the unequal power relationship between English and Spanish. I agree with Ana Zentella in her counter to Ricardo Otheguy's recommendation of excising the term from people's speech (for Otheguy "Spanglish" seems to be "a jumbled up mix" of sounds and words). Even if this could be done, and I don't believe it possible, the issue for me is not the term itself but the cultural, sociolinguistic, and economic forces of domination, including the oppression that comes with nativist language policies, on the speakers of the various forms of spoken and written "Spanglish." For a summary of the debate on "Spanglish" between Otheguy and Zentella, see Otheguy.

23. First published in 1985, the source text *Puppet* is already a bilingual original, with a slant toward Spanish. It resists translation because it demands high-level bilingual readers. The book is unintelligible to monolingual and bilingual readers on the lower-end of the bilingual spectrum. The book subverts the unilingual book because readers must flip the book to encounter the other language. When first picking up the book, one is unclear whether it is the original or the English translation. Diana Tey Rebolledo's "Foreword" to the translation, however, only appears on the English side,

suggesting that English, all things considered, is the privileged language. The word "Puppet," the title of the original book, is left untranslated in the English translation. For further details, see Rebolledo's "Foreword" and Fagan (12).

24. My thanks to Marc Zimmerman for alerting me to the added connotation.

25. The broad historical meaning of pachuco refers to Mexican-American marginalized youths of 1940s urban Los Angeles. The pachuco is linked to the zoot suiter of the 1940s, or those pachucos who converted the white man's business suit by exaggerating its characteristics to symbolize Chicano resistance, especially to the draft of World War II. The caló dialect is often linked to the pachuco and zoot suiters (those who wore the flamboyant suits) of the 1940s.

CHAPTER 2: THE "NEW" STATUS OF THE SPANISH LANGUAGE IN THE UNITED STATES

1. The same PEW reported that "[t]he overall share of those across all generations who speak Spanish at home rose to 78% at the peak of the immigration wave in 2000 but has since tailed off, dropping to 73% in 2013" (Adams).

2. For figures of the Spanish-speaking population at the time of the Mexican–American war, Crawford refers to Carey McWilliams's *North from Mexico: The Spanish-Speaking People of the United States*: " . . . [A]n estimated 75,000 Spanish-speakers lived in the Southwest: 60, 999 in New Mexico, 7,500 in California, 5,000 in Texas, 1,000 or so in Arizona, and 1,500 in Colorado" (*Language* 58). Massey (645) says that fewer than 50,000 Mexicans in the conquered territory became U.S. citizens.

3. Despite Article IX of the Treaty of Guadalupe Hidalgo of 1848 that many interpret to have guaranteed legally the cultural rights (including language) of the Mexican population (Crawford, *Language* 51–52), English was imposed in California. Some credit is due to New Mexico: the Spanish-speaking population was numerically substantial at the time the state constitution was ratified, and its official statutes were published in two languages (Crawford, *Language* 59). English was imposed on the majority Spanish-speaking Puerto Rican population at the time of conquest. (Crawford, *Language* 50). Cervantes-Rodriguez and Lutz in "Coloniality of Power" discuss how the Spanish language becomes a subaltern language as part of a "great world systemic formation" (525) which, in modern times, led to the development of an English-Spanish asymmetry in a global system of languages and language regulating mechanisms in the United States. They highlight the Mexican–American and Spanish–American wars (and I will add the massive migration resulting from the Mexican Revolution) as the historical core of power relations that racialized the "Hispanic" population in the United States (527) and made Spanish a racial marker of a minority community (525).

4. Massey says that immigration from Mexico "mushroomed from 50,000 in the first decade of the century, to 220,000 in the second, to 460,000 in the third" (636).

5. Zentella states that over 50,000 Puerto Ricans left each year between 1945 and 1955 ("Language Situation" 140).

6. Massey quotes 200,000 Cubans, 100,000 Dominicans, and 70,000 Colombians (637).

7. The formation of Pérez's Zapotec identity involved an association of Spanish, the public, high-prestige language and majority national language, with his father, and Zapotec, the indigenous minority language, with his mother. His primary and secondary education was in Spanish (email correspondence August 17, 2011):

"En mi comunidad—Macuiltianguis- el zapoteco se aprende porque es la lengua común, no hay una escuela donde se vaya a tomar clases. Muy al contrario, hace muchos años, cuando la escuela de nivel primaria—creo que es lo equivalente a primero a sexto grado en USA—se estableció en mi pueblo, las maestras que llegaron no eran bilingües, entonces tenían dificultades para su enseñanza. Como remedio, desculturizante, en una asamblea, dieron la sugerencia a que en casa, los padres evitaran hablar zapoteco con los hijos. En mi caso, con mi madre siempre era en zapoteco pero con mi padre siempre era en español." (In my community—Macuiltianguis—we learn Zapotec because it is the common language, there is no school where we can take classes. In fact, many years ago, when the primary school—I believe this is the equivalent of first to sixth grade in the United States—was established in my community, the teachers who arrived were not bilingual, they, therefore, found it difficult to teach us. In an assembly, they suggested that our parents refrain from speaking Zapotec in the home. In my case, I always spoke Zapotec with my mother but Spanish with my father. [trans. mine])

8. The writing and translations of the Cuban-born Jose Martí and other Latin Americans living on the East Coast in the late nineteenth century interjected cultural and political commentary into an assumed Anglo-American empire's expansion into the Global South. For extensive discussions on how Martí's writing reexamined and expanded the definition of U.S. literature and its perspective on modernity, see Lomas, *Translating Empire*.

9. The U.S. federal government has never codified the English language as an "official" language, but it is the de facto national language of the United States. See Shell, "Babel" 104, n. 6. Molesky ("Understanding") makes interesting points about the silence of the Constitution on language policy: on the one hand, there is freedom because having no official policy, ironically, allows for tolerance of linguistic rights, but on the other hand, the lack of an explicit policy provides a space for conservative restrictions on language (34–35).

10. According to the CBO (Congressional Budget Office, February 2011), the destination of the largest amount of remittances from the United States was Mexico. Between 1990 and 2000, an estimate of remittances from the United States to Mexico

alone rose from five to fourteen billion. In 2009, they reached close to 20 billion. Re-mittances are one of the top three sources of revenue (in addition to oil and tourism) in the Mexican economy. See Congressional Budget Office.

11. Electronic mediation and mass migration are two global mechanisms that have brought the United States into a "transnational era" (Giles 46–7).

12. I define these idiolects and vernaculars in chapter 1.

13. As Meléndez notes, modern technological innovation, in the form of the first printing presses, arrived in 1834 in Santa Fe, New Mexico and Monterrey, California. They were brought to the territories by native influential citizens and ecclesiastical leaders by producing a variety of materials in Spanish, mitigating the region's cul-tural isolation and its lack of communication with Europe, Mexico, and the rest of the Spanish Américas. They helped to establish the beginnings of a culture of print among Spanish-speaking communities whose roots lay primarily in oral preliterate culture (*So All is Not Lost* 16). Kent and Huntz (1996) provide a useful summary from the early development in 1848 to 1992: San Francisco and Brownville were two main centers for newspaper publishing (447–448); *El nuevo mexicano* and *El boletín popu-lar*, using lower-case letters here follows the Spanish rule; *mexicano* is not upper-case both from Santa Fe, were published well into the 1900s (448); Los Angeles and Santa Fe also boasted Spanish-language newspapers (448); newspapers appeared in Cali-fornia, the Upper Rio Grande Valley, and South Texas (449); *El heraldo de México* (1916–1920) in Los Angeles provided news from Mexico to the working-class Mexican audience who had settled in Los Angeles during and after the Mexican Revolution. Rodríguez reports that throughout the nineteenth and well into the twentieth centu-ry, Spanish-language newspapers were primarily a community business supported by immigrant enclaves (359).

Veciana-Suarez explains that on the east coast, the Miami daily newspaper *Diario las Americas* started in 1953, six years before several thousand Cubans fled from the Cuban Revolution to the city (30). Its founder, Horacio Aguirre-Baca, a Nicaraguan, predicted accurately that though sparse in the 1950s, Miami's Spanish-speaking pop-ulation would make the city a strategic geographical location for a Spanish-language market (30). She adds that in 1976, an English-language newspaper, *Miami Herald*, was the first to publish a Spanish-language insert with a bilingual title, *El Herald* (36).

14. In 2011, Guskin and Mitchell reported that according to the 2010 census, "the Latino population grew to more than 50 million, more than double its size in 1990, and up 46.3% since 2000. In the same report, they noted that "English-speaking Hispanics continue to watch Spanish-language TV. Almost a quarter of Hispanics who speak English mostly at home, 24%, watch between one and three hours of Spanish-language TV a day, according to data from Nielsen Media Research."

15. Pratt argues that the idea and use of "'Foreignness' equally misapplies to French, Cantonese, Italian, or Japanese—to say nothing of Lakota, Navajo, or Cree.

Following the tradition of the MLA, let us agree on the term *modern languages* and put an end to another lexical legacy of the Cold War" (*Comparative Literature* 64).

16. Stavans writes in protest of the Trump administration's removal of the Spanish-language side of the White House website. Writing in 2017, Stavans put the United States at number five among the world's Spanish-speaking countries. The Spanish-based Instituto Cervantes in 2015 put it at number 2, with 41 million native Spanish speakers and 11.6 million who are bilingual for a total of a little less than 53,000,000, ahead of Colombia (48 million) and Spain (46 million), only Mexico has more (121 million). See "US Now Has More Spanish." It seems likely that the numbers in the United States would be higher than fifth in the world.

17. Arteaga argues: "History is not written chronologically but, rather from East to West so that Spanish is encountered by the likes of Austin and Fremont during the Western expansion late in U.S. history; it appears *historically* after English" (25).

18. LOTE and LOTS are acronyms used in the contexts of languages, literature, and education.

19. "As a result of mass migration following the 1961 labor recruitment agreement, workers from Turkey brought the language to Germany" (144). There are some striking parallels between Turkish migration to Germany and Mexican migration to the United States: both were initiated by major revolutions in the home country, forcing each group to move or die, and both constitute the backbone of imported labor. See Seyhan (99–106).

20. My thanks to Ana Celia Zentella for alerting me to this difference. This was corroborated to me by Dr. Michael Daxtner, Professor of Sociology and University President emeritus (Oldenburg) in an email June 11, 2017. See also Pavlenko, "We Have Room" 165.

21. For an extensive discussion of how dominant listening practices operate in mainstream perception, see Stoever-Ackerman, "Splicing."

22. Writing in 2004, Crystal says that "Spanish is the fastest growing mother tongue at present" (*Language Revolution* 22).

23. On this point, Pratt writes: the idea that the world is becoming more English-speaking is misleading. "The world is becoming increasingly bilingual" ("What's Foreign" 1287). Esther Allen notes that while Mandarin Chinese is the "first language of the greatest number of speakers on earth," its reach might not be wide enough for the Chinese themselves. English-speakers in China will surpass the number of speakers of English as a first language in the rest of the world. She cites the UK former prime minister Gordon Brown's 2005 statement in Beijing: "In twenty years this appears as I have it in the source time, the number of English speakers in China is likely to exceed the number of speakers of English as a first language in all the rest of the world." ("Translation" 17).

24. In 2008, the Oklahoma Republican senator James Inhofe introduced the Na-

tional Language Act that declared "English as the national language of the Government of the United States, and for other purposes." See Lennon (188, note 38). In addition to Hawaii and Alaska, Oklahoma is one of three states with co-official native languages. See *Business Wire*.

25. According to Marc Shell, before Hayakawa's efforts, the "twentieth-century legal movement to make 'American' the official language of the United States dates from about 1923, when Congressman Washington J. McCormick introduced a bill to Congress that, though it died in committee, was later adopted by Illinois." ("Babel," note 82, 123–24).

26. For example, the rights of minority groups to use the ethnic language and to claim language education services, according to Title VI of the Civil Rights Act of 1964 (Wong, esp. 371–72), and to bilingual election ballots, according to the 1978 amendment to the Voting Rights Act of 1965. See Woolard 126.

27. Santorum's perspective supports the historically held view of U.S. policy. Crawford explains that ever since 1898, United States policy dictated English "as the language of government and education" of Puerto Rico and went so far as to officially anglicize the pronunciation and spelling of its name into "Porto Rico," until 1932. The policy, after much resistance by Puerto Ricans, was finally scrapped in 1949, "an acknowledged failure" (*Hold Your Tongue* 50–51).

28. The *Wall Street Journal* (April 30, 2010) reported that "[t]he Arizona Department of Education recently began telling school districts that teachers whose spoken English it deems to be heavily accented or ungrammatical must be removed from classes for students still learning English." See Jordan.

29. Allen, nonetheless, provides a comment on NY bookstores off sync with the reality of the city. "[A]nyone who has ever ridden the New York subway has plunged into an environment probably as multilingual as any on earth. But if that same subway rider goes back up to the street and strolls into a bookstore, she'll find little there that can help her win entry into the alien tongues that were ringing in her ears a few seconds earlier—almost everything there will have been written in English" ("Translation" 31).

30. Though Spanish had been spoken before in the U.S. Senate, Kaine's speech was historic in that he was the first to deliver an entire speech in Spanish on the Senate floor (Border Security, Economic Opportunity, and Immigration Modernization Act of 2013; see Matthews).

31. Yildiz notes that monolingualism, rather than multilingualism, is a relatively more recent (but "highly successful") development. Multilingualism has a longer existence in world history, and now is a fact of a global age, but the effectiveness of a monolingual paradigm has tended to becloud its social reality, then and now (Yildiz 2).

32. A monolingual paradigm "first emerged in late-eighteenth century Europe" alongside the formation of the modern nation-state (Yildiz 2–3). The two phenome-

na—monolingual paradigm and modern nation-state—emerged in Europe at the same time and consolidated one another. It was no different in the United States. Though the reality of the sociolinguistic character of the revolutionary colonies was polyglottism, Marc Shell comments that by 1917, President Theodore Roosevelt had advocated the "swift assimilation of the aliens [America] welcomes to her shores." He declared "we must . . . have but one language. That must be the language of the Declaration of Independence." (See Shell 111 and note 35). English was the language of the Declaration of Independence but what may seem inevitable to us now, was not so at the time of the revolutionary colonies and throughout the eighteenth and even the nineteenth centuries. See Shell's interesting historical article on U.S. multilingualism and the social language engineering toward English monolingualism or the anglicization of the United States.

CHAPTER 3: *POCHO EN ESPAÑOL*

1. All page references to the source are to the 1989 English extant edition and all references to the translation text to the 1994 Spanish edition of Cantú's *Pocho En Español*.

2. In this sense, Cantú's multilingualism recalls Bakhtin's notion that no language is a "flat" language ("Language. . .is never unitary") as might be conveyed by the general usage of "monolingual" ("Discourse on the Novel" 288, also 262 and 301-331). We might say that foreignness is already present in the language we think we know/own because we never comprehend everything in one ("our") language. All languages have internal varieties of linguistic registers within one language (including the standard register, dialects, popular vernacular, slang, accents, and regionalisms). Bakhtin's term is "heteroglossia" for the differentiated social voices in the context of one language. Rainer Grutman, in contrast, offers the term of "heterolingualism" to describe the foregrounding of different languages in literary texts (Grutman, *Refraction* 18–19). My usage of "multilingual" and "multilingualism" are closer to Grutman's "heterolingual" and "heterolingualism."

3. In a different article, "Translation Theory," Gentzler says, "I am particularly interested in unequal cultural exchanges carried out in translation or repressed by non-translation, especially between large hegemonic cultures such as the United States or China, and small language groups within those nation-states, such as the Spanish-speaking Chicanos or Chicanas, or French-speaking Cajun and Louisianans in the United States" (107). Not all Chicanos/as are Spanish-speaking. They span a range of linguistic practices, from monolingual English to bilingual and biliterate competencies. Many are bicultural.

4. "The purpose of, say, a poetry translation is not, as it is usually said, to give the foreign poet a voice in the translation-language. It is to allow the poem to be heard in the translation-language, ideally in many of the same ways it is heard in the original language" (Weinberger 8).

5. Two others are "destruction of rhythms" (284) and "the effacement of the superimposition of languages" (287–289). In "Translation," Berman cautions that his "deforming tendencies" (280) are relevant not only to French but "in fact they bear on all translating, at least in the western tradition" (280), found just as often in "English translators as in Spanish or German, although certain tendencies may be more accentuated in one linguistic cultural space than in others" (280). He asks: "[H]ow to preserve the Guarani-Spanish tension in Roa Bastos? Or the relation between Spanish from Spain and the Latin American Spanishes in *Tirano Banderas*?" (288).

6. According to Sobarzo, *pochi* is derived from ópata (referring to peoples native to the northern Mexican border state of Sonora) and can refer to the act of cutting or yanking (*arrancar*) a plant from its ground. It can also refer to a shortened piece of cloth, as in a boy's or man's pants after shortening (258).

7. García Canclini's coined the term to mean the economic and cultural transformation of traditional high and popular forms in a context of modern processes. Mary Louise Pratt expands García Canclini's concept in its cultural sense: cultural reconversions are "transpositions where knowledges, practices, or symbols of one society or institution get processed into the contents of another" ("Traffic" 33).

8. Although sometimes classified as loan words or anglicisms—English words appropriated by different national cultures into their own language systems—*pochismos* are different. Unlike anglicisms, pochismos are specific to contact between English and Spanish, and they traditionally carry a stigma attributed to marginal citizens. In Mexico, *la computadora*, *el computador*, *cheque* (as noun or verb [*chequear*]), *la internet*, *el garage* (not *el garaje*, a *pochismo*) are anglicisms used by many; pochismos are summarily dismissed as undesirable by the status quo or middle-class society, especially at the time *Pocho* appeared.

9. See also Lefevere's "Literary Theory," 12+.

10. The broad historical meaning of pachuco refers to Mexican-American marginalized youths of 1940s urban Los Angeles. The pachuco is linked to the zoot suiter of the 1940s, or those pachucos who converted the white man's business suit by exaggerating its characteristics to symbolize Chicano resistance, especially to the draft of World War II. The caló dialect is often linked to the pachuco and zoot suiters (those who wore the flamboyant suits) of the 1940s.

11. The word "intend" is the operative word. I am speaking here of possible audiences, especially in the case of a Mexican audience. In its original and translated format, this text is available to a Mexican audience, since most books are available worldwide on the Internet. However, Roberto Sánchez, professor at the Universidad de Michoacán and a visiting scholar at ASU 2008–2009, with whom I had numerous conversations about this translation, assured me that it is not read in Mexico, suggesting that it is more than availability that determines whether a book is read or not.

12. The gesture *"en Español"* is comparable to *"traduit en Québécois"* in Quebec, Canada, or *"traduit en Occitan"* in Southern France, two intranational contexts. See Brisset 346.

CHAPTER 4: UNFORGETTING THE FORGETTING

1. See my Introduction (p 00) and Chapter 1 (pp. 00).

2. "The language I mostly speak is English" (trans. mine).

3. "How much Spanish [she] I had forgotten" (trans. mine).

4. "I was forced to relearn the language of my childhood" (trans. mine).

5. "The life I tell in this life was lived in Spanish but was initially written about in English" (trans. mine).

6. Jacques Derrida speaks about the ban of Berber and Arabic in his school in Algeria as a "pedagogical mechanism" in *Monolingualism of the Other.* Berber and Arabic were forbidden as alien languages, "a strange kind of alien language as the language of the other, but then, of course, and this is the strange and troubling part, the other as the nearest neighbor" (37).

7. Zentella offers other examples from her own life growing up in New York. "My *bildin* [building] was in the middle of our *bloque* [block], across the street from *la candistor* [the candy store]. It had *un faya ejquéi* [a fire escape] where we sat on steamy nights, and a four stair *estup* [stoop] where we played stoopball, *y donde jangueába-mos* [and where we used to hang out]." See "Growing Up" 4. Other English words pronounced with a Spanish accent and written accordingly in a Puerto Rican popular lexicon (and which overlap with *pochismos*) are *lonchar* (from "to lunch"), *chequear* (from "to check"), and *yarda* (from "yard," signifying "patio").

8. Domínguez Miguela ("La puertorriqueñidad en tela de juico") comments simi-larly on the title: "El título de esta autobiografía es lo primero que choca a los lectores. . . . El tiempo pretérito del título sugiere que la autora ya no es puertorriqueña, que una vez lo fue, sino que se asimiló más tarde convirtiéndose en norteamericana" (230). "The autobiography's title is the first thing that troubles readers. . . . The title's past tense suggests that the author is no longer Puerto Rican, what she once was, but that she later assimilated becoming a North American girl" (my trans.).

9. "What was there about this book that called out from its cover that the author was no longer Puerto Rican" (trans. mine).

10. "But more than the cover, the *Was* of the title attracted me. Here the author states that she is no longer Puerto Rican. And why is she no longer Puerto Rican? What is she now? Why no longer?" (trans. mine).

11. Also spelled *gíbaro*. The *g* and *j* were used interchangeably until *j* prevailed in the modern period. Note spelling of Manuel Alonso's *El gíbaro: Cuadro de costumbres de la isla en Puerto Rico*, a book of poetry and prose about Puerto Rican customs origi-nally published in 1849. Although jíbaros are mainly associated with Puerto Rico and,

to some extent, mainland New York, a group of highland peasants, contracted to work the plantations, migrated from the island to Hawaii in the early 1900s. Their descendants to this day maintain jíbaro musical and dance genres. For a study on Hawaii's jíbaros, see Solís "Jíbaro Image." The term is similar analogously to *guajiro* in Cuba or *quisqueya* in the Dominican Republic.

12. For the English translation of González' essay, see Guinness. González, of mixed race (son of a white Puerto Rican father and a mestizo Dominican mother), proposes the architectural metaphor of a mansion to describe Puerto Rican history and culture. It consists, he says, of four *pisos* (storeys or tiers), or periods of a population's cultural coexistence. The first "storey" is the co-presence of the Taíno, African, and Spanish cultures, of which the most important for him is the African. The second storey consists of a first wave of migrants in the early nineteenth century from different Latin American countries then in formation, followed by migrants from Ireland, England, France, and Holland; a second wave is from Catalunia, Mallorca, and Corsica. The third storey corresponds to an urban professional class superimposed by the 1898 or the North American invasion by the United States (Lo que pasó en 1898 fue que la invasión norteamericana empezó a echar un tercer piso, sobre el segundo todavía mal amueblado; González 27). Then what happened in 1898 was that the American invasion began to add a *third* storey to a second which was still not inhabitable (Guinness 15). The fourth storey corresponded to a managerial class resulting from Luis Muñoz Marín's economic policies leading up to El Estado Libre Asociado in the 1950s. (Marín was Puerto Rico's first governor, considered the father of modern Puerto Rico). González believed that *cultura nacional* or "national culture" was made and defined "from below," rather than "from above," by a white minority. The national culture as defined in Puerto Rico by a white minority in the modern period, therefore, belonged to the dominant class. See also Alvarez Nazario (*El habla campesina*) who suggests the jíbaro resulted from the sexual union of Spanish colonizers and "las mujeres de la raza indígena del país" (native women of the island; 20). The jíbaro and not the jíbara dominated discussions and was the exclusive image of the PPD (*Partido Popular Democrático*) that I discuss further on in this section. For a brief discussion of the jíbara, see Guerra, *Popular Expression* 110–17.

13. "Don't be a *jíbara*" (12).

14. "we have so many ignorant jibaros" (139)

15. "The necessity of searching who we are: of defining ourselves, of knowing what we are and what we are like" (trans. mine).

16. "What yesterday was a pejorative name, today is a high-class title that all of us would like to own" (trans. mine).

17. Guerra does a thorough study of the jíbaro in relation to Puerto Rican nationalism and popular expression.

18. Two major Puerto Rican writers who took issue with Pedreira's representa-

tion of the jíbaro (read "white) as key to Puerto Rico's national identity were Luis Pales-Matos and José Luis González. These two writers brought African culture and the black slaves into the national equation. González affirms that the idea of a Puerto Rican national culture promulgated by Puerto Rican intellectuals, like Pedreira and his generation, is the culture of the dominant class. It is important to note, in fairness, that this established class resisted notions of Puerto Ricanness that in turn had excluded them.

19. Although Muñoz Marín shared in the "ideological affiliation to the *jíbaro* as the center of the Puerto Rican soul" (Guerra 77), long before reading Markham's poem, he credited "The Man with the Hoe" for reinforcing his identification with the Puerto Rican laborer who tilled the land receiving no rest or reward. Markham himself had been inspired to write his poem upon seeing the painting by Jean François Millet "*L'homme à la hue*." Muñoz Marín met Markham in New York and with his permission translated the poem (Aitken 68). He also translated the poetry of Walt Whitman and Carl Sandburg.

20. "an enlightened jíbaro" (trans. mine)

21. "But many times I feel the pain of having left my little island, my people, my language. And sometimes that pain turns to hate, to resentment, because I did not choose to come to the United States. I was brought here" (trans. mine).

22. "How am I to explain what *jíbaro* means? What word in English has the same meaning as our *cocotazo*?" (trans. mine).

23. *Fogón* is pronounced "foh-góhn," *quinque* is "Keen-kéh," and *morivivi* is "mohr-ee-vee-vee". See Santiago's glossary in *When I Was* (271–274).

24. *Vaguadas* is pronounced "vah-goo-ah-dahs" and *dignidad* is "deeg-nee-dad". See Santiago's
glossary in *When I Was* (271–274).

25. Ironically, the editing of the transliterations in both English and Spanish perform the action of *suppressing* the word ("suppress") denoted in the original phrasing.

26. To transmit the feeling of foreignness to readers, Bellos argues, ". . . is a peculiarly hard and rather paradoxical thing" for a translator to attempt ". . . unless you can call on conventions that the target language already possesses for representing the specific 'other' associated with the culture of the language from which the source text comes" (51).

27. See pp. 88.

28. "I returned to live with my family in Bayamón thinking they would all be proud of me. But I learned that no one considered me sufficiently Puerto Rican; they considered me Americanized" (trans. mine).

29. In her article of 2006, Zentella says that newer generations of Puerto Ricans assert "it is not necessary to speak Spanish to be Puerto Rican" ("Growing Up" 8). Those who no longer speak Spanish still insist they are Puerto Rican: they "feel" and "act"

Puerto Rican. They challenge "a narrow territorial and language-based definition" (8) of what it means to be Puerto Rican.

30. *Los Americanos invaden a macún* (69-91)

31. Gloria D. Prosper Sánchez ("Washing Away") identifies this type of linguistic interference between original and translation. The interference, she argues, results from the tension between Santiago's academic English and her experience with colloquial Spanish. The colloquialisms occur mainly in the dialogue, not in the narration. Prosper Sánchez's article is in Spanish, but see also Martínez-San Miguel "Bitextualidad" 32.

32. "So *Negi* means I'm black?" (13).

33. Speaking about growing up Puerto Rican in New York (Nuyorican), Zentella points out that the English "Negro" did not have any positive connotations, as *negro* did/does in Puerto Rican Spanish, albeit alongside the negative" ("Growing Up" 5).

CHAPTER 5: I MAY SAY "WETBACK" BUT I REALLY MEAN *MOJADO*

1. All quotations in English indicated by page number are from *Diary*; all quotations in Spanish indicated by page number are from *Diario*. In addition to the shortened titles *Diary* and, I use *Guerrilla* to refer to *Diary of a Guerrilla*, a third text by Pérez. Ramón "Tianguis" Pérez is henceforth simply Pérez.

2. *El Mundo* was a Spanish-language newspaper in Houston. Licón's Zopilote cartoon, "Zopilote, Meet Mr. Migra," appeared in 1985 in *Texas Monthly* (118, 120).

3. Many translation theorists now critique this tradition. See Venuti's *Rethinking Translation*. The history of the nation-state model allows for one language only, and this language is the mother-tongue of individuals who make up the culture of the national collectivity. Though her frame of reference is specifically a German and German-Turkish national circumstance, Yildiz's discussion of the linkage between an individual's mother-tongue and a national language is also helpful in a U.S. context. See Yildiz 2–3.

4. Some theorists and writers about translation recognize translation as a phenomenon that occurs within the same language. George Steiner is one well-known example. In *After Babel,* he discusses similar processes of communication in interlingual and intralingual translation. See p. 47.

5. In the introduction, I mentioned Lori Chamberlain's article on the gender implications (author codes male and translator coded female) of the "original-copy" dichotomy.

6. See note 4 of Introduction for Nicolás Kanellos's explanation of the change in title.

7. Filmmaker David Riker estimates that in 2014 there were three million Oaxacans: 1 million in California, another million in Oaxaca City, and a third million in the villages and rural towns of Oaxaca.

8. When enacted in 1987, the IRCA, popularly called the Amnesty law, conferred legal status on three million people. Among the reasons Pérez gives in *Diario* for

declining to apply and leave the United States are: he had achieved his objective of saving money to improve the life of his Zapotec family, he did not believe that the IRCA would make a substantial difference in his ability to qualify for more than a minimum-wage job, and life in the United States was too routinized and alienating for him.

9. I interpret Benjamin's "elsewhere" to mean different national spaces, but in Pérez's case both original and translation are published inside the same national space.

10. A Spanish original of *Guerrilla* was never published anywhere.

11. After primary school, Pérez was selected by educators who came to his village to attend a boarding school in Oaxaca City where his public education continued in Spanish. Zapotec was the language of his village. To this day, Pérez's Zapotec-Mexican identity involves an association of Spanish, the public, high-prestige language and majority national language, with his father, and Zapotec, the indigenous minority language, with his mother. See note 7, chapter 2, for Perez's reflections in his own words about his Zapotec-Spanish bilingualism. Public education in Zapotec was not the norm during Pérez's primary educational years. Lynn Stephen in *Transborder Lives* comments that "[b]y 2004 the linguistic norm in Teotitlán [the center of Zapotec culture] was bilingualism in Spanish and Zapotec, with a significant sprinkling of English learned while living and working in the US" (293). Similarly, Pratt says that "in Mexico, indigenous writers are establishing modern poetry in languages like Zapoteco, Mixteco, and Yucatec Maya, while in Guatemala Quiché Maya today is becoming the lingua franca for a broad indigenous revival (Pratt, "Comparative Literature and the Global Linguascape" 279).

12. Yildiz situates "mother tongue" at the center of the monolingual paradigm. She calls it the "affective knot," implying "corporeal intimacy"; it "relies heavily on the invocation of the maternal, without however necessarily referencing actual mothers" (10). Weinrich refers to the first language ('mother tongue') as "absorbed with mother's milk" (Weinrich 1339).

13. "'*Estadu*' [sic] because that's the way that '*Estado*' or state, is pronounced in Zapotec, our language" (*Diary* 14).

14. *Diario* had a total of 4,500 copies and *Diary* a total of 9,000 copies printed. I am grateful to Marina Tristan and Nicolás Kanellos of Arte Público Press for this information.

15. The earliest date the OED gives for "wetback" is 1929 in a context of U.S.-Mexican affairs. But later I note that the linguist William Randle l finds its usage in this same context as early as 1924 (Randle 78–80).

16. Samora notes that in the late nineteenth century, "[a]s a result of the Chinese Exclusion Law in 1882, the primary border problem became the issue of the smuggling of Chinese rather than the entry of Mexicans. In the eyes of immigration authorities, the Chinese were the first 'wetbacks,' and it was in the interest of excluding Chinese that the first efforts were made to establish a border guard" (34). He does not say specif-

ically that the Chinese were called "wetbacks," just that they fulfilled the same occupational function as Mexicans did several decades later. See also González-Quiroga (35).

17. See Jorge Bustamante, cited in Spener 4.

18. Jorge Rodríguez, a visiting professor at Arizona State University from Mexico, 2012–2013, informed me that some Mexicans jokingly pun on "wetback" to suggest that a "wet" is sent "back" to Mexico. No comparable verbal play is possible with espalda mojada.

19. Even though espalda is feminine, this epithet is probably assigned a masculine designation because historically most undocumented immigrants have been men, especially in the first half of the twentieth century.

20. Although the River is the primary context for the origin of "wetback" and mojado, another popular hypothesis maintains that English and Spanish speakers used them to refer to migrants working in the fields whose "back" became wet from sweat and toil.

21. See also Bustamante: "El mojado . . . viola una ley extranjera que es legal y socialmente sancionada en los Estados Unidos, pero en México no. 'Irse de mojado' no tiene ninguna consecuencia estigmatizante en México para el que se lo propone o para el que ha regresado" (The mojado breaks a law in the United States, but not in Mexico. To "be a mojado" has no stigmatizing effect for the one who leaves or the one who returns; 144, trans. mine).

22. The historian David Montejano suggested to me that middle-class exiles of the Mexican Revolution in Texas, and those after this period, might have employed this label to express their disdain for their less fortunate compatriots. If this is so, they did not use it before "wetback" obtained popular currency (personal communication, August 23, 2011).

23. However, I think the sting of the label pocho to suggest betrayal of nation is stronger; mojado may convey to Mexicans a person who is trying to make due, trying to survive.

24. Ngai cites an INS official who expressed the conventional association between wetbacks and criminality: "The 'wetback' starts out by breaking the law; therefore 'it is easier and sometimes appears even more necessary for him to break other laws since he considers himself to be an outcast, even an outlaw'" (149). See note 19 for Bustamante's explanation on the mojado's perspective on the law.

25. In the late 1940s, espalda mojada and mojado became part of the Mexican common vocabulary in the late 1940s. The classic *Las aventuras de Don Chipote, o, cuando los pericos mamen* (*The Adventures of Don Chipote or When Parrots Breastfeed*) originally published in Mexico in 1928 (and republished in Spanish by Arte Público in 1999), does not use the word, nor does the English translation (2000), even though the book's central theme is Mexican migration. (See Kanellos's Introduction in English or Spanish). The phrase espaldas mojadas appears in several instances in *La Prensa*, a San Antonio Spanish-language newspaper, in the early 1950s.

26. Rene Cardona's films, *La china Hilaria* (1938) and *Adiós mi chaparrita* (1939), took up the subject of Mexican migration into the North almost twenty years before Galindo's *Espaldas mojadas*. Norma Iglesias explains that the unlike Galindo's film. they did not visually depict *la frontera* but, also importantly, showed the impact upon those left behind by the men who came north (vol.1, 23–29).

27. Spota writes, "Lo que aquí [Murieron a mitad del río] se narra es auténtico. Lo he vivido personalmente y puedo dar fe de ello. Conozco los campos de Texas y los he trabajado, de Brownsville a Corpus Christi. En dos ocasiones crucé el río Bravo sin papeles, como lo hacen, cada noche, cientos y cientos de hombres a todo lo largo de la frontera líquida que separa México de Estados Unidos—de Matamoros a Ciudad Juárez." (What I narrate here [*Murieron a mitad del río*] is true. I have personally lived it and can testify to it. I know the Texas fields and I have worked them, from Brownsville to Corpus Christi. On two occasions I crossed the río Bravo without papers, as is done, each night, by hundreds and hundreds of men all along the liquid border that separates México and the United States, from Matamoros to Ciudad Juárez; trans. mine). These words appear in the book's opening pages.

28. "Now his feet did not step on his country's land . . . they were no longer on this side but on the other side. He felt the sting of fear; he now knew the risk of being a *mojado*, an illegal immigrant" (trans. mine).

29. Ngai explains that the Bracero Program, although established to solve problems of illegal immigration, actually increased the numbers of illegal migrants. Among other reasons was that Texas, Arkansas, and Missouri, due to prior history of discrimination against Mexicans, were ineligible to use *braceros*, but they nonetheless found ways to attract illegal labor (147–148).

30. Around this same period, Reavis had authored and published *Without Documents*, a book on U.S.–Mexican immigration aimed at a US general audience.

31. Medrano-Mederos was a participant and survivor of 1960s and 1970s *campesino* movements in Guerrero and Morelos led by the school teachers, Génaro Vásquez and Lucio Cabañas, who were turned guerrilleros and assassinated in 1972 and 1974, respectively. These campesino insurgents, like the folk hero and leader Medrano-Mederos, anticipated the Zapatistas in Chiapas and their world-known leader Sub-Comandante Marcos of the 1990s. In *Fuerte es el silencio*, first published in 1980, Elena Poniatowska tells five testimonial narratives that capture the voices and personal histories of disenfranchised segments of society and that official Mexican history would sooner relegate to silence. Among these is the foundation and later destruction of Medrano-Mederos's grassroot social movement in the 1970s. See pp. 181–278.

32. Ramón Pérez was born and raised in San Pablo Macuiltianguis, a remote village in the Sierra Norte Juárez region of Oaxaca, about a three-hour drive from Oaxaca City, the state's capital. He tells us in *Diary* (1991) that Macuiltianguis has been "sit-

ting there for centuries, always in the same position, even though history didn't notice the town until a little more than four hundred years ago" (Reavis 4). "Tianguis" is an abbreviation of Macuiltianguis, which means "five plazas." "Macuil" and "tianguis" are Nahuatl: the former means "five," the latter a *mercado* or market, is well-known in the United States.

33. The specific passage is: "'*Compañero* Tianguis,' he [Medrano] said when he came back. . . . Now besides being a *compañero*, I was also *Compañero* Tianguis. I had been baptized again!'"

34. Pérez confirmed this suspicion to me in my interview with him. I thank Reavis for granting me permission to use his name in this essay.

35. "Ya en Nuevo Laredo me fui directamente a una caseta de teléfono y pedí una llamada de larga distancia. Hablé con mi amigo informándole de los acontecimientos" (*Diario* 54).

36. Reavis told me this detail in a phone conversation.

37. I agree with Spener (1) who regards "undocumented immigrant" as an "alternative that responds to the concerns of human rights activists who have insisted that no human being is either 'illegal' or an 'alien.'"

38. "Esta forma de vida comenzó cuando el rumor del programa de braceros llegó a nuestro pueblo. Eso fue diez años antes de que se trazara la carretera federal" (*Diario* 18).

39. "compré un diccionario de inglés-español. . . . Durante más de una hora estuve sobre una mesa de un puesto de hamburguesas buscando los significados de cada palabra. Cuando los descifré, no me sentí tan orgulloso como al principio" (*Diario* 66).

40. "Seguramente sabían que estaban siguiendo a un mojado" (*Diario* 144).

41. "¿Por qué no vas a la iglesia de la Virgen de Guadalupe? . . . Según he escuchado, ahí ayudan a los mojados a encontrar 'jale' [jobs]" (*Diario* 86).

42. "¿Es verdad que aquí ayudan a los mojados?"

43. "una mujer de estatura alta y de unos treinta y cinco años de edad, vestida con un traje de color verde suave" (*Diario* 88).

44. "Perdón—dije, dirigiéndome a ella—¿Es aquí donde ayudan a los mojados?" (*Diario* 88–89).

45. "Mi tirada era irme de mojado . . . 'espalda mojada'" (*Diario* 6).

46. It is used only one other time, a peculiarity in the translation since words such as *coyote, chivos, patero*, and the less familiar *perreras* (dog houses) are used more frequently in their untranslated Mexican idiom.

47. "pero los había abierto ya en redondo como si le costara trabajo verme y sus labios estaban apretados" (*Diario* 89).

48. "No!—contestó tajante y fría—Aquí no hay mojados" (*Diario* 89).

49. "Aquí no hay mojados" (*Diario* 89).

50. "Trabajador indocumentado, es el término correcto" (*Diario* 89).

51. Mexican Americans do not fare well in the books. The man who takes advantage of Pérez with the social security card seems to be a Mexican American, as is the police officer who stops Pérez later in his travels, in the chapter titled "*El choquecito*" (*Diario* 267–70) "The Fender-Bender" (*Diary* 213–16) because he suspects him of being "undocumented."

52. I am playing with Harish Trivedi's metaphor about the change in the traditional relationship between the disciplines of translation studies and comparative literature: "it is the translational tail (he means translation studies) now that wags the comparative dog (Comparative Literature)." See Trivedi 281.

WORKS CITED

Adams, David. "English is on the Rise Among U.S. Latinos but Spanish Still Valued." *Univision News.* April 20, 2016. Web. November 5, 2017.

Aitken, Thomas Jr. *Poet in the Fortress.* New York: New American Library, 1964. Print.

Albarran, Alan B., and Brain Hutton. "A History of Spanish-Language Radio in the United States." *Center for Spanish-Language Media.* Arbitron. Denton, Texas: U of North Texas, 2009: 3–24. Web. October 25, 2017.

Allen, Esther. "Translation, Globalization, and English." *To Be Translated or Not To Be.* PEN/IRL. Report on the International Situation of Literary Translation. Ed. Esther Allen. Barcelona: Institut Ramon Llul, 2007: 17–33. Print.

Allen, Esther. "The Will to Translate: Four Episodes in a Local History of Global Cultural Exchange." *In Translation: Translators on their Work and What It Means.* Eds. Esther Allen and Susan Bernofsky. New York: Columbia UP, 2013: 82–104. Print.

Allende, Isabel. *La casa de los espiritus.* HarperCollins Rayo, 2001. Print.

Alonso, Carlos. "Spanish: The Foreign National Language." *ADFL Bulletin* 37.2–3 (2006):15–20. Print.

Alonso, Manuel. *El gíbaro: Cuadro de costumbres de la isla de Puerto Rico* [A Description of Customs in the Island of Puerto Rico]. 1849. San Juan: Academia Puertorriqueña de la Lengua Española, Plaza Mayor, 2007.

Alvarez, Julia. *How the García Girls Lost Their Accents.* New York: Penguin, 1992. Print.

Alvarez, Julia. *De cómo las muchachas García perdieron el acento.* Trans. Mercedes Guhl. New York: Vintage Español RH, 2007. Print.

Alvarez Nazario, Manuel. *El habla campesina del país: Orígenes y desarrollo del español en Puerto Rico.* Rio Piedras: Editorial de la Universidad de Puerto Rico, 1992. Print.

Ambrosio, Daniel. "Ello hires marketing chief in 'Pivotal Year.'" 2015. *Burlington Free Press.* Web. October 21, 2017.

Anaya, Rudy. *Bless Me, Ultima.* 1972. Warner Books, 1994. Print.

Anaya, Rudy. *Bendíceme Última.* Grand Central Pub. Hachette Book Group, 1992. No translator named. Print.

Anderson, Benedict. *Imagined Communities.* Rev. ed. London: Verso, 2006. Print.

Anzaldúa, Gloria. *Borderlands: La frontera*. San Francisco: Aunt Lute Books, 1987. Print.

Aparicio, Frances. "On Sub-versive Signifiers: U.S. Latina/o Writers Tropicalize English." *American Literature*, 66.4 (1994): 795–801. Print.

Arias, Ron. *The Road to Tamazunchale*. Tempe: Bilingual Review P, 1978/1987. Print.

Arias, Ron. *El camino a Tamazunchale*. Trans. Beth Pollack and Ricardo Aguilar Melantzón. Tempe: Bilingual Review P, 2002. Print.

Arteaga, Alfred. "An Other Tongue." *An Other Tongue*. Ed. Alfred Arteaga. Durham: Duke UP, 1994. 1–33. Print.

Asad, Talal. "The Concept of Cultural Translation in British Social Anthropology." *Writing Culture: The Poetics and Politics of Ethnography*. Ed. James Clifford and George E. Marcus. Berkeley: U California P, 1986. 141–64. Print.

Asad, Talal. "A Comment on Translation, Critique, and Subversion." *Between Languages and Cultures: Translation and Cross-Cultural Texts*. Eds. Anuradha Dingwaney and Carol Maier. Pittsburgh: U of Pittsburgh P, 1995. Print.

Bakhtin, Mikhail. "Discourse on the Novel." *The Dialogic Imagination: Four Essays*. Trans. Caryl Emerson and Michael Holquist. Austin: U of Texas P, 1982. 259–422. Print.

"Ballad of an Unsung Hero." Dir. Isaac Artenstein. Producer-Writer Paul Espinosa. Cinewest and KPBS-TV, 1984. Television.

Bandia, Paul. "Postcolonial Literary Heteroglossia: A Challenge for Homogenizing Translation." *Perspectives: Studies in Translatology* 20.4 (Dec. 2012): 419–31. Print.

Bardales, Aída. "HarperCollins and Planeta Launch Joint Venture; HarperCollins Publishers and Spain's Grupo Planeta Announced Copublishing Agreement." *Criticas*. Web. October 1, 2006.

Barradas, Efraín. "Telémaco Criollo." *The Latino Review of Books* Spring/Fall 1997: 73–75. Print.

Barradas, Efraín. "Esmeralda Santiago o como dejar de ser puertorriqueño." *Partes de un todo: Ensayos y notas sobre literatura puertorriqueña en los Estados Unidos*. San Juan: Editorial de la Universidad de Puerto Rico, 1998. 199–202. Print.

Bassnett, Susan. "The Translation Turn in Cultural Studies." *Constructing Cultures: Essays on Literary Translation*. Eds. Susan Bassnett and André Lefevere. Clevedon: Multilingual Matters, 1998. 123–40. Print.

Bearden, Michelle. "Buenos días, USA." *Publishers Weekly* August 28, 1995: 77+. Print.

Bearden, Michelle. "Esquivel's Spanish Primer." *Publishers Weekly* October 3, 1994: 40–42, 43. Print.

Bellos, David. *Is That a Fish in Your Ear?* New York: Faber and Faber, 2011. Print.

Benjamin, Walter. "The Task of the Translator." 1923. Trans. Harry Zohn. Ed. Hannah Arendt. *Illuminations*. New York: Schocken, 1969, 69–82. Print.

Berman, Antoine. "Translation and the Trials of the Foreign." *Translation Studies Reader*. Ed. Lawrence Venuti. 2nd ed. New York: Routledge, 2004, 276–89. Print.

Besemeres, Mary. *Translating One's Self: Language and Selfhood in Cross-Cultural Autobiography*. Oxford: Peter Lang, 2002. Print.

Border Security, Economic Opportunity, and Immigration Modernization Act of 2013. S. R. 4071, 159th Congress, June 11, 2013.

Brisset, Annie. "The Search for a Native Language: Translation and Cultural Identity." Trans. Rosalind Gill and Roger Gannon. 2nd ed. *The Translation Studies Reader*. Ed. Lawrence Venuti. New York: Routledge, 2004, 337–68. Print.

Brito, Aristeo. *The Devil in Texas/El diablo en Texas*. 1976. Trans. David W. Foster. Tempe: Bilingual P, 1990. Print.

Business Wire. "Oklahoma Voters Approve State Official English Law." *Business Wire*. November 2010. Web. October 25, 2017.

Bustamante, Jorge. "El espalda mojada, informe de un observador-participante." [The Wetback, a Participant-Observer's Report]. *Chicanos: Antología histórica y literaria* [Chicanos: A Historical and Literary Anthology]. Ed. Tino Villanueva. México: Fondo de Cultura Económica, 1980, 144–87. Print.

Cantú, Roberto. Introduction. *Pocho en Español*. New York: Random House. 1994, 1–10. Print.

Cantú, Roberto. *Pocho en Español*. New York: Random House. 1994. Print.

Cardoso, Lawrence. A. *Mexican Emigration to the United States 1897–1931*. Tucson: U of Arizona, 1980. Print.

Carreira María. "The Media, Marketing, Critical Mass, and other Mechanisms of Linguistic Maintenance." *Southwest Journal of Linguistics* 21.2 (2001): 35–54. Print.

Casanova, Pascale. "What is a Dominant Language? Giacomo Leopardi: Theoretician of Linguistic Inequality." *New Literary History* 44.3 (2013): 379–99. Print.

Casanova, Pascale. *The World Republic of Letters*. Trans. M.B. Debevoise. Cambridge MA: Harvard UP, 2004. Print.

Casillas, Dolores Ines. *Sounds of Belonging. U.S. Spanish-language Radio and Public Advocacy*. New York: New York UP, 2014. Print.

Cassin, Barbara. Introduction. *Dictionary of Untranslatables: A Philosophical Lexicon*. Trans. Steven Rendall et al. Ed. Barbara Cassin. New Jersey: Princeton UP, 2013, xvii–xx. ProQuest E-book.

Castillo, Ana. *The Mixquiahuala Letters*. Binghamton, N.Y.: Bilingual P, 1986. Print.

Castillo, Ana. *Las cartas de Mixquiahuala*. No translator named. Consejo Nacional para la Cultura y las Artes México, D.F. Editorial Grijalbo, 1994. Print.

Cervantes-Rodríguez, Ana Margarita and Amy Lutz. "Coloniality of Power, Immigration, and the English-Spanish Asymmetry in the United States." *Nepantla: Views from the South*. Durham: Duke UP 4.3 (2003): 523–60. Print.

Céspedes Diógenes, Silvio Torres-Saillant and Junot Díaz. "Fiction is the Poor Man's Cinema: An Interview with Junot Díaz." *Callaloo* 23.3 (Summer 2000): 892–907. Print.

Chamberlain, Lori. "Gender and the Metaphorics of Translation." *Rethinking Translation: Discourse, Subjectivity, Ideology*. Ed. Lawrence Venuti. London: Routledge, 1992, 57–74. Print.

Chavez, Denise. *Face of an Angel*. New York: Farrar, Straus, and Giroux, 1994. Print.

Cheyfitz, Eric. *The Poetics of Imperialism: Translation and Colonization from The Tempest to Tarzan*. New York: Oxford UP, 1991. Print.

Cisneros, Sandra. *The House on Mango Street*. New York: Random House, 1991. Print.

Cisneros, Sandra. *La casa en Mango Street*. Translated by Elena Poniatowska. New York: Random House, Vintage Español, RH 1991. Print.

Cisneros, Sandra. *Woman Hollering Creek*. New York: Random House, Vintage Books, 1991. Print.

Cisneros, Sandra. *El arroyo de la llorona*. Translated by Liliana Valenzuela. New York: Random House, Vintage Español, 1996. Print.

Clinton. Bill. *Mi Vida*. New York: Random House, Vintage Español 2005. Print.

Clyne, Michael. "Multilingualism." *Handbook of Sociolinguistics*. Ed. Florian Coulmas. Oxford: Blackwell Publishing, 1997, 301–314. Print.

Congressional Budget Office. Feb 2011. Web. <https://www.cbo.gov/sites/default/files/112th-congress-2011–2012/reports/02–24-remittances_chartbook.pdf/>.

Coolidge Toker, Emily Brown. "What Makes a Native Speaker? Nativeness, Ownership and Global Englishes." *Minnesota Review* 78. 1 (2012): 113–29. *Project Muse*. Web. DOI 10.1215/0026 5667–1550680.

Córdova, Nathaniel I. "In his Image and Likeness: The Puerto Rican *jíbaro* as Political Icon." *CENTRO Journal* 17.1 (Fall 2005): 170–191.

Cota-Cárdenas, Margarita. *Puppet: A Chicano Novella* [*Puppet: Una novella Chicana*]. Bilingual Edition. Trans. Barbara D. Riess and Trino Sandoval. Albuquerque: U of New Mexico P, 2000. Print.

Crawford, James. *Hold Your Tongue: Bilingualism and the Politics of "English Only."* Reading, MA: Addison-Wesley Publishing, 1992. Print.

Crawford, James, ed. *Language Loyalties: A Source Book on the Official English Controversy*. Chicago: U of Chicago P, 1992. Print.

"Create Relevant Literature for Future Gen: Junot Díaz." *Times of India*. January 22, 2011. Web. October 27, 2017.

Crystal, David. *The Language Revolution*. Cambridge: Polity Press, 2004. Print.

Davila, Arlene. *Latinos Inc. The Marketing and Making of a People*. Berkeley: U of California P, 2001. Print.

DEA (Diccionario de la Real Academia). Edición del Tricentenario. Web. October 30, 2017.

De Courtivron, Isabelle, ed. Introduction. *Lives in Translation: Bilingual Writers on Identity and Creativity*. New York: Palgrave, 2003. Print.

Derrida, Jacques. *Monolingualism of the Other, or the Prosthesis of Origin*. Trans. Patrick Mensah. Stanford: Stanford UP, 1998. Print.

Díaz, Junot. *Drown*. New York: Riverhead Books, 1996. Print.

Díaz, Junot. *Negocios*. Trans. Eduardo Lago. New York: Random House: Vintage Español, 1997. Print.

Díaz, Junot. *La breve y maravillosa vida de Óscar Wao*. Trans. Achy Obejas. Random House Vintage Español, 2008. Print.

Díaz, Junot. *The Brief and Wondrous Life of Oscar Wao*. New York: Riverhead Books, 2007. Print.

Dominguez Miguela, Antonia. "La puertorriqueñidad en tela de juicio: *When I was Puerto Rican* de Esmeralda Santiago," in *Pasajes de ida y vuelta: La narrativa puertorriqueña en Estados Unidos.* Huelva: Universidad de Huelva, 2005. 228–54. Print.

Duany, Jorge. "Dominicans." *Oxford Encyclopedia of Latinos and Latinas in the* United States. Eds. Suzanne Oboler and Deena J. González. Oxford: Oxford UP, 2005. Web.

Espaldas mojadas. Prod. J. Elvira and dir. A. Galindo. Urban Vision Entertainment, 1953. Film.

Esquivel, Laura. *Like Water for Chocolate. [Para agua como chocolate].* Trans. Carol Christensen and Thomas Christensen. New York: Doubleday 1992/1993. Print.

Fagan, Allison E. "Negotiating Language." *The Routledge Companion to Latino/a Literature.* Eds. Suzanne Bost and Frances Aparicio. New York: Routledge, 2013, 207–15. Print.

Fermino Jennifer. "Mayor Bloomberg Defends NYPD's English-only Policy." *Daily News.* June 24, 2013. Web. October 28, 2017.

Finegan, Edward. "English." *The world's major languages* (2nd ed.). Ed. B. Comrie. London, UK: Routledge. 2011. Literati by Credo. Web. October 28, 2017.

Fishman, Joshua. "Positive Bilingualism: Some overlooked rationales and forefathers." *Georgetown University Round Table on Languages and Linguistics.* Eds. James E. Alatis. Washington D.C.: Georgetown UP, 1978, 42–52. Print.

Flaherty, Colleen. "Not a Small World After All." February 11, 2015. *Inside Higher Ed.* Web. October 28, 2017.

Fornoff, Fredrick, H. *The Underdogs.* Pittsburgh: U of Pittsburgh P, 1992. Print.

Foster, David. "On Translating Miguel Méndez." *Bilingual Review* 9.3 (September–December, 1994): 83–88. Print.

García, Diana. *When Living Was A Labor Camp.* Tucson: U of Arizona P, 2000. Print.

García-Canclini, Néstor. "Cultural Reconversion." *On Edge: The Crisis in Contemporary Latin American Culture.* Ed. George Yúdice. Minneapolis, MN: U of Minneapolis P, 1992, 29–43. Print.

García-Márquez, Gabriel, *Memorias de mis putas tristes.* New York: Random House, Vintage Español, 2004. Print.

Geertz, Clifford. *The Interpretation of Cultures.* New York: Basic Books, 1973. Print.

Genette Gerard. *Paratexts. Thresholds of Interpretation.* Trans. Jane E. Lewin. Cambridge: Cambridge UP, 1997. Print.

Gentzler, Edwin. "Translation Theory: Monolingual, Bilingual or Multilingual?" *Journal of Translation Studies* 9.1 (2006): 105–23. Print.

Gentzler, Edwin. "What is Different about Translation in the Americas? *CTIS (Centre for Translation and Intercultural Studies) Occasional Papers* 2 (2002): 7–19. Print.

Gentzler, Edwin. *Translation and Identity in the Americas.* London: Routledge, 2008. Print.

Gikandi, Simon. Editor's Column: "From Penn Station to Trenton: The Language Trains." *PMLA* 128.4 (2013): 865–871. Print.

Giles, Paul. "The Deterritorialization of American literature." *Shades of the planet.* Ed. Wai Chee Dimock and Lawrence Buell. Princeton, NJ: Princeton UP, 2007, 39–61. Print.

González, José Luis. "El país de cuatro pisos." *El país de cuatro pisos y otros ensayos*. Río Piedras: Ediciones Huracán, 1980, 11–44. Print.

González-Quiroga, M.A. "Conflict and Cooperation in the Making of Texas-Mexico Border Society, 1840–1880." Eds. B.H. Johnson & A.R. Graybill. *Bridging National Borders in North America*. Durham: Duke UP, 2010. 33–58. Print.

Gramling, David. "On the Other Side of Monolingualism: Faith Akin's Linguistic Turn(s)." *German Quarterly* 83.3 (2010): 353–72.

Grande, Reyna. *Across 100 Mountains*. New York: Atria Books, 2006. Print.

Grande, Reyna. *A través de cien montañas*. Translated by Reyna Grande. New York: Atria Books, 2007. Print.

Grande, Reyna. *The Distance Between Us*. New York: Atria Books, 2012. Print.

Grande, Reyna. *La distancia entre nosotros*. Translated by Reyna Grande. New York: Atria Books, 2013. Print.

Grutman, Rainier. "Refraction and Recognition: Literary Multilingualism in Translation." *Target* 18.1 (2006): 17–47.

Grutman, Rainier. "Multilingualism and Translation." *Routledge Encyclopedia of Translation Studies*. 2nd Edition (Revised and Extended). Eds. Mona Baker and Gabriela Saldanha. London–New York: Routledge, 2009, 182–85. Print.

Guerra, Lillian. *Popular Expression and National Identity in Puerto Rico: The Struggle for Self, Community, and Nation*. Gainesville: UP of Florida, 1998. Print.

Guinness, Gerald, translator. "Puerto Rico: The Four-Storeyed Country." *Puerto Rico: The Four-Storeyed Country*. Princeton, NJ: Marcus Wiener Publishing, 1993. Print.

Guskin, Emily and Amy Mitchell. "New Study: Hispanic Media: Faring Better than the Mainstream Media." *Pew Research Center's Project for Excellence in Journalism. The State of the News Media 2011. Hispanic PR Blog*. Web. October 28, 2017.

Guzmán, Martín Luis. *El aguila y la serpiente*. Madrid, M. Aguilar, 1928. Print.

Guzmán, Martín Luis. *La sombra del caudillo*. Madrid: Espasa-Calpe, S.A., 1929. Print.

HarperCollins Publishers. "HarperCollins Publishers Expands Rayo Publishing Program Offering Greater Range of Titles to Latino Market." Press Release. 2004. Web. October 28, 2017.

Hernández, Ramona. "Dominican Americans." 2013. *Oxford Bibliographies*. Web. October 28, 2017.

Hendricks, Frances Kellam and Beatrice Berger. *Two Novels of the Mexican revolution: "The Trials of a Respectable Family" and "The Underdogs."* San Antonio: Trinity UP, 1963. Print.

Herrera, Juan Felipe. *Notebooks of a Chile Verde Smuggler*. Tucson: U of Arizona P, 2002. Print.

Hijuelos, Oscar. *The Mambo Kings Play Songs of Love*. New York: Farrar, Straus, and Giroux, 1989. Print.

Hijuelos, Oscar. *Los reyes de mambo tocan canciones de amor*. Trans. Alejandro García Reyes. New York: Harper Libros, 1996. Print.

Hill, Jane. *The Everyday Language of White Racism*. Malden, MA & Oxford: Wiley-Blackwell, 2008. Print.

Hinojosa-S., Rolando. *Estampas del valle*. Berkeley: Quinto Sol, 1973. Print.

Hinojosa-S., Rolando. *Klail City/Klail City y sus alrededores*. Houston, Arte Público P, 2014. Print.

Hinojosa-S. Rolando. *This Migrant Earth*. Houston, Arte Público P, 1987. Print.

Homel, David and Sherry Simon, eds. *Mapping Literature: The Art of Politics of Translation*. Montréal: Véhicule P, 1988. Print.

Iglesias, Norma. *Entre yerba, polvo y plomo* [*Amidst Weeds, Dust, and Lead*] 1–2. Tijuana: El Colegio de la Frontera Norte, 1991. Print.

Index Translationum. <http://www.unesco.org/xtrans/bsform.aspx/>.

Jordan, Miriam. "US News: Arizona Grades Teachers on Fluency—State Pushes School Districts to Reassign Instructors with Heavy Accents or Other Shortcomings in Their English." *Wall Street Journal* April 30, 2010: A.3. Web. October 28, 2017.

Kanellos, Nicolás. Introduction. *The Adventures of Don Chipote, or, When Parrots Breast-feed*. Tr. Ethriam Cash Brammer. Houston: Arte Público P, 2000, 1–17. Print.

Kanellos, Nicolás. Introducción. *Las aventuras de Don Chipote, o cuando los pericos mamen*. Houston: Arte Público P, 2004, v–xvi. Print.

Kent, Robert B and Maura E. Huntz. "Spanish-Language Newspapers in the United States." *Geographical Review* 86.3 (1996) 446–56. Print.

Krosgstad, Jens Manuel and Ana Gonzalez-Barrera. "A Majority of English-Speaking Hispanics in the U.S. are Bilingual." *Pew Research Center*, May 24, 2015. Web. October 28, 2017.

Lefevere, André. "On the Refraction of Texts." *Cultura Ludens: Mimesis in Contemporary Theory—An Interdisciplinary Approach*. Eds. Guiseppe Mazzota and Mihai I. Spariousu. vol. 1. The Literary and Philosophical Debate. Amsterdam NLD John Benjamins Publishing Co., 1984, 217–37. Print.

Lefevere, André. "Literary Theory and Translated Literature," *Dispositio* (The Art and Science of Translation) 7.19–21 (1982): 3–22. Print.

Lennon, Brian. *In Babel's Shadow: Multilingual Literatures, Monolingual States*. Minnesota: U of Minnesota P, 2010. Print.

Levine, Ben and Julia Schulz. Letter. *New Yorker*, May 4, 2015: 3. *Fluent comprehenders*. Print.

Levine, Caroline. "The Great Unwritten: World Literature and the Effacement of Orality." *Modern Language Quarterly* 74.2 (June 2013): 217–37.

Like Water for Chocolate. Dir. Alfonso Arau. Miramax Films, 1993. Film.

Limón, Graciela. *In Search of Bernabé*. Houston: Arte Público P, 1993. Print.

Limón, Graciela. *En busca de Bernabé*. Trans. Miguel Angel Aparicio. Houston: Arte Público P. 1997. Print.

Lomas, Laura. 2008. *Translating Empire: José Martí, Migrant Latino Subjects, and American Modernities*. Durham: Duke UP, 2. Print.

Lomas, Laura. "Thinking-Across, Infiltration, and Transculturation," José Martí's Theory and Practice of Post-Colonial Translation." *Translation Review* 81.1 (2011): 12–33. DOI: 10.1080/07374836.2011.10555800.

López, Gustavo. "Hispanics of Dominican Origin in the United States." *Pew Research Center*. September 15, 2015. Web. October 28, 2017.

López, Gustavo. "Hispanics of Salvadoran Origin in the United States, 2013." *Pew Research Center.* September 15, 2015. Web. October 28, 2017.

Lopez, Mark Hugo and Ana Gonzalez Barrera. "What is the Future of Spanish in the United States." *Pew Research Center.* September 5, 2013. Web. October 28, 2017.

Lopez, Mark Hugo and Ana Gonzalez-Barrera. PEW Research Center. June 19, 2013. "Salvadorans May Soon Replace Cubans as Third-Largest U.S. Hispanic Group." *Pew Research Center.* June 19, 2013. Web. October 28, 2017.

Martí, José. "Nuestra América." *El Partido Liberal,* January 30, 1891. *Obras completas.* vol. 6. La Habana: Editorial Nacional de Cuba, 1963, 15–23. Print.

Martí, José. "Our America." *José Martí: Selected Writings,* ed. and trans. Esther Allen. New York: Penguin, 2002, pp. 288–96. Print.

Martínez-San Miguel, Yolanda. "Bitextualidad y bilingüismo: Reflexiones sobre el lenguaje en la escritura latina contemporánea." *CENTRO Journal* 12.1 (Fall 2000): 19–34. Print.

Massey, Douglas. 1995. "The New Immigration and Ethnicity in the United States." *Population and Development Review* 21.3, 631–52. Print.

Matthews, Dylan. "Tim Kaine Delivered the First-Ever Senate Speech all in Spanish." Vox. July 22, 2016. Web.

McKee Irwin, Robert and Mónica Szurmuk. "Cultural Studies and the Field of 'Spanish' in the US Academy." *Journal on Social History and Literature in Latin America* 6.3 (2009): 36–60. Web. October 28, 2017.

Meléndez, A. Gabriel. *So All Is Not Lost: The Poetics of Print in Nuevomexicano Communities 1834–1958.* Albuquerque: U of New Mexico P, 1997. Print.

Méndez, Miguel. *Peregrinos de Aztlán.* 1974. Tempe: Bilingual P, 1991. Print.

Méndez, Miguel. *Pilgrims in Aztlán.* Trans. David W. Foster. Tempe: Bilingual P, 1992. Print.

Mignolo, Walter. "The Role of the Humanities in the Corporate University." *PMLA* 115.5 (2000) 1238–45. Print.

Molesky, Jean. "Understanding the American Linguistic Mosaic: A Historical Overview of Language Maintenance and Language Shift." *Language Diversity: Problem or Resource?* Cambridge: Newbury House, 1988, 29–68. Print.

Molloy, Sylvia. "Bilingual Scenes." *Bilingual Games: Some Literary Investigation.* Ed. Doris Sommer. New York: Palgrave, 2003, 289–96. Print.

Morales, Alejandro. *The Brick People.* Houston: Arte Público P, 1988. Print.

Morales, Alejandro. *Hombres de ladrillo.* Trans. Isabel Díaz Sánchez. Houston: Arte Público P, 2010. Print.

Munguía, Enrique E. *The Underdogs.* 1929. New York: Signet, 1962. Print.

Navarro, Mireya. "Is Spanish the Measure of 'Hispanic'?" *New York Times.* Religion. June 8, 2003. Web. October 28, 2017.

Neate, Wilson. "Unwelcome Remainders, Welcome Reminders." *New York Times.* 19.2 (Summer 1994): 17–34. *New York Times.* August 4, 2017. Web.

Ngai, Mae M. *Impossible Subjects: Illegal Aliens and the Making of Modern America.* Princeton: New Jersey: Princeton UP, 2004. Print.

Niranjana, Tejaswini. *Siting Translation: History, Post-structuralism and the Colonial Context.* Berkeley: U of California P, 1992. Print.

Oder, Norman. "S & S, Harper Launch Spanish Lines for Spring." BookNews. *Publishers Weekly* 242.1(January 2, 1995): 31–32. Web. October 28, 2017.

Ojito, Mirta. "Publisher Tries Literary Lightning Rod to Attract Latino Writers and Readers." *NY Times*. September 10, 2002. Web. October 28, 2017.

Otheguy R. and Ana Celia Zentella. "Debate about the Term 'Spanglish,'" 22nd Conference on Spanish in the United States, Coral Gables, FL, 2009. Web. October 28, 2017.

Onwuemen, Michael C. "Limits of Transliteration: Nigerian Writers' Endeavors toward a National Literary Language." *PMLA* 114.5 (1999): 1055–66.

Ospina, Carmen. "Harper Collins To Expand Rayo Imprint." *Publishers Weekly* 251.38 (September 20, 2004).

Ospina, Carmen. "Random House Expands Spanish Line at Vintage; Vintage Español Celebrates its 10th Anniversary by Expanding its Publishing Program and Naming a New Director." News. *Criticas*. (January 1, 2005): 5. *Lexis Nexis Academic*. Web. October 28, 2017.

Paredes, Américo. "The Problem of Identity in a Changing Culture: Popular Expressions of Culture Conflict along the Lower Rio Grande Border." Ed. R. Bauman. *Folklore and Culture on the Texas-Mexican Border*. Austin: U of Texas P, 1993, 19–47. Print.

Paredes, Américo. *With a Pistol in His Hand*. Austin: U of Texas P, 1959. Print.

Pavlenko. Aneta. *Emotions and Multilingualism*. Cambridge: Cambridge UP, 2005. Print.

Pavlenko. Aneta. "'We have Room but for One Language Here': Language and National Identity in the US at the Turn of the Twentieth Century." *Multilingua* 21.2–3 (2002): 163–96. Print.

Pedreira, Antonio. "La actualidad del jíbaro." *El jíbaro de Puerto Rico: Símbolo y figura*. Eds. Enrique Laguerre and Esther M. Melón. Sharon, Conn. Troutman P, 1968, 7–24. Print.

Pellón, Gustavo. *The Underdogs with Related Texts*. Indianapolis: Hackett, 2006. Print.

Pérez, Ramón "Tianguis." *Diario de un mojado*. Houston: Arte Público P, 2003. Print.

Pérez, Ramón "Tianguis." *Diary of a Guerrilla*. Trans. Dick J. Reavis. Houston: Arte Público P, 1999. Print.

Pérez-Firmat, G. *Tongue Ties: Logo-Eroticism in Anglo-Hispanic Literature*. New York: Palgrave MacMillan, 2003. Print.

Poniatowska, Elena. *Fuerte es el silencio*. 3rd edition. México: Era, 1981. Print.

Pratt, Mary Louise. "Comparative Literature and Global Citizenship." *Comparative Literature in the Age of Multiculturalism*. Ed. Charles Bernheimer. Baltimore: Johns Hopkins UP, 1995, 58–65. Print.

Pratt, Mary Louise. "Comparative Literature and the Global Languagescape." *A Companion to Comparative Literature*. Eds. Ali Behdad and Dominic Thomas. MA: John Wiley & Sons, 2011, 273–95. Web. November 12, 2017.

Pratt, Mary Louise. "Translation Studies Forum: Cultural translation." *Translation Studies* 3.1 (2010): 94–96. doi: 10.1080/14781700903338706. http://dx.doi.org/10.1080/14781700903338706. Web. October 28, 2017.

Pratt, Mary Louise. "What's Foreign and What's Familiar?" *PMLA* 117.5 (2002): 1283–87. Print.

Pratt, Mary Louise. "The Traffic in Meaning: Translation, Contagion, Infiltration." *Profession*, 2002, 25–36. Print.

Prosper Sánchez, Gloria D. "Washing Away the Stain of the Plantain: Esmeralda Santiago y la constitución del relato autobiográfico bilingüe." Actas del "Congreso en torno a la cuestión del género y la expresión femenina actual." Ed. Carmen Cazurro García de la Quintana. Aguadilla: Universidad de Puerto Rico, 1998, 131–38. Print.

Rabassa, Gregory. *If This Be Treason: Translation and Its Discontents*. New York: New Directions, 2005. Print.

Rafael, Vicente. *Contracting Colonialism: Translation and Christian Conversion in Tagalog Society under Early Spanish Rule*. Durham: Duke UP, 1993. Print.

Ramos Jorge. *La otra cara de América: Historia de los inmigrantes que están cambiando a Estados Unidos*, Grijalbo, 2000. Print.

Ramos Jorge. *The Other Face of America: Chronicles of the Immigrants Shaping Our Future*. Trans. Patricia Duncan. New York: HarperCollins Rayo, 2002. Print.

Randle, William. "'Wetback': An Extension Usage." *American Speech* 36.1 (1961): 78–80. Print.

Reavis, Dick, trans. *Diary of an Undocumented Immigrant*. [*Diario de un mojado*]. Houston: Arte Público P, 1991. Print.

Reavis, Dick. *Without Documents*. New York, Condor, 1978. Print.

Rebolledo, T.D. Foreword. *Puppet*. Albuquerque: U of New Mexico P, 2000, xiii–xxii. Print.

Rivera, Tomás. *. . . y no se lo tragó la tierra* [*. . . and the Earth Did not Swallow Him.*] 1971. Trans. Evangelina Vigil-Piñón. Houston: Arte Público P, 1992. Print.

Robe, Stanley L. *Azuela and the Mexican Underdogs*. Berkeley: U California P, 1979. Print.

Robinson, Douglas. Review of *The Subversive Scribe* by Suzanne Jill Levine and *Rethinking Translation* by Lawrence Venuti *Genre* 4.24 (1991): 467–475. Print.

Robinson, Douglas. *Translation and Empire: Post-colonial Theories Explained*. Manchester, UK: St. Jerome, 1997. Print.

Rodríguez, América. "Creating an Audience and Remapping a Nation: A Brief History of Spanish-Language Broadcasting (1930–1980). *Quarterly Review of Film and Video* 16.3–4 (1999): 357–74.

Romero, Simon. "Spanish Thrives in the U.S., Despite an English-Only Drive." *New York Times*. August 23, 2017. Web. October 28, 2017.

Rosa, Jonathan and Nelson Flores. "Unsettling Race and Language." *Language in Society*. Cambridge UP, 2017, 1–27. doi:10.1017/S0047404517000562. Web. October 28, 2017.

Rudin, E. *Tender Accents of Sound: Spanish in the Chicano Novel in English*. Tempe: Bilingual P. 1996. Print.

Ruiz-Mantilla, Jesús. "Más 'Speak Spanish' que en España." Cultura. *El País* (October 6, 2008). Web.

Ruiz, Richard. "Orientation in Language Planning," in *Language Diversity: Problem or Resource, A Social and Educational Perspective on Language Minorities in the United States.* Eds. Sandra Lee Mckay and Sua-Ling Wong. Cambridge: Newbury House Publishers, 1988, 3–25. Print.

Ryan, Camille. "Language Use in the United States: 2011." American Community Service Reports. August, 2013: 1–13. *Census.gov.* October 28, 2017.

Sakai. Naoki. "How do we count a language? Translation and Discontinuity." *Translation Studies* 2.1 (2009): 71–88. Print.

Samora, Julian. *Los mojados: The Wetback Story.* Notre Dame: U of Notre Dame P, 1972. Print.

Sánchez, Marta. "La Malinche at the Intersection: Race and Gender in Piri Thomas's *Down These Mean Streets.*" *PMLA* 113.1 (January, 1998): 117–29. Print.

Sánchez, Marta. *Pocho en español: The Anti-Pocho Pocho. Translation Studies* 4.3 (2011): 310–324. Print.

Sánchez, Marta. "'I may say wetback but I really mean mojado': Migration and Translation in Ramón 'Tianguis' Pérez's *Diary of an Undocumented Immigrant.*" *Perspectives: Studies in Translatology* 22.2 (2014): 161–78. Routledge. DOI: 10.1080/0907676X.2013.824490.

Santiago, Esmeralda. *When I Was Puerto Rican.* New York: Random House, 1994. Print.

Santiago, Esmeralda. *Cuando era puertorriqueña.* Trans. Esmeralda Santiago. Random House, Vintage Español, 1994. Print.

Santorum Rick. "Santorum to Puerto Rico: Speak English if You Want Statehood." *Reuters.* Web. October 28, 2017.

Sarmiento, Domingo Faustino. *Life in the Argentine Republic in the Days of the Tyrants; or, Civilization and Barbarism.* New York: Hurd and Houghton, 1868. Print.

Seyhan, Azade. *Writing Outside the Nation:* Princeton, Princeton UP, 2001. Print.

Shnayerson, Michael. "The Four Amigas." *Vanity Fair* 57.9 (September, 1994): 128. Print.

Shell Marc. "Babel in America: or The Politics of Language Diversity in the United States." *Critical Inquiry* 20.1 (Autumn 1993): 103–27. Print.

Shell, Marc and Werner Sollors, eds. *The Multilingual Anthology of American Literature: Reader of Original Texts with English Translations.* New York: New York UP, 2000. Print.

Simon, Sherry. Introduction. *Culture in Transit: Translating the Literature of Quebec.* Ed. Sherry Simon. Montreal: Véhicule P, 1995, 7–15. Print.

Simon, Sherry. "The Language of Cultural Difference: Figures of Alterity in Canadian Translation." *Rethinking Translation: Discourse, Subjectivity, Ideology.* Ed. Lawrence Venuti. London: Routledge 1992, 159–76. Print.

Sobarzo, Horacio. *Vocabulario sonorense.* Mexico: Editorial Porrúa, 1966. Print.

Solís, Ted. "Jíbaro Image and the Ecology of Hawai'i Puerto Rican Music Instruments." *Latin American Music Review* 16.2 (Fall/Winter 1995): 123–53.

Spanish Language Domains. "The Numbers of Spanish-Speakers in the World Exceeds 500 Million." 2014. *Spanish Language Domains.* Web. October 28, 2017.

Spener, David. "Some reflections on the Language of Clandestine Migration on the Mexico-U.S. Border." *Trinity.edu.* 2009. Web. October 28, 2017.

Spota, Luis. *Murieron a mitad del rio* [Death in Midstream] (6th ed.). México, DF: B. Costa-Amic Editor, 1977. No page given but stated in book's opening pages.

Stavans Ilan. "Bilingual Nation: Spanish-Language Books Since the 1960s." *A History of the Book in America*, vol. 5 *The Enduring Book: Print Culture in Postwar America*. Eds. David Paul Nord, Joan Shelley Rubin, and Michael Schudson. Chapel Hill: U of North Carolina P, 2009, 389–406. Print.

Stavans Ilan. Introduction. *Spanglish: The Making of a New American Language*. New York: Harper Collins, 2003, 1–54. Print.

Stavans Ilan. "Trump, the Wall, and the Spanish Language." Op-Ed. *New York Times.* January 30, 2017. Web. October 28, 2017.

Steiner, George. *After Babel: Aspects of Language and Translation*, 1992. 2nd ed. New York: Oxford UP, 1992. Print.

St. John, Rachel. *Line in the Sand: A History of the Western U.S.-Mexico Border.* Princeton, NJ: Princeton UP, 2011. Print.

Stephen, Lynn. *Transborder Lives: Indigenous Oaxacans in Mexico, California, and Oregon.* Durham: Duke UP, 2007. Print.

Stoever, J.L. "The Noise of SB1070: or do I Sound Illegal to You?" The Sound Strike on Facebook. August 19, 2010. Web. <http://soundstudiesblog.com/2010/08/19/the-noise-of-sb-1070/>. Web. October 28, 2017.

Stoever, J.L. "Splicing the Sonic Color-Line: Tony Schwartz Remixes Postwar Nueva York." *Social Text* 102.28.1 (Spring 2010): 59–85. DOI 10.1215/01642472-2009-060.

Suga, Keigo. "Translation, Exophony, Omniphony." *Voices from Everywhere*. Ed. Douglas Slaymaker, 27 (2007): 21–33.

Taylor Diana. *The Archive and the Repertoire: Performing Cultural Memory in the Americas.* Durham: Duke UP. 2003. Print.

Taylor, Paul, et al. "Language Use Among Latinos." *Pew Hispanic.* April 4, 2012. Web. November 11, 2017.

Texas Monthly. May 1985: 118, 120. *Google Books.* Web. October 28, 2017.

Thomas, Piri. *Down These Mean Streets.* 1967. New York: Random House, Vintage Books, 1995. Print.

Thomas, Piri. *Por estas calles bravas.* Trans. Suzanne Dod Tomás. New York: Random House, Vintage Español, 1998. Print.

Torres-Robles, Carmen L. "Esmeralda Santiago: Hacia una (re)definición de la puertorriqueñidad" *Bilingual Review* 23 (September-December, 1998): 206–213. Print.

"Toyota to Reach Out to Hispanics in Super Bowl." 2007. Associated Press, 2013. *NBC News.* Web. October 28, 2017.

Trivedi, Harish. "Translating Culture vs. Cultural Translation." *In Translation: Reflections, Refractions, Translations.* Eds. Paul St-Pierre and Prafulla C. Kar. Amsterdam/Philadelphia: John Bejamins Publishing. May 15, 2007, pp. 277–87. Web. October 28, 2017.

Tymoczko, Maria and Edwin Gentzler, eds. *Translation and Power.* Amherst: U of Massachusetts P, 2002. Print.

"US Now Has More Spanish Speakers Than Spain—only Mexico Has More." *Guardian US News*. June 29, 2015. Web. October 28, 2017.

Valdés, Guadalupe. "Language Situation of Mexican Americans." *Language Diversity: Problem or Resource? A Social and Educational Perspective on Language Minorities in the United States*. Cambridge: Newbury House Publishers, 1988, 111–39. Print.

Vallejos, Tomás. "Jose Antonio Villarreal." 2005–2006. BookRags Biography, 1–14. Print.

Vasconcelos, José. "Asoma el pochismo." *La Tormenta* Part II *Ulises criollo*. México, Ediciones Botas, 1937, 73–77. Print.

Veciana-Suarez, Ana. *Hispanic Media, USA: A Narrative Guide to Print and Electronic Hispanic News Media in the United States*. Washington DC: The Media Institute, 1987. Print.

Velazquez-Monoff. "The Meaning of 'Despacito' in the Age of Trump. *New York Times*, August 4, 2017. Web. October 28, 2017.

Venegas, Daniel. *Las aventuras de don Chipote, o cuando los pericos mamen* Houston: Arte Público P, 1998. Print.

Venegas, Daniel. *The Adventures of Don Chipote, or When Parrots Breastfeed*. Trans. Ethriam Cash Brammer. Houston: Arte Público P, 2000. Print.

Venuti, Lawrence. *The Translator's Invisibility: A History of Translation*. New York: Routledge, 1995. Print.

Venuti, Lawrence. *Scandals of Translation: Towards an Ethics of Difference*. New York: Routledge, 1998. Print.

Venuti, Lawrence. *Rethinking Translation: Discourse, Subjectivity, Ideology*. Ed. Lawrence Venuti. London: Routledge, 1992. Print.

Villarreal, José Antonio. *Pocho*. New York: Anchor Books (1959, 1970, 1987). Print.

Villarreal, José Antonio. *Pocho en Español*. Trans. Roberto Cantú. New York: Anchor Books, 1994. Print.

"Vintage Español Enters into Joint Venture with Random House Mondadori: Publisher to Become Spanish-Language Market Leader in U.S." Press Release. The Knopf DoubleDay Group. 2009. <http://www.penguinrandomhouse.biz/media/pdfs/Vin tageEspanol_RHMondadori.pdf/>. Web. October 30, 2017.

Walkowitz, Rebecca. *Born Translated: The Contemporary Novel in an Age of World Literature*. New York: Columbia UP, 2015. Print.

Waisman, Sergio. "Borges on Translation: The Development of a Theory." *Borges and Translation: The Irreverence of the Periphery*. Lewisburg: Buckness UP, 2005, 41–83. Print.

Wechsler, Robert. *Performing Without a Stage: The Art of Literary Translation*. North Haven, CT. Catbird Press, 1998. Print.

Wei, Li. "Dimensions of Bilingualism," *The Bilingualism Reader*. Ed. Li Wei. New York, Routledge: 2000, 3–25. Print.

Weinberger, Eliot. "Anonymous Sources: A Talk on Translators and Translation" *Encuentros* 39. Cultural Center, Intl. Development Bank, Nov. 2000, 1–14. Print.

Weinrich, Harold. "Chamisso, Chamisso Authors and Globalization." *PMLA* 19.5 (Oct, 2004) 1339–1346. Print.

Woolard, Kathryn A. "Voting Rights, Liberal Voters and the Official English Movement: An Analysis of Campaign Rhetoric in San Francisco's Proposition 'O.'" *Perspectives on Official English: The Campaign for English as the Official Language of
the USA*. Eds. Karen L. Adams and Daniel T. Brink. Berlin: Mouton de Gruyter,
1990, 125–37. Print.

Wong, Sau-ling Cynthia. "Education Rights of Language Minorities." *Language Diversity: Problem or Resource*? Cambridge: Newbury House Publishers, 1988, 367–
86. Print.

Yáñez, Agustín. *Al filo del agua*. México, Editorial Porrúa, 1947. Print.

Yildiz, Yasemin. 2012. *Beyond the Mother Tongue: The Postmonolingual Condition*.
New York: Fordham UP. Print.

Zentella, Ana Celia. "Growing Up Nuyorican." *Hispanic Education in the United
States*. Ed. Lourdes Díaz-Soto. Westport, CT: Greenwood Pub, 2006, 1–8. Print.

Zentella, Ana Celia. "Bilinguals and Borders: California's *Transfronteriz@s* and Com-
peting Constructions of Bilingualism." *Int'l Journal of the Linguistic Association of
the Southwest* [*IJLASSO*] 32.2, 15–46. [IN PRESS]

Zentella, Ana Celia. "Language Situation in Puerto Rico." McKay, Sandra Lee and
Sau-Ling Cynthia Wong, eds. 1988. *Language Diversity: Problem or Resource? A
Social and Educational Perspective on Language Minorities in the United States*.
Cambridge: Newbury House Publishers 1988, 140–65. Print.

"Zopilote, Meet Mr. Migra." *Texas Monthly*, 1985, 118–21. Print.

INDEX